Volume I · Ouroboros

The Birds That Fly Backwards

DAVID WEDDLE

Roll the Hard Six Press
WWW.DAVIDOWEDDLE.COM

The Birds That Fly Backwards
Volume I: Ouroboros
Copyright © 2026 by David Weddle

double three by Roberto Blanco
from thenounproject.com (CC BY 3.0)

Printed in the United States of America

Roll the Hard Six Press
28128 Pacific Coast Hwy. #262
Malibu, CA 90265
www.davidoweddle.com

LCCN: 2026905733
ISBN: 979-8-234-01571-6

To my brother, James Weddle,
who blazed a trail for me to follow.

Whether he's writing formidable sci-fi and what-if fiction (*Battlestar Galactica, For All Mankind*) or fearless biographies of the director Sam Peckinpah (*If They Move… Kill 'Em*) and the city of Beverly Hills (*Among the Mansions of Eden*), David Weddle digs beneath surface grit and glitter to unearth the crucibles where characters are made. In *The Birds That Fly Backwards* he uses a screenplay/memory play form to look back in anger, and in love, at 60 years of American life. It's a self-portrait of an artist and his influences (from Red Skelton and Ken Kesey to Buster Keaton and Sam Peckinpah) that's also a turbulent group portrait of a conflicted middle-class family. Weddle grapples with the highs and lows of the "Greatest Generation"—and the generation that followed it—with a raw cunning that brings it all to frank, unruly life."

—MICHAEL SRAGOW,
author of *Victor Fleming: An American Movie Master*, former film critic
for *The New Yorker, The Atlantic,* and *Rolling Stone.*

"Weddle has the keen instincts of a journalist, the meticulous eye of a historian, and the unfettered imagination of a screenwriter. He is a unique voice in Hollywood, a truly gifted and passionate storyteller."

—NAREN SHANKAR,
writer-producer for *The Expanse, God of War, For All Mankind,* and *CSI.*

"David Weddle has created something really extraordinary here — a kaleidoscopic journey into the heart of his own family that, in its specificity, empathy and honesty, is the antithesis of self-indulgent. It's universal. It is essential. Weddle bravely uses his incredible power as a screenwriter to make us see, hear, and feel every moment of this story, which spans decades. As we read it, we are right there with the Weddles, in all their vulnerability, humor, cruelty, longing, creativity and, more than anything, their love for one another. Is this a limited series? A novel in script form? However you want to classify it, *The Birds That Fly Backwards* is a stunning and deeply personal work of art."

—LIZ PHANG,
writer/producer for *Foundation, Yellowjackets, Locke & Key,
The Haunting of Hill House,* and *The Strain.*

"Weddle is an unflinchingly honest writer, one who's unafraid to expose truths without concern for how they reflect on him or his ancestors. He is candid to a fault."

—DREX HEIKES,
former editor of *Los Angeles Times Magazine*

"After a storied career ranging from his seminal biography of Sam Peckinpah to brilliant work on television series including *Battlestar Galactica* and *For All Mankind*, David has now crafted his most personal work. I could not recommend it more highly! *The Birds That Fly Backwards* tells a deeply emotional story of David's family and especially his relationship with his father, written in screenplay style by a master storyteller. Prepare yourself for a roller coaster of highs and lows that will stick with you in ways you might not expect."

—MARK VERHEIDEN,
screenwriter of *The Mask*, *Timecop*, and *My Name Is Bruce*; writer/producer for such television series as *Battlestar Galactica*, *Falling Skies*, *Heroes*, *Swamp Thing*, *Daredevil*, and *Constantine*.

"In *The Birds That Fly Backwards* Weddle has created something sleek and new while reaching back through time to mine the veins of long-buried memory and the hopes and dreams of a young, white, middle-class boy in mid-20th century America. Time and again, David's love of books and movies proves to be the only respite or reliable guide he can count on as he weathers the vicissitudes of family life dominated by an all-too-human father deeply scarred by his time in the Marines fighting on Guadalcanal in the Second World War. Weddle's writing is as elegant as John Cheever's photographic short stories, and as raw and even joyful as the poetry and lyrics of Patti Smith. The choice the author has made of how to tell his tale is no less chimeric. The sometimes laugh-out-loud descriptions of David's adolescent and familial tribulations are a humorous addition to what could very well be called a "Script Novel" for the way Weddle uses the ribs of the screenplay to support this deeply felt story of one boy's life."

—JOHN LANG,
author of *All the Darkness Holds*, songwriter for Mr. Mister,
Miles Davis, and Tupac Shakur.

"David Weddle is a B2 stealth bomber. He is also a dramatist, biographer, journalist and yarn spinner. His style is clean and simple. You don't hear him coming but, when the goods are delivered, they bring fire and thunder and no one is safe. David's an emotional writer and he hides it from the reader...until he doesn't. He's also an honest writer and that's the kind you have to watch out for."

—MICHAEL NANKIN,
director for *Battlestar Galactica*, *The Good Lord Bird*, *Hell on Wheels*,
Terminator: The Sarah Connor Chronicles, and *CSI*.

Acknowledgements

I would like to thank my wife, Risa Parness, who was the first to read each of the episodes in this book. Risa listened to me obsess over my creative struggles through dinners and lunches and sleepless nights, and she helped me formulate solutions to them. Liz Phang, Toni Graphia, John Lang, Suzanne Peter, and Lee Landey also gave detailed feedback and instilled me with the confidence to see this through to the very last word. Howard Libes did the same. Howard has been deeply involved with every major piece of writing I have done in my career. He has devoted countless hours over the last 35 years to every project I've worked on, and thus is one of my closest friends.

Last, and most importantly, I would like to thank my sister, Tracey Weddle, and brother, James Weddle, who not only read the material but contributed many powerful ideas that elevated the story at every turn and twist in its journey.

—David Weddle
Malibu, California, October 17th, 2025

In the Valley of Shadow

BLACKNESS

A man's voice can be heard on a scratchy AUDIO RECORDING. It
is a deep voice, hoarse with sickness and age.

                    MAN (RECORDING)
          Where are you? I'm here all alone.
          Hoping to reach you. But you're
          out on the town, I suppose...
          Well, I just wanted you to know I'm
          thinking about you. Missing you.
          But I guess you've forgotten all
          about me...

FADE IN:

EXT. SANTANELLA CONVALESCENT HOSPITAL - DAY

DAVID WEDDLE (40) pulls his 1991 grey HONDA ACCORD into the
parking lot. He is of medium build, thin, with long bushy
red hair. Turns off the engine, pulls up the parking break,
then pauses to stare at the building's facade, tension
clenching his face. He does not want to go in there and do
this, but knows he must. Opens the door and gets out,
wearing a tie-dyed t-shirt and cargo shorts.

SUPER: **AUGUST, 1996.**

INT. SANTANELLA CONVALESCENT HOSPITAL - ENTRYWAY - DAY

David walks through what passes for a lobby: A COUPLE OF
MISMATCHED CHAIRS and AN END TABLE that offers year-old
issues of LOS ANGELES MAGAZINE, the covers creased and
curling up at the corners.

THE HEAD NURSE glances up from the window that frames her
desk, recognizes David as a regular visitor, and drops her
eyes back to her PAPERWORK.

INT. SANTANELLA CONVALESCENT HOSPITAL - HALL - DAY

David continues down a hall paved with linoleum that gleams
like a sheet of beige ice. Past open doors to rooms that
house TWO AND THREE BEDS, most half-shrouded by green
curtains. WITHERED LEGS on crumpled sheets. LABORED
COUGHING from fluid-filled lungs. THE BLAST OF DAYTIME TV --
glimpses of CATHODE RAY TUBES beaming color-faded 70's
SITCOMS, their SOUNDTRACKS unleashing GREAT WAVES OF CANNED
LAUGHTER.

THE DOOR TO HIS MOTHER'S ROOM. Weddle peeks in.

INT. SANTANELLA CONVALESCENT HOSPITAL - GLORIA'S ROOM - DAY

GLORIA WEDDLE'S BED is empty. A frayed brown bedspread. At
the foot of the mattress, a neatly folded NEW YELLOW
COMFORTER.

A PARTICLE BOARD ARMOIRE rests against the far wall, its
warped doors ajar, revealing Gloria's paltry wardrobe -- a
couple of flower-print DRESSING GOWNS. TWO PAIRS of worn
SLIPPERS.

A DOZEN SNAPSHOTS thumbtacked to the green plaster wall
beside the bed -- of Gloria's granddaughter, KACEY (3), of
David and his sister, TRACEY, taken a decade ago. And one
FRAMED PHOTO of Gloria and her husband, JAMES WEDDLE, taken
ten years ago, on a cruise of the South Pacific. Both are
tanned and relaxed. Jim is shirtless, with grey stubble on
his rugged cheeks. Gloria grips his chin with her thumb and
forefinger. Although Jim is 66 and Gloria 55, their slightly
glassy, almost giddy eyes seem to belong to a pair of
lovestruck teenagers. Even then, Gloria Weddle was an
extraordinarily beautiful woman, with sandy blond hair, an
elegant up-turned nose and warm hazel eyes. David regards
the photo for a moment, then ducks back to the hall to resume
the search for his mom.

INT. SANTANELLA CONVALESCENT HOSPITAL - HALL - DAY

David passes a CORK BULLETIN BOARD WITH NOTICES OF VARIOUS
UPCOMING EVENTS -- a screening of GRUMPY OLD MEN, an exercise
class for the wheelchair bound, a group therapy session to be
led by a visiting psychologist, PICTURES OF A FOURTH OF JULY
PARTY featuring a gallery of ravaged faces wearing glittering
party hats. Weddle is both eager to find his mom, and
dreading the prospect, tension mounting inside him as he
continues on to...

INT. SANTANELLA CONVALESCENT HOSPITAL - DINING HALL - DAY

David steps into the fluorescent-lit chamber, scanning the
FORMICA TABLES. ONE HUNDRED ELDERLY PEOPLE in WHEELCHAIRS,
sitting before CAFETERIA TRAYS, mechanically shoveling FOOD
into their mouths. Faces expressionless, eyes like burnt-out
filaments. The silence is eerie. Not one word of
conversation passes between these people. They don't even
look at each other, only the food before them.

Weddle doesn't see his mom. He moves down the aisle between
the tables. Pinpricks of sweat break out on his forehead.
Walks all the way to the end of the room before deciding she
must not be here. Pivots and heads out.

As he passes a pair of old women, one of them, with thick
glasses, eyes David's ass and murmurs to her companion.

                    OLD WOMAN
          There's a nice one...

She reaches to grab Weddle's butt, but he's experienced and
deftly skips beyond her hungry fingers. He's almost out the
door when he hears a familiar bleat...

                    GLORIA
          Hi...

David turns and spots GLORIA (64), in a corner in her
WHEELCHAIR. Her grey curly hair is still damp from her late
morning trip to the shower room, the thin shiny skin of her
cheeks stitched with blue webs of broken blood vessels. The
bib tied over her blue floral housecoat splotched with LUMPS
OF BEEF STROGANOFF AND LEMON JELL-O. A DAB OF GRAVY clings
to the curly whiskers on her chin. She attempts to take a
last bite of Jell-O, but her hand shakes so violently she has
trouble getting it in her mouth.

                    DAVID
          Hello, Mom, how are you?

Gloria shakes her head, tears of joy forming in the corners
of her eyes.

                    GLORIA
          I should say!

David leans down to stroke her hair and kiss her cheek. She
makes soft kissing sounds.

                    DAVID
          Did you have a good lunch?

                    GLORIA
          I should say! The hamburger is
          very American.

                    DAVID
          Good.

David undoes her bib and wipes off her chin.

                    DAVID (cont'd)
          How about if we go out to the patio
          and sit and talk for a while,
          wouldn't that be nice?

                    GLORIA
          Oh, don't you know it!

David wheels her chair out the door.

EXT. SANTANELLA CONVALESCENT HOSPITAL - PATIO - DAY

David pushes his mother into the dusty enclosed space. Trees
shade most of the concrete. TABLES AND CHAIRS are scattered
about. A couple of them are occupied by VISITORS chatting
quietly with their WHEELCHAIR BOUND PARENTS AND GRANDPARENTS.

David wheels his mother beneath a tree, and sits opposite
her. His mother has begun to weep, the small strangled sobs
of a child. David takes her blue, trembling hand. The
polish on her once immaculate nails is chipped and cracked.

                    DAVID
          What's wrong, Mom?

                    GLORIA
          I don't...

                    DAVID
          You don't what?

                    GLORIA
          Understand why this happened to me.

                    DAVID
          There is no why.

                    GLORIA
          It's not fair!

                    DAVID
          You're right. It's not. It's
          hard, I know. It's very hard.

Gloria continues to sob. David struggles to work up his
courage, then...

                    DAVID (cont'd)
          Listen, you know what I'm going to
          do? I've decided I'm going to
          bring you back to my house to stay
          with me. How does that sound?

Her sobs subside. She looks at him and nods. David's not
certain she understands. He needs to make sure she does.

                    DAVID (cont'd)
          Remember your favorite spot? At
          the end of my street, on the bluff,
          overlooking the ocean?
                    (off her nod)
                    (MORE)

                    DAVID (cont'd)
          I'm going to take you back there.
          I'm going to wheel you out to that
          bench and you'll sit and look out
          at the ocean. Then I'll take you
          back to my house, my room. You'll
          be with me and Tracey. I'm going
          to take you off of the drugs, Mom.
          You'll be able to let go. You'll
          die at home, in my room, with me
          and Tracey right there. How does
          that sound?

Gloria looks at him, her gaze suddenly steady and focused.

                    GLORIA
          Yes. I'd like that. I'm tired...
          I've had... it is... Enough.

Her lips begin to tremble, tears gather again in the corners
of her eyes.

                    GLORIA (cont'd)
          Scared.

Her grip on his hand tightens with surprising strength.
David leans forward and strokes the crinkly discolored skin
of her forearm.

                    DAVID
          I know, Mom. It's very
          frightening. But I'll be there
          with you and so will Tracey. We'll
          be right by your side the whole
          time.

Gloria regards him with piercing intensity.

                    GLORIA
          Where would I have been without
          you?

David's eyes moisten. He struggles to respond, but can find
no words.

EXT. DAVID'S TRAILER - MALIBU - NIGHT

A single-wide trailer on a bluff. Rows of SINGLE AND DOUBLE
WIDE TRAILERS stretch down the street to the edge of a cliff,
which overlooks the Pacific Ocean, glistening silver-blue
under a 3/4 MOON.

INT. DAVID'S TRAILER - KITCHEN - NIGHT

David's on a CORDLESS PHONE, pacing in the narrow kitchen,
which has a basic STOVE and a SMALL FORMICA TABLE with FOUR
WOODEN FOLDING CHAIRS.

                    DAVID
          She agreed.

His fiancé, RISA (47), a striking brunette with an upturned
nose and a strong Brooklyn accent, is washing the DISHES FROM
DINNER in a small sink and listening as David talks to...

                              INTERCUT WITH:

INT. TRACEY'S HOUSE - KITCHEN - NIGHT

TRACEY WEDDLE (37) also paces while talking on an much newer
CORDLESS PHONE. Tracey has a rich mane of blond hair and is
incredibly fit. Her kitchen is large, opulent, and outfitted
with the latest appliances. She's struggling to accept what
David has just told her.

                    DAVID
          I'll arrange for an ambulance to
          bring her here, Monday morning.

                    TRACEY
          You sure she understood you?

                    DAVID
          Yeah, I am. I asked the question
          multiple ways and she said yes
          every time. I worried she was just
          agreeing with me, no matter what I
          said. So I changed it up and asked
          if she would like to stay in the
          nursing home and continue taking
          her meds and she said no. Very
          forcefully.

                    TRACEY
          Okay... Then I guess we're
          actually going to do this.

                    DAVID
          It's the right thing, Tracey.

                    TRACEY
          I know. I just...
               (starts crying)
          I gotta go...

She hangs up. END INTERCUT. David frowns, worried. Risa
turns to look at him.

                    RISA
          How'd she take it?

                    DAVID
          Not great. But she agreed it's
          time.

INT. DAVID'S TRAILER - BEDROOM - NIGHT

The small bedroom is decorated with a huge poster of SAM
PECKINPAH'S *THE WILD BUNCH,* and PHOTOS OF BUSTER KEATON AND
LAUREL AND HARDY. And a PAINTING OF MCKEESPORT, Pennsylvania
in the 1930s -- in it, two Bessemer FURNACES belch volcanic
flames into an obsidian sky, illuminating the fetid waters of
the Monongahela River.

David's reading Ken Kesey's *JAIL JOURNAL,* the cover slathered
with incandescent psychedelic images from the five months
Kesey was incarcerated in a Federal work farm for possession
of Marijuana. Risa lies beside him, her eyes closed. David
sets the book down and switches off the light. The room's
bathed in SILVER-BLUE MOONLIGHT streaming through the sliding
glass door that leads to the back yard.

David emits a stressed-out sigh.

                    RISA
          What's wrong?

Her eyes are open now, watching him with concern.

                    DAVID
          Nothing... Everything...

                    RISA
          It's the right thing. You know it
          is.

                    DAVID
          I do...

                    RISA
          Then what is it?

                    DAVID
          I don't know... I... I looked into
          her room today, at that shitty
          armoire they gave her.

                    RISA
          Okay...

She waits patiently for him to elaborate.

                    DAVID
          All she's got are three flimsy
          dresses. And three pairs of
          slippers.

He falls silent.

                    RISA
          And?

                    DAVID
          And it made me start time tripping
          again. I mean, three years ago my
          parents had two houses, three cars,
          six televisions, a dog. Closets
          full of clothes, a massive oak
          dining table, two sets of patio
          furniture, enough paintings to fill
          a gallery... A whole world that
          revolved around these two people.
          And now it's vanished, as if it
          never existed. And in a week, that
          will be true of my mother, too.

                    RISA
          No it won't. You and your sister
          will remember her. So will I. And
          Peg.

                    DAVID
          But in a few years we'll all be
          gone, too.

                    RISA
          A few years? Don't know about you,
          but I intend to hang around longer
          than that.

                    DAVID
          But in the grand scheme of things,
          when you think about all of the
          people who lived from the time
          humans first stood upright on the
          plains of Africa till now, it won't
          be so long at all. The blink of an
          eye. And when we're all gone,
          there will be no one left who
          remembers her. It will be as if
          she never lived.
                    (MORE)

"IF THEY MOVE...KILL 'EM!"

SAM PECKINPAH

DAVID WEDDLE

                    DAVID (cont'd)
          Maybe years from now strangers will
          run across some of our family
          photos on a table in a swap meet
          somewhere and wonder who the hell
          these people in the faded pictures
          were. And there will be no one to
          tell them.

Risa takes his hand.

                    RISA
          Nothing lasts.

                    DAVID
          I've known that for a long time.
          Intellectually. Abstractly.

                    RISA
          But now it's visceral.

David doesn't answer, his gaze fixed on the ceiling.

EXT. NEW YORK - LINCOLN CENTER - NIGHT

AN ILLUMINATED POSTER OUTSIDE THE DOORS TO THE THEATER
proclaims **SAM PECKINPAH'S *THE WILD BUNCH***. It features the
long shadowed silhouettes of EIGHT OUTLAWS striding away from
camera, armed to the teeth.

A LONG LINE OF MOVIE BUFFS moves out of the cold and into the
warmth of the posh theater.

SUPER: **FEBRUARY, 1995 (SIXTEEN MONTHS EARLIER)**

INT. LINCOLN CENTER - THEATER - NIGHT

PEOPLE are packed to the rafters. A PODIUM WITH A MICROPHONE
has been set up before the great white slab of a MOVIE
SCREEN. A dapper and charismatic STEVEN GAYDOS (45) steps up
to the lectern. The small talk dies and people turn their
attention to him.

                    STEVEN GAYDOS
          Good evening. My name is Steven
          Gaydos. I am the executive editor
          of *Variety*, and a longtime fan of
          Sam Peckinpah's films, and of this
          one in particular, which is widely
          regarded as his masterpiece. It
          has been 25 years since anyone has
          seen the director's cut of this
          extraordinary movie.
                    (MORE)

                    STEVEN GAYDOS (cont'd)
          A few weeks after it was released
          in the summer of 1969, Warner
          Brothers cut 10 minutes from the
          picture so they could increase the
          number of showings per day in
          theaters. The scenes they removed
          obliterated crucial backstory and
          motivations for the characters and
          reduced the scope and emotional
          range of the movie. Peckinpah was
          devastated. I think it's fair to
          say he never recovered from the
          mutilation of his greatest film.
          But now the director's cut has been
          restored to its former glory and
          released to theaters across the
          country, thanks to the efforts of
          the man I am about to introduce.
          David Weddle.

Gaydos gestures to a STACK OF BOOKS on a nearby DISPLAY
TABLE.

                    STEVEN GAYDOS (cont'd)
          Mr. Weddle has also written the
          critically acclaimed biography, *"If
          They Move... Kill 'Em!" The Life
          and Times of Sam Peckinpah.*
          Let's give a big hand to David
          Weddle.

David bounds onto the stage in a pin-striped suit and tie,
riding a surge of adrenaline in this moment of triumph,
blissfully unaware of what the future holds. The audience
welcomes him with THUNDEROUS APPLAUSE.

AT THE BACK OF THE THEATER, Gloria (62) sits with her best
friend, PEG SHAW (73), and Risa. Gloria's immaculately
dressed, her hair elegantly coiffed, a gold charm bracelet
dangling from her wrist, a gold wedding band on her finger,
with a diamond engagement ring. Gloria's surprised by the
way the accolade for her son builds and builds, until people
begin rising to give him a standing ovation. Gloria stands
too, clapping so hard her palms sting and tears fill her
eyes.

ON STAGE, David has taken possession of the podium. He waits
for the applause to subside.

                    DAVID
          Thank you. It's a privilege to be
          here.
                    (MORE)

16

                    DAVID (cont'd)
          We have some honored guests in the
          audience this evening, who appeared
          in the movie. Ernest Borgnine...

ERNEST BORGNINE stands and waves to the applauding audience.

                    DAVID (cont'd)
          Jaime Sanchez... Bo Hopkins... L.Q.
          Jones... R.G. Armstrong...

The actors stand, wave and nod to fresh gusts of applause.
As the clapping subsides, Weddle continues...

                    DAVID (cont'd)
          The film you are about to see was
          first unveiled 25 years ago at a
          sneak preview in Kansas City. The
          spring of 1969 was a blood soaked
          moment in our nation's history.
          Every night, TV news broadcasts
          pumped scenes of ghastly carnage
          into American living rooms. The
          Vietnam War was raging, and our
          cities were burning as anti-war and
          civil rights protests exploded with
          spasms of violence. The people who
          came to see this movie hoped to
          escape the madness by watching a
          good old fashioned western with
          clearly defined good guys and bad
          guys, and an easily digestible
          moral to the story that would help
          them forget their troubles. But
          the hope for a simple diverting
          entertainment died before the
          opening credits ended, because
          Peckinpah was determined to force
          people to face the truth about
          themselves. When I watch this
          movie today, I like to imagine
          myself in that Kansas City audience
          and think about how I would have
          reacted. Anyway, I hope you enjoy
          the picture.

Weddle leaves the podium, and signals the projectionist to
kill the lights and roll the film.

AT THE BACK OF THE THEATER, Gloria claps along with the
RAPTUROUS APPLAUSE for her son as the lights begin to fade.

INT. LINCOLN CENTER LOBBY - NIGHT

David sits at a FOLDING TABLE. A POSTER FOR HIS BOOK rests
on a nearby EASEL. Risa stands behind him, observing
proudly. A LINE OF PEOPLE, each of them holding a copy of
David's book, snakes across the lobby. David signs a copy
for Howard, a giddy Peckinpah head.

                    HOWARD
          I've read all of the books on him.

                    DAVID
          Seriously? Last time I counted
          there were more than a dozen.
          You're pretty committed.

                    HOWARD
          You bet! I thought I knew
          everything about the man, but your
          book opened my eyes. You really
          brought him to life.

                    DAVID
          Thank you. That means a lot,
          coming from a die hard fan.

Risa taps David's shoulder.

                    RISA
          Your mother's leaving. She wants
          to say good-bye.

David looks at the next person in line, a MIDDLE-AGED WOMAN.

                    DAVID
          Excuse me for just a moment.

The woman nods as David walks over to his mother, standing
off to one side.

                    DAVID (cont'd)
          Hey, Mom. Did you enjoy the movie?

                    GLORIA
            (euphoric)
          Oh, I should say so. I could not
          believe all those people giving a
          standing ovation to <u>my</u> <u>son</u>. It
          was... amazing.

                    DAVID
          I was pretty blown away myself.

                    GLORIA
          I wish your father lived to see it.
          He would have been so proud.

                    DAVID
               (melancholy sigh)
          I know... But you're here, and that
          means everything to me. Are we
          still on for dinner tomorrow night?

                    GLORIA
          I should say so. What time?

                    DAVID
          I made a reservation for seven
          p.m.

                    GLORIA
          Perfect. At The Five Crowns,
          right?

David's confused and unsettled.

                    DAVID
          The Five... No, Mom. We're meeting
          at the Waldorf, like you wanted.

Gloria's embarrassed by her mistake and slightly
discombobulated.

                    GLORIA
          Right. Of course... What time do
          you want to meet there?

                    DAVID
          Seven p.m.

                    GLORIA
          Okay. I'll make a reservation.

                    DAVID
               (disturbed)
          No, Mom, I just told you. I made a
          reservation already. Seven p.m.

                    GLORIA
          Okay. Great! See you then!

Gloria hurries off, worried she'll make another mistake.
David's eyes meet Risa's. They are both uneasy about what
they just witnessed.

INT. WALDORF ASTORIA - DINING ROOM - NIGHT

David, Gloria, Risa, and Peg finish shoveling the last of a
CHOCOLATE MOUSE CAKE into their mouths. Peg, like Gloria, is
elegantly dressed, and wears a high end, CURLY RED WIG.

                    DAVID
          That was a religious experience.

                    RISA
          So am I to take it you believe in
          God now?

                    DAVID
          Not god. But I am a devout
          believer in chocolate mouse.

Gloria and Risa's spoons head for the last piece, almost
colliding before they both pull back.

                    RISA
          You go ahead, Gloria.

                    GLORIA
          No, you take it, Risa. Please.

Risa smiles and eats the last piece as the WAITER delivers
the CHECK.

                    WAITER
          Thank you, everyone.

Gloria reaches for it, but David snatches it before it lands
on the table.

                    DAVID
          I got it.

                    PEG
          Whoah. Look at Mr. Big Shot,
          picking up the tab.
              (smiles warmly)
          Thank you, honey.

                    DAVID
          My pleasure, Peg. Thank you for
          coming all the way out here for
          this.

                    PEG
          Are you kidding? I wouldn't have
          missed it for the world. Your
          father would have wanted me to be
          here.

Gloria has grown agitated. She picks up her LOUIS VUITTON
PURSE and looks at Peg.

                    GLORIA
          We better get going. Got a long
          drive to the desert.

Everyone looks at her with concern.

                    DAVID
          Mom... We're not in California.
          We're in New York, remember?

Gloria laughs, but her eyes are gripped with panic.

                    GLORIA
          Oh yes, of course. I know. I
          meant we're... what you said. I
          agree.

INT. WALDORF ASTORIA - LOBBY - NIGHT

Gloria heads to THE LADIES ROOM door, waving to Peg.

                    GLORIA
          Be right back.

                    PEG
          Take your time. We'll be right
          here.

As soon as she's gone, David turns to Peg, deeply worried.

                    DAVID
          You see what I mean?

                    PEG
          She's just tired. Hardly slept
          because she was so excited about
          your event. She'll be right as
          rain once she gets some sleep.

But David's not convinced.

EXT. WALDORF ASTORIA - NIGHT

The VALET holds a TAXICAB door open. Gloria and Peg wave to
David and Risa, who stand on the red carpet, waiting for the
next cab.

                    GLORIA
          Bye, honey.

                    DAVID
          Bye, Mom. Peg.

                    RISA
          See you tomorrow.

After their cab departs, David turns to Risa with a worried
expression.

                    RISA (cont'd)
          Stop catastrophizing. You heard
          Peg. She's tired, and frankly the
          two of them have been drinking
          since they got here. Your mom will
          be fine after a good night's sleep.
          You'll see.

                    DAVID
               (shakes his head)
          Something's wrong. I'm gonna call
          my sister.

                    RISA
               (exasperated sigh)
          Do what you want.

INT. TRACEY'S HOTEL ROOM - NIGHT

Tracey's on the PHONE, nervously pacing. Her SUITCASE lies
open on a FOLD-OUT RACK, CLOTHES and TOILETRIES scattered on
a nearby DESK. PRODUCTION MEMOS litter the bed.

                    TRACEY
          I agree. Something's off. Before
          she flew to New York she called me
          from Palm Desert. She had gone to
          the mall and couldn't remember
          where she parked. Ended up walking
          around the parking structure for
          more than an hour before she found
          her car.

                                        INTERCUT WITH:

INT. DAVID'S HOTEL ROOM - NIGHT

David's pacing with the PHONE in his hand. Risa's in bed,
reading a BOOK about the opera star RICHARD TUCKER.

                    DAVID
          I do that kind of thing all the
          time.

                    TRACEY
But it's part of a larger pattern.
She can't find the right words for
things. And she keeps forgetting
stuff and asking me to repeat it.

                    DAVID
She did that tonight. You... Do
you think she could've had a
stroke?

                    TRACEY
It's possible. But there's no
paralysis, no slurred speech.
Don't you usually get that with a
stroke?

                    DAVID
I thought so. But then again, what
do I know about strokes? She's
walking fine, and she looks good.
Scarfed down her dinner tonight in
record time. You think the new
blood pressure medicine could be
affecting her?

                    TRACEY
What new medicine?

                    DAVID
Her doctor changed her medication a
couple of weeks ago. She mentioned
it to me.

                    TRACEY
I didn't know that. Fuck! I
thought she was on top of all that.

                    DAVID
Me too. I mean, I've never even
talked to her doctor. Maybe we
need to get more involved.

                    TRACEY
Definitely.

                    DAVID
Okay, look. As I said, she seems
strong. Healthy, physically.
Maybe the thing to do is for me to
go down to Palm Desert when we get
back. Go with her to see her
doctor, hear first hand what she
has to say about this.
                    (MORE)

                    DAVID (cont'd)
And if her doctor thinks we should
do some tests, I will stay for
those, too.

                    TRACEY
What kind of tests?

                    DAVID
I don't know. Blood work. MRIs.
Whatever we need to do to get to
the bottom of this.

                    TRACEY
Agreed. I may come down to the
desert, too.

                    DAVID
Okay, then we have a plan of
action. That makes me feel better.

                    TRACEY
Oh, hey, how did it go last night?

                    DAVID
I got a standing ovation.

                    TRACEY
No shit?

                    DAVID
     (laughs)
Yes, shit.

                    TRACEY
That's so great! You deserve it.
You sacrificed so much for so many
years. It's nice to see you
getting your due. I just wish Dad
coulda been there.

                    DAVID
Me too. How's the commercial
going?

                    TRACEY
The director's a flaming asshole.
But nothing I haven't dealt with
before.

                    DAVID
I'm sure you can handle him. Just
don't let him get inside your head.

                    TRACEY
          Easier said than done. But yeah,
          that's the goal. Okay, I'll talk
          to you when I finish this
          commercial and get back to
          California.

David hangs up. END INTERCUT. STAY WITH DAVID as he turns
to Risa.

                    DAVID
          You heard all that?

                    RISA
               (nods)
          How do you feel?

                    DAVID
          Better. I know you think it's
          nothing, but we need to be sure.

                    RISA
          I agree. You know her much better
          than me. If she doesn't seem like
          herself, you should definitely get
          her checked out.

David gets into bed with her. Risa puts her book down.

                    DAVID
          Could be that new blood pressure
          medicine, causing side effects.

                    RISA
          Then you'll talk to her doctor and
          change the medication.

                    DAVID
          Absolutely. I feel much better
          now.

                    RISA
          Me too.

He SWITCHES OFF THE LIGHT. The room plunges into blackness.
A long pause, then...

THE PHONE RINGS. A blurry-eyed David turns on the light.
Glances at the clock. 7:33 a.m. He answers it, struggling
to clear the cobwebs.

                    DAVID
          Hello?

                    PEG (ON THE PHONE)
          David. It's Peggy. You need to
          get over here right now.

                    DAVID
          What's going on?

                    PEG (ON THE PHONE)
          I don't know. But something's
          definitely wrong. She's in the
          bathroom. I've been waiting for my
          chance to call.

                    DAVID
          Okay. I'm on my way.

                    PEG (ON THE PHONE)
          Hurry, David.

                    DAVID
          I will.

He hangs up, jumps out of bed and frantically yanks on his
clothes. Has trouble getting into his pants.

                    DAVID (cont'd)
          Fuck!

Risa sits up.

                    RISA
          What's wrong?

                    DAVID
          Mom. Come on, we've got to get
          over to her hotel.

Risa gets up and begins to dress.

INT. W HOTEL - HALLWAY - DAY

David and Risa, both unbearably tense, step up to a hotel
room door. David gently knocks. After a moment, Peg
answers, dressed for the day, but her face drained by a
harrowing night.

                    PEG
               (hushed voice)
          She's in the shower. Come on in.

HAPPY BRT

INT. W HOTEL - GLORIA'S ROOM - DAY

They enter a posh hotel room with TWO QUEEN BEDS. The
BATHROOM DOOR is shut. Behind it, the SOUND OF RUNNING
WATER.

                    DAVID
               (softly)
          So what's going on?

                    PEG
          I don't know if she's had a stroke,
          or it's Alzheimer's --

                    DAVID
          Alzheimer's doesn't hit you all of
          a sudden, out of nowhere. This has
          only developed over the last month
          or so.

                    RISA
          You don't know that. You aren't
          with her all the time. Maybe she
          was able to hide her symptoms.

                    DAVID
               (to Peg)
          So what are the symptoms?

                    PEG
          She was up all night. Pacing.
          Packing and unpacking her suitcase.
          Wringing her hands. I mean,
          literally like this.

Peg imitates Gloria's hand wringing. It almost looks like a
caricature.

                    DAVID
          Did she say what was making her
          anxious?

                    PEG
               (shakes her head)
          Only that she wanted to go home. I
          kept telling her everything was
          fine. Then...

                    DAVID
          Then what?

                    PEG
          She called her house.

                    DAVID
          In Palm Desert?
               (off Peg's nod)
          But no one's there.

                    PEG
          She thought your father was. When
          he didn't pick up, she got even
          more agitated.

David's stomach plummets. Risa's face drains of color.

Suddenly, the bathroom door opens. Gloria emerges in a
luxurious terrycloth robe, her hair damp. She beams when she
sees David and Risa, displaying none of the angst Peg
described.

                    GLORIA
          Well, hello there! You ready to
          get some breakfast?

                    DAVID
          Um... in a while. How are you
          feeling, Mom?

                    GLORIA
          Terrific! I'm starved. Just give
          me a moment to get dressed.

She heads for her SUITCASE, which lies open on a FOLD-OUT
RACK, but David gently touches her arm.

                    DAVID
          Mom, wait. Sit down for a moment.
          We need to talk.

                    GLORIA
          What's wrong?

                    DAVID
               (gestures to the bed)
          Sit. Please.

                    GLORIA
          What?
               (to David and Risa)
          Have you two been fighting?

                    DAVID
          No. It's not that.

                    GLORIA
          What then?

                    DAVID
          We're concerned about you.

                    GLORIA
               (shocked)
          Me? What on earth are you talking
          about? I feel great.

                    DAVID
          Mom, you have not been acting
          normal.

                    GLORIA
          I don't understand.

                    DAVID
          You've been forgetful --

                    GLORIA
          Hah. Wait till you're my age.
          You'll see --

                    DAVID
          No, it's more than that. You use
          the wrong words for things, you
          don't know where you are sometimes,
          and Peg tells us you were up all
          night --

Gloria turns on Peg, her face puckered with anger.

                    GLORIA
          You've been talking to them behind
          my back? Telling them lies --

                    PEG
               (near tears)
          Glo, why would I tell lies about
          you? You're the best friend I have
          in this world. Remember how
          anxious you were last night?

                    GLORIA
          What are you trying to do, Peg,
          turn my own son against me?

                    DAVID
          It's not just Peg, Mom. We've all
          been noticing it. Risa, too.

Gloria's eyes shift to Risa.

                    RISA
          That's right. I have.

                    DAVID
          And Tracey. I talked to her last
          night on the phone, and she agrees
          we need to get you checked out.

                    GLORIA
          Checked out by who?

                    DAVID
          A doctor. We need to find out
          what's causing this.

Gloria struggles to understand.

                    GLORIA
          So you think something's wrong with
          my mind?

                    DAVID
          Yes, I do.

                    GLORIA
          Oh, I don't believe this! Of all
          the things. Can't believe you're
          pulling this on me.

                    DAVID
          No one's pulling anything. We're
          trying to help you.

David steps to the PHONE on a nearby DESK.

                    GLORIA
          Who are you calling? I don't want
          you worrying your father with this
          nonsense.

David freezes. Gloria shifts uneasily as she sees all three
of them staring at her with alarm.

                    GLORIA (cont'd)
          What? Land's sake, what did I say
          now?

                    DAVID
          Dad's been dead for more than a
          year.

Gloria blushes and becomes flustered.

                    GLORIA
          I know... I was only trying to
          say... Wait, who are you calling?

David has already dialed a number. He speaks into the phone.

                    DAVID
          Hello, this is David Weddle. I'm
          calling from Gloria Weddle's room,
          number 262. Gloria is my mother,
          and I think she may have had a
          stroke.

                    GLORIA
          A stroke? Oh, you've got to be
          kidding me!

Peg motions for Gloria to be quiet.

                    DAVID
          Do you have a doctor on call?...
          Oh, thank god. Could he come up
          here to examine her?

TIME CUT: CLOSE ON GLORIA'S EYE as a PEN LIGHT SHINES INTO
IT, CAUSING THE PUPIL TO CONTRACT.

                    DR. MOISE
          Now, again, follow the light as I
          move it.

DR. MOISE moves the light to the right and left. Gloria's
eye follows it.

                    DR. MOISE (cont'd)
          Very good, Gloria. Thank you.

Moise turns to the others, who have been waiting expectantly.

                    DAVID
          Well?

                    DR. MOISE
          Her pupils contracted normally and
          her eye movements are also normal.
          She's got good balance.
               (to Gloria)
          You are remarkably fit for a 63-
          year-old woman.

                    GLORIA
          So I'm okay.

                    DR. MOISE
          I did not say that. Your
          difficulty in answering some of my
          questions, your struggle to choose
          the correct words, and your
          confusion indicate something's
          wrong.

                    GLORIA
          With my brain.

                    DR. MOISE
          I think so.

                    GLORIA
               (agitated)
          Oh, that's great. Just great!

                    DAVID
          So what do we do?

                    DR. MOISE
          We need to run tests to pinpoint
          exactly what the problem is.
          I'm going to call the emergency
          room at Lenox Hill Hospital. It's
          the best in the city. They'll be
          waiting for her. I suggest you
          take her at once.

                    GLORIA
          The hospital? Oh, this is
          ridiculous.

                    DAVID
          No, it's not, Mom. We're going.

INT./EXT. TAXICAB - MANHATTAN - DAY

David and Gloria are in the back of the cab, headed for the
hospital. Gloria's now dressed. They pass RADIO CITY MUSIC
HALL. TOM JONES IS ON THE MARQUEE.

                    GLORIA
          Oh look! Tom Jones! My favorite!
          Did you get good tickets? I want
          to see him shake his baked potato!

                    DAVID
          No, Mom, we're not going there.

                    GLORIA
          (shocked)
     We're not?... Where are we going?

                    DAVID
     To the hospital.

                    GLORIA
     Why?

                    DAVID
     We need to have some tests done.

                    GLORIA
     What's wrong, honey? Aren't you
     feeling well?

                    DAVID
     Not tests on me. We need to do
     some tests on you.

                    GLORIA
     Me? But I feel perfectly fine.

                    DAVID
     No, you are not. Remember what the
     doctor said? We need to take some
     MRI's of your brain.

                    GLORIA
     My brain? Are you telling me
     something's wrong with my mind?

                    DAVID
     Yes. And we need to find out
     exactly what it is.

                    GLORIA
     Oh, for Pete's sake. I don't
     believe this. First you tell me
     we're going to see a show --

                    DAVID
     I never told you that.

                    GLORIA
     Yes, you did! Now you're pulling
     this stunt. Wait till your father
     finds out. He'll hit the roof!

                    DAVID
     Dad's dead, Mom. Remember?

                    GLORIA
               (struggles to remember)
          Dead... Oh, yes, of course...

Gloria's distracted as they pass TIFFANY'S JEWELRY STORE.

                    GLORIA (cont'd)
          Oh, look! Tiffany's. Can we stop?
          I want to get something for Tracey.

                    DAVID
          No. We need to get to the
          hospital.

                    GLORIA
          What hospital?

OFF DAVID, feeling the strain of this bizarre Beckett-like
conversation.

INT. LENOX HILL HOSPITAL - ER - DAY

Gloria is now lying in a hospital gown on a GURNEY. There
are SEVEN OTHER GURNEYS in the room, most of them occupied.
David stands beside her, tightly gripping the gurney's side
rail.

                    GLORIA
          I don't like this place. I want to
          go back to the hotel.

                    DAVID
          You can't.

                    GLORIA
          Why not?

                    DAVID
          Because we need to do some tests.

                    GLORIA
          What kind of tests?

                    DAVID
          I'll explain later. Right now I
          need to fill out your admission
          forms. So I want you to stay here
          and I'll be back as soon as I can.
          Okay?

                    GLORIA
          If you say so.

INT. LENOX HILL HOSPITAL - ADMITTING OFFICE - DAY

David sits in the small space, surrounded by glass windows
that look out on the LOBBY. On the other side of the desk
sits an ADMITTING CLERK.

                    ADMITTING CLERK
          Does she have insurance?

                    DAVID
          Yes. Blue Shield.

                    ADMITTING CLERK
          Can I please see her insurance
          card?

                    DAVID
          Of course. Let me just...

David rummages through Gloria's PURSE. Finds her WALLET.
Searches through a chaotic CLUSTER OF CREDIT CARDS, AN AUTO
CLUB CARD, HER MEMBERSHIP CARD FOR IRONWOOD COUNTRY CLUB --
but finds no insurance card. Shit! He opens another pocket
of the purse and finally locates it, his blood pressure
dropping as he hands it over.

                    ADMITTING CLERK
          Thank you.

As the clerk types the information into Gloria's computer
file, David's eyes drift up and he sees....

THROUGH THE WINDOW, Gloria walks out of the ER, through the
lobby, and onto the street.

                    DAVID
          Excuse me for a moment.

David races out to...

EXT. LENOX HILL HOSPITAL - DAY

David catches up to his mother, who is headed down the street
in her hospital gown. New Yorkers pass her without so much
as a glance. David grabs his mom's arm.

                    DAVID
          Mom! What are you doing? You have
          to go back --

                    GLORIA
               (indignant)
          I'm not staying in that place.
          It's disgusting.

                    DAVID
          You need to.

                    GLORIA
          Why?

                    DAVID
               (weary)
          I'll explain. Now, come on.

He gently guides her back to the hospital.

INT. LENOX HILL HOSPITAL - HALLWAY - MRI LAB - DAY

ON A WALL CLOCK THAT READS 4:30.

                    GLORIA
          How much longer?

REVEAL GLORIA'S GURNEY parked in the corridor outside a door
with a sign: **MRI LAB**. An exhausted and frazzled David stands
beside her.

                    DAVID
          I don't know. We have to finish
          these tests. Then, hopefully, a
          doctor will come and give us a
          diagnosis.

                    GLORIA
          For what?

                    DAVID
          Your condition.

                    GLORIA
          What condition? I feel fine.

                    DAVID
          Your mental condition.

                    GLORIA
          Mental...
               (quiet outrage)
          Are you trying to tell me there's
          something wrong with my brain?

                    DAVID
          Yes. That's what I'm telling you.

                    GLORIA
          Well, I never. I wish you had told
          me about this before.

                    DAVID
          I did tell you.

A PAIR OF ORDERLIES APPEAR.

                    ORDERLY
          Okay, we're ready for her.

One orderly opens the door to the MRI Lab. The other steers
Gloria's gurney toward it.

                    GLORIA
               (alarmed)
          Wait. Where are you taking me?

                    DAVID
          They're going to give you an MRI.
          It's just a test. It won't hurt.

                    GLORIA
          Don't leave me!

                    DAVID
               (to an orderly)
          Can I come?

The orderly shakes his head.

                    DAVID (cont'd)
          I can't, Mom. I'll see you
          afterward.

                    GLORIA
          Oh, I don't believe this. Of all
          the dirty...

She disappears into the lab. The orderlies shut the door
behind her. David feels relieved. He's been on his feet for
six hours, answering the same questions from his mother over
and over again. But the relief is quickly followed by a pang
of guilt.

INT. LENOX HILL HOSPITAL - GLORIA'S ROOM - NIGHT

A private room with A VIEW OF THE ILLUMINATED SKYSCRAPERS OF
MANHATTAN. David sits in a CHAIR beside his mother's BED.

On the TABLE before her is a PLASTIC TRAY OF FOOD: A SCRAWNY
BOILED CHICKEN BREAST, SHRIVELED PEAS, A FEW WITHERED HOME
FRIED POTATOES, and a SQUARE OF LIME JELLO WITH PIECES OF
FRUIT SUSPENDED IN IT. Gloria ignores the PLASTIC KNIFE AND
FORK, picks up the chicken breast with her hands, and takes a
bite.

                    DAVID
          How's it taste?
               (off Gloria swallowing)
          Is it good?

                    GLORIA
          No.

                    DAVID
          Would you like me to see if I can
          get you something else?

                    GLORIA
          When can I go home?

                    DAVID
          I don't know. We have to wait for
          the neurologist...

                    DR. COTTLE
          That would be me.

David turns to see DR. COTTLE stepping through the door with
a MANILLA ENVELOPE. He has curly brown hair and a set of
oversized tortoiseshell glasses.

                    DR. COTTLE (cont'd)
          Hello, I'm Dr. Cottle. Are you
          Gloria?
               (off her nod)
          Pleased to meet you.

                    GLORIA
          I want to go home.

                    DR. COTTLE
          I understand. Unfortunately, we
          can't let you go just yet.

                    DAVID
          I'm her son, David. Did you get a
          chance to review her MRI's?

                    DR. COTTLE
          I did.

Cottle removes a PAIR OF MRI TRANSPARENCIES from the manilla
envelope, places them on a LIGHT BOX ON THE WALL, and
switches it on so they can see cross sections of Gloria's
brain. He points to a DARK SHADOW ON THE LEFT SIDE.

                    DR. COTTLE (cont'd)
          See this dark spot here?

                    DAVID
          What is it?

                    DR. COTTLE
          Blood.

                    DAVID
          So she had a stroke?

                    DR. COTTLE
          That's what it looks like. It's
          located in the left temporal lobe --
          the part of the brain that
          processes language. That's why
          your mother has trouble
          communicating.

                    DAVID
          Is it causing her memory issues as
          well?

                    DR. COTTLE
          Probably.

                    DAVID
          So what do we do about it?

                    DR. COTTLE
               (to Gloria)
          We're going to put you on some
          steroids to reduce the
          inflammation. That should then
          allow the blood to get reabsorbed
          in your system.

                    DAVID
          How long will that take?

                    DR. COTTLE
          A few days. We're starting her on
          the steroids tonight. If we're
          lucky, we should see some
          improvement as early as tomorrow..

Tears of relief fill David's eyes.

                    DAVID
          Wow! That's great news! If it
          works, will I be able to take her
          on a plane back to California? I'd
          like to get her with her own
          doctors so they can supervise
          whatever rehab she needs.

                    DR. COTTLE
          Let's not get ahead of ourselves.
          We'll see what tomorrow brings.

                    DAVID
          Got it.

                    DR. COTTLE
          Okay, Gloria. I need to see some
          other patients, but I will look in
          on you tomorrow morning to see how
          you're progressing.

David effusively shakes Cottle's hand.

                    DAVID
          Thank you, Doctor. Thank you so
          much!

Cottle quickly disengages and turns for the door. David
pivots to Gloria, who's frowning.

                    DAVID (cont'd)
          You hear that, Mom?

                    GLORIA
          I want to go home.

                    DAVID
          That's what he's saying. If the
          steroids work, you can.

EXT. MARRIOTT HOTEL - DAY

A VALET, in a long coat with gold epaulettes, loads Risa's
LUGGAGE into a TAXI. David and Risa stand nearby.

                    RISA
          Any idea when you'll be back in
          L.A.?

                    DAVID
          If the steroids work, maybe a
          couple of days.
                         (MORE)

                    DAVID (cont'd)
               (betraying worry)
          If not...

                    RISA
          They'll work. You'll see.

                    DAVID
          At least we know what it is now.
          And it's treatable. Thank god for
          that.

The valet approaches Risa.

                    VALET
          All set, Ma'am.

David slips a $20 into the valet's gloved hand.

                    VALET (cont'd)
          Thank you, sir.

David and Risa kiss. She climbs into the cab and waves
through the open window.

                    RISA
          See you soon!

INT. LENOX HILL HOSPITAL - HALLWAY - GLORIA'S ROOM - DAY

David approaches the open door to his mother's room and sees
her talking with Dr. Cottle. Her gaze is clear and focused
and her voice strong and coherent.

                    GLORIA
          Do you think the plane flight made
          it worse?

                    DR. COTTLE
          It didn't cause the stroke, but it
          could have exacerbated your
          symptoms.

                    GLORIA
               (sees David enter)
          Hi, honey!

                    DAVID
          How are you feeling?

                    GLORIA
          Much better! A thousand percent.

                    DAVID
          That's great, Mom!

                    GLORIA
          You're telling me!

He hugs her, his spirits soaring.

                    DAVID
          Do you remember what you went
          through the last couple of days?

                    GLORIA
          Not really. It's pretty foggy.

                    DAVID
          We were here all day yesterday,
          doing tests. You asked me the same
          questions over and over again for
          more than 12 hours.

                    GLORIA
          I remember you standing there, but
          can't remember what we talked
          about. I am so lucky you got me to
          the hospital right away.

                    DAVID
            (to Cottle)
          So the steroids worked.

                    DR. COTTLE
          They did indeed.

                    DAVID
          When can I fly her home?

                    DR. COTTLE
          If she continues to improve,
          possibly Thursday.

                    GLORIA
          Thank God!

                    DR. COTTLE
          I've got other patients to see.
          We'll do another MRI this afternoon
          to determine what's going on in
          there. But from everything we're
          seeing here, I'm very optimistic.

David shakes his hand.

                    DAVID
          Thank you, Doctor. We so
          appreciate everything you've done.

Cottle nods and departs. David turns to his mother with a
huge grin.

                    DAVID (cont'd)
          Wow. What a difference a day
          makes.

                    GLORIA
          I'll say.

                    GLORIA (cont'd)
          I am so lucky. So, so lucky.

                    DAVID
          We all are.

INT. LENOX HILL HOSPITAL - HALLWAY - DAY

David's on a PAY PHONE.

                    DAVID
          ...I know, the steroids worked.
          The neurologist says I can fly her
          home Thursday.

                                        INTERCUT WITH:

EXT. ATOP A DESERT MESA - UTAH - DAY

Tracey is talking on a SATELLITE PHONE. A FILM CREW behind
her prepares another CAMERA SET-UP for a FORD BRONCO
commercial. GRIPS AND GAFFERS lug EQUIPMENT while the
director, CALEB, screams unintelligibly at a panicked COSTUME
DESIGNER. Tracey holds a finger in her other ear to block
out Caleb's spew of invective.

                    TRACEY
          So you don't think I need to come
          out there?

                    DAVID
          No. I'll get her back to Palm
          Desert, go with her to see her
          doctor on Friday, and find out
          where we go from there.

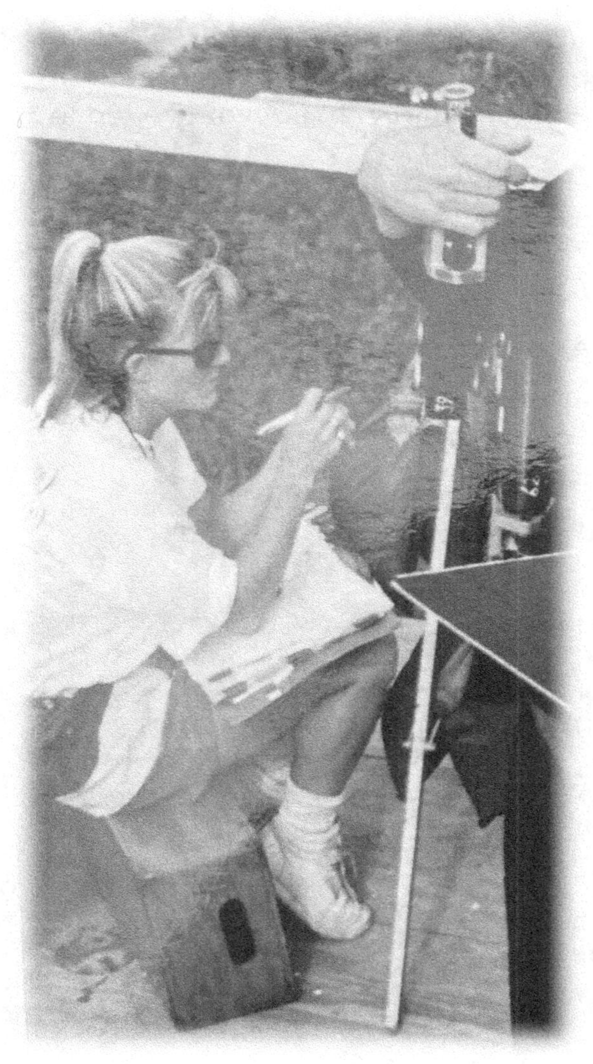

                    TRACEY
          I feel guilty that this all landed
          on you.

                    DAVID
          Why? I'm the one who invited her
          to come with me to New York. Have
          to take the good with the bad.

                    TRACEY
          But still --

                    DAVID
          Come see her when you get back to
          California. You can help
          coordinate whatever tests she
          needs, and figure out the next
          steps -- if she has to see some
          specialists, or start rehab --

                    TRACEY
          Whatever it takes to get her back
          to normal.

                    DAVID
          Exactly.

JEFF FORESTER, the assistant director, approaches Tracey.

                    FORESTER
          Caleb's ready to roll.

                    TRACEY
               (to David)
          Okay, I gotta go.

She terminates the call. END INTERCUT AND STAY WITH TRACEY
as she hands the phone to Jeff.

                    FORESTER
          You know how Caleb feels about
          personal calls from the set.

                    TRACEY
          Sorry, it was an emergency. Won't
          happen again.

As she walks toward the CAMERA, Caleb glares at her.

                    CALEB
          You done having phone sex?

                    TRACEY
          It was my brother.

                    CALEB
          Ooh, kinky. If it's all right with
          you, and not too much of an
          imposition, can we please roll now?

                    TRACEY
          Of course.

                    CALEB
          Awesome! Hey gang, Tracey's ready.
          Isn't that fantastic?

Tracey slides into her CHAIR beside the CAMERA, face red with
humiliation and sublimated anger.

INT. LENOX HILL HOSPITAL - HALLWAY - GLORIA'S ROOM - DAY

David approaches his mother's room. Her door is closed.
Outside it, Dr. Cottle stands with DR. ANTHONY MORENO (45) --
handsome, supremely confident, bordering on arrogant. Cottle
stiffens when he sees David.

                    DR. COTTLE
          Mr. Weddle, this is Dr. Moreno.
          He's the head of neurosurgery here
          at Lenox Hill.

David shakes Moreno's hand, sensing tension.

                    DAVID
          Hi. What's up?

                    DR. MORENO
          Mr. Weddle, I've had a look at your
          mother's latest MRIs and I'm sorry
          to tell you she has a brain tumor.

David's face flushes. Pinpricks of sweat start on his
forehead as he fights a surge of nausea. His eyes shift to
Cottle, hoping he will somehow contradict this.

                    DAVID
          But you said --

                    DR. COTTLE
          I was wrong. Dr. Moreno has a much
          greater level of expertise in these
          matters.

                    DAVID
                (quiet desperation)
          Can I still take her home Thursday?
          I'd like to have her treated --

                    DR. MORENO
          Absolutely not. You put her on a
          plane, she could have a seizure.

David fights to maintain his composure.

                    DAVID
          So... uh... what do we do?

                    DR. MORENO
          Operate. As soon as possible.

                    DAVID
          Tonight?

                    DR. MORENO
          No, tomorrow morning. Come on down
          to my office so we can discuss it.

                    DAVID
               (shell shocked)
          Okay.

David follows Moreno down the hall, away from Cottle, who
wears an expression of profound regret. Pulse pounding in
his ears, David puts one foot in front of the other, too
overwhelmed to feel anything.

INT. LENOX HILL HOSPITAL - DR. MORENO'S OFFICE - DAY

A dark, wood-paneled room. Moreno sits behind a polished
MAHOGANY DESK. David sits opposite. In the center of the
desk is a PLASTIC BRAIN ON A SMALL STAND. At the front of
the desk is a PLACARD: **ALL FEES MUST BE PAID IN ADVANCE.**

Moreno takes a gleaming STAINLESS STEEL PEN and points to a
section of the brain.

                    DR. MORENO
          The tumor's located here, in the
          left temporal lobe.

                    DAVID
          Is it malignant?

                    DR. MORENO
          We won't know until we do a biopsy.
          I suspect it's a secondary tumor.
          The cancer probably originated
          somewhere else in her body then
          metastasized and spawned this one.

                    DAVID
               (despondent sigh)
          Swell. Where do you think it
          started?

                    DR. MORENO
          Probably in one of her breasts. We
          see this quite often. Breast
          cancer spawns tumors in the brain
          and elsewhere. The good news is
          it's treatable with radiation and
          chemotherapy. Her chances of
          survival are quite good.

                    DAVID
               (anxiety easing)
          Thank god for that... So... are you
          going to tell her all this?

                    DR. MORENO
          I think you should be the one to
          tell her.

Sweat beads on David's pale forehead.

                    DR. MORENO (cont'd)
          You okay?

                    DAVID
          No. But... I'll do it... It's
          just...

                    DR. MORENO
          What?

                    DAVID
          My father died of lung cancer a
          year and a half ago. Mom was just
          putting her life back together, and
          now this.

Moreno's expression softens to something approaching empathy.

                    DR. MORENO
          Boy, you've really been through it,
          haven't you?

                    DAVID
          Yeah.

                    DR. MORENO
               (back to business)
          Anyway, the first step is removing
          this tumor and doing a biopsy.
                              (MORE)

                    DR. MORENO (cont'd)
          You can arrange payment with my
          receptionist.

A DROP OF SWEAT cuts a lethargic path down David's right
temple as he wonders if this means instant bankruptcy. But
he tries to sound calm.

                    DAVID
          Okay... uh, how much is that going
          to be, exactly?

                    DR. MORENO
          Ten thousand. That's for my
          services.

                    DAVID
          What about the rest of your team?
          The anesthesiologist, and the --

                    DR. MORENO
          We'll bill your insurance. But I
          need my fee up front. Then we'll
          send the paperwork to your
          insurance and they'll reimburse
          you.

                    DAVID
          Got it. Thanks.

David shuffles out the door as Moreno punches some numbers on
the keypad of his PHONE.

INT. LENOX HILL HOSPITAL - GLORIA'S ROOM - DAY

David stands before his mother. He's just updated her.
Gloria struggles to come to terms with it.

                    GLORIA
          A tumor? In my brain?

                    DAVID
          That's right.

                    GLORIA
          But Dr. Cottle said it was a
          stroke.

                    DAVID
          Apparently there was so much
          inflammation and blood in the first
          set of MRIs, he couldn't see the
          tumor. This Moreno is one of the
          best neurosurgeons in the country.
                    (MORE)

                    DAVID (cont'd)
          I believe he knows what he's
          talking about.

                    GLORIA
          So he's going to cut open my head?
          Into my brain?

                    DAVID
               (nods)
          To remove the tumor. Then he'll
          sew you up. He says the recovery
          time is pretty quick. We should be
          able to fly home in a week or so.

                    GLORIA
          I'll be stuck here for another
          week?

                    DAVID
          I'm afraid so.

                    GLORIA
          And there may be more tumors in my
          breasts, or Lord knows where?

                    DAVID
          Yes. But the others should be
          treatable with chemotherapy and
          radiation. He thinks you stand an
          excellent chance of making a full
          recovery.

OFF GLORIA, wanting to believe this.

INT. LENOX HILL HOSPITAL - HALLWAY - DAY

David's on the PAY PHONE.

                    DAVID
          I think you should get on a plane
          ASAP. They're operating on her
          tomorrow morning.

                                        INTERCUT WITH:

EXT. ATOP A DESERT MESA - UTAH - DAY

Tracey's on the SATELLITE PHONE. The commercial CREW and
FORD BRONCO are in the background.

                    TRACEY
          But I'm in the middle of shooting
          this commercial. I can't just walk
          off the set before they find
          someone to replace me.

Behind her, Forester, the AD, calls out.

                    FORESTER
          Tracey! We're waiting on you!

She waves him off.

                    DAVID
          I wouldn't ask you to do it if I
          didn't think it was important.

                    TRACEY
          Why can't we stick to our original
          plan? Wait till she gets back
          home, and then I'll --

The director, Caleb, is stalking toward Tracey, livid about
the delay. The other crew members move out of his way.

                    CALEB
          Tracey! What the hell are you
          doing?

                    DAVID
          Suppose there are complications
          during the surgery? Anything could
          happen, and if it does, you need to
          be here. If you're not, you'll
          never forgive yourself.

                    TRACEY
          Okay, okay. All right. I'll get
          on a flight tonight.

She terminates the call. END INTERCUT AND STAY WITH TRACEY
as she turns to find Caleb standing there, apoplectic.

                    CALEB
          Everyone's waiting on you. The
          script supervisor. Again. I know
          it's difficult to tear yourself
          away from your boyfriend, but --

                    TRACEY
          It was my brother. My mother's
          sick --

                    CALEB
          Don't pull the sick mother card on
          me. You think I give a damn about
          your Mommy? We have a film to
          finish.

                    TRACEY
               (explodes)
          FUCK YOU! YOU PREENING
          NARCISSISTIC PIECE OF SHIT! TAKE
          THAT CAMERA AND SHOVE IT UP YOUR
          ASS!

Caleb's knocked back on his heels. No one has ever talked
like this to him. The other crew members avert their gazes,
some to conceal their horror, others to conceal their grins.
Tracey walks away, calling over her shoulder to Caleb.

                    TRACEY (cont'd)
          And it's not a film, it's a fucking
          commercial. You haven't made a
          feature in five years, so stop
          acting like an auteur, because
          you're not and never were!

Chastened by her fury, and even a little turned on by it,
Caleb calls after her.

                    CALEB
          Wait, is your Mom really sick?

Tracey doesn't answer as she heads toward the BASE CAMP -- a
dusty collection of TRAILERS, TRUCKS, and LAND ROVERS. She
catches the eye of a TEAMSTER.

                    TRACEY
          I need a ride to the airport. Now.

                    TEAMSTER
               (smiles warmly)
          You got it, kid.

EXT. LENOX HILL HOSPITAL - DAWN

David climbs out of a TAXI. Grey light filters down through
the steel and stone spires of Manhattan. He glances across
the street at the warm welcoming light of a BODEGA and makes
his way along the CROSSWALK.

INT. BODEGA - DAY

David enters and checks his WALLET. He's down to a COUPLE OF
DOLLAR BILLS, but has a neat stack of TRAVELER'S CHECKS.
Turns to the CASHIER, servicing a LINE OF PATRONS.

                    DAVID
          Do you take traveler's checks?

                    CASHIER
          Sure.

                    DAVID
          Great!

David wanders down an aisle to a GLASS ENCLOSED PASTRY
CABINET with an ARRAY OF SWEET ROLLS. He slips a couple into
a PAPER BAG, then heads off to...

ANOTHER AISLE. A RACK OF REFRIGERATED BEVERAGES. David
grabs a BOTTLE OF FRESH SQUEEZED ORANGE JUICE. Heads to...

THE CHECK OUT LINE. David steps up to the cashier. As the
clerk rings up the items, David signs a $100 traveler's
check. Hands it to the cashier, who frowns.

                    CASHIER
          One hundred dollars? I can't cash
          that.

David glances at the customers lined up behind him, already
beginning to simmer with impatience.

                    DAVID
          Swell. Thanks.

David walks out of the bodega, leaving the items for the
cashier to re-shelve.

INT. LENOX HILL HOSPITAL - CASHIER WINDOW - DAY

David stands in another line of PEOPLE. The window's
operated by a dour woman, ALIA (40). Finally, it's his turn.
He steps up the METAL GRATE that allows him to speak to her.

                    DAVID
          Do you cash traveler's checks?
              (off her nod)
          Awesome.

He slides the check through the slit at the bottom of the
window. Alia peers at it, then looks up, eyeing David as if
he's a dangerous criminal.

                    ALIA
          You already signed it.

                    DAVID
          I know. You see, I --

                    ALIA
          It states quite clearly here on the
          check, "Must be countersigned in
          presence of payee."

                    DAVID
          Yes, I understand. But you see --

She starts to slide the check back through the slit, but
David blocks it with his palm.

                    DAVID (cont'd)
              (rapidly)
          Please. I'm from out of town. My
          mother's about to undergo emergency
          surgery. I tried to cash this at
          the market across the street. The
          clerk said he would cash it, but
          then he saw it was for $100, and
          refused --

                    ALIA
          That is not my --

                    DAVID
          I'm a stranger here, do not know
          the city, you would really be
          helping me if you cashed it. I
          need to get upstairs to surgery.
          I'll sign it again, if you want.
          See, here's my driver's license.

He slips his DRIVER'S LICENSE through the slit. Alia peers
at it.

                    ALIA
          This is a California license. Not
          valid here.

                    DAVID
          Okay, here's my passport.

He pushes his PASSPORT THROUGH THE SLIP. She scrutinizes
it, page by page.

                    DAVID (cont'd)
          Please, I want to see my mom before
          she goes into the operating room.
              (MORE)

                    DAVID (cont'd)
          If you could make an exception this
          one time, I would greatly
          appreciate it.

Alia examines the check for signs of counterfeiting, decides
it looks genuine.

                    ALIA
          Okay, This once. But in the
          future, you must sign in the
          presence of the payee.

                    DAVID
          I understand. Thank you.

She slides a $100 bill through the slit, along with his
passport and driver's license.

                    DAVID (cont'd)
          Thank you so much. Sorry for the
          inconvenience.

He rushes off to the ELEVATORS.

INT. LENOX HILL HOSPITAL - GLORIA'S ROOM - DAY

Tracey stands beside Gloria's bed as TWO NURSES unhook her
from the MONITORING EQUIPMENT.

                    GLORIA
          Can't believe you left your job and
          came all this way. I am so sorry --

                    TRACEY
          Don't be. I wanted to be here.

                    GLORIA
          Did your director understand?

                    TRACEY
          Oh yeah. I made sure of that.

                    GLORIA
          Where's David?

Tracey casts an anxious glance at her watch.

                    TRACEY
          I called him at his hotel this
          morning. He was on his way out the
          door. Must've gotten hung up in
          traffic.

                    GLORIA
          I hope he --

                    DAVID
          I'm here!

David arrives, sweating and out of breath.

                    DAVID (cont'd)
          Sorry. Tried to get some
          breakfast, but... Never mind. Not
          important.

                    NURSE
          Okay.   We're ready to go.

David and Tracey stiffen, exchanging an apprehensive glance
as the nurses wheel Gloria's bed out the door.

EXT. LENOX HILL HOSPITAL - CORRIDOR - SURGERY - DAY

The nurses wheel Gloria into a wide entry area before a set
of DOUBLE DOORS with a sign proclaiming: **NEUROSURGERY**. Dr.
Moreno awaits them.

                    DR. MORENO
          Hello, Gloria. You ready to do
          this?

                    GLORIA
          As ready as I ever will be, I
          guess.

                    TRACEY
          I'll see you on the other side,
          Mom.

                    GLORIA
          Okay, sweetie.

Tracey hugs her mother tight, struggling to contain her
tears. Then steps aside so David can hug her, too.

                    DAVID
          I'll be here when you come out.

                    GLORIA
              (emotional)
          Thank you, honey. For everything.

David nods, unable to muster more words.

The nurses wheel Gloria through the doors and she's gone.

Moreno lingers to talk to David and Tracey.

                    DR. MORENO
          The surgery should take about two
          hours. I'll do a biopsy
          immediately afterward. If you wait
          right here, I'll come out and give
          you the results.

                    DAVID
          We'll be here.

Moreno starts to turn away.

                    DAVID (cont'd)
          Does anyone ever die during a
          surgery like this?

                    DR. MORENO
          Not my patients.

                    DAVID
          Good to know. Thanks.

Moreno disappears through the double doors.

David and Tracey eyeball the stark space that they will
inhabit for the next couple of hours. Beige linoleum floor.
STRIPPED GURNEYS line the far wall. A blurry WINDOW stained
from decades of rain, snow, and smog. Not a couch or chair
in sight.

                    TRACEY
          Well, I guess there's nothing to do
          now, but wait.

                    DAVID
          Sorry I pressured you to come
          here...

Tracey waves off his apology.

                    TRACEY
          I'm glad you did. When I think
          about how she was always there for
          me as a kid, holding my head every
          time I threw up. With me in the
          hospital when I had my tonsils
          out...

                    DAVID
          And when I had my appendix out.
          She was there for two days
          straight. Didn't see Dad once.

                    TRACEY
          (trace of bitterness)
     God knows where he was... Anyway,
     I'm glad I could be here for her
     now.

                    DAVID
     Me, too.

David glances up at the clock. 8:06 a.m.

A HIGH ANGLE LOOKING DOWN at the two small figures of brother
and sister, looking very much alone in the sterile space.

TIME CUT: ON THE CLOCK, NOW READING 10:45 a.m.

Tracey stares out the grimy window at the fuzzy skyscrapers.
David lies on one of the gurneys, staring up at the green
plaster ceiling.

The surgery doors fly open. Tracey turns. David sits up.
Moreno appears in his scrubs. David slides off the gurney.
Brother and sister move to meet the surgeon, searching for
clues in his expression about how it went, but he's
impossible to read.

                    DR. MORENO
     Your mother came through the
     surgery just fine. She's in
     recovery and awake.

                    DAVID
     Did you do the biopsy?

                    DR. MORENO
     We did. It's not a secondary
     tumor.

                    DAVID
          (relieved)
     So it didn't metastasize from
     somewhere else in her body. This
     is the only one.

                    DR. MORENO
     Correct. It's a glioblastoma,
     which means it's growing out of the
     brain itself, so I couldn't get all
     of it without further damaging her
     brain.

                    TRACEY
     Glio... what kind of tumor is that?

                    DR. MORENO
          A Stage Four. Very aggressive,
          fast growing.

                    TRACEY
          Okay... uh... so how do we treat
          it?

                    DR. MORENO
          First thing you need to understand
          is that there is no cure. All we
          can do is try to impede the tumor's
          growth and buy your mother as much
          time as possible.

David and Tracey are shocked. They don't quite know how to
respond.

                    DAVID
          What... how?...

                    DR. MORENO
          The most common treatment is
          blasting it with a gamma knife.
          That sends a very highly
          concentrated, micro-targeted beam
          of radiation into the tumor to kill
          as much of it as we can. Then we
          follow this up with a daily regimen
          of Tamoxifen.

                    DAVID
          What are the side effects?

                    DR. MORENO
          The Tamoxifen will not cause any
          side effects. It's a mild and safe
          form of chemotherapy.

                    DAVID
          Okay... How much time will this buy
          her?

                    DR. MORENO
          A year. Maybe less. Maybe more.
          Perhaps as long as two years.
          Depends on the individual. But
          it's important for you to know that
          radiation does some collateral
          damage to the brain. So your
          mother will live longer, but with
          significant impairment.

                    DAVID
          How significant?

                    DR. MORENO
          Hard to say. It varies with each
          individual.

                    TRACEY
          What if we do nothing?

                    DR. MORENO
          She'll be dead in three months.

Tracey doubles over, as if punched in the stomach. Falls
back against the wall and slides to the floor, crying.

David struggles to stay focused. Moreno ignores Tracey and
addresses David.

                    DR. MORENO (cont'd)
          There is an alternative to
          radiation. I have a lab in
          Westchester County that's
          experimenting with new forms of
          chemotherapy. Now they're very
          aggressive, and might cause some
          severe side effects, but they could
          buy your mother more time. Are you
          open to exploring that option?

Tracey's convulsive sobs echo off the plaster walls and
ceiling.

                    DAVID
          Sure. Let's try it.

                    DR. MORENO
          Okay. I'll prepare a tissue sample
          from your mother's tumor that you
          can take to the lab. Now, would
          you like to see her?

Tracey's sobs slow. She looks up, her face wet with tears
and snot running down from her nose.

                    DAVID
          Yes. Have you told her all this?

                    DR. MORENO
          No. And don't tell her. It would
          be too much of a shock. Tell her
          tomorrow, after she's had time to
          rest.

                    DAVID
          Tracey, you want to come?

                    TRACEY
          Yes.

David offers his hand and helps her up.

Moreno leads them toward the double doors.

                    DR. MORENO
          Remember, keep it positive, for
          now.

INT. LENOX HILL HOSPITAL - RECOVERY AREA - DAY

Moreno leads them along a hallway.

                    DR. MORENO
          Make it brief.

They round a corner to a large room where A HALF-DOZEN POST
SURGERY PATIENTS are stationed on GURNEYS.

David and Tracey spot Gloria, sitting up, attached to an IV
and some MONITORING EQUIPMENT. The LEFT SIDE OF HER HEAD HAS
BEEN SHAVED AND A LARGE FRANKENSTEIN-LIKE SCAR runs up her
temple with THICK BLACK STITCHES, OOZING SMALL DROPS OF
BLOOD. Tracey and David swallow their horror and
overcompensate with manic grins.

                    DAVID
          Hi, Mom!

                    TRACEY
          Mom, you did great! It's all done!

They each briefly hug her.

                    GLORIA
          Am I okay?

                    DAVID
          Yeah, they took it out!

                    TRACEY
          You'll be able to go home soon!

Gloria sees the anguish in their eyes.

                    GLORIA
          You're not telling me everything.

David fights to maintain his composure as he pivots and heads
back the way he came.

                    DAVID
          Okay, we gotta go! See you when
          you get back to your room!

Tracey swiftly follows David out.

                    TRACEY
          See you soon, Mom!

                    GLORIA
          What aren't you telling me?

David and Tracey escape around the corner.

                    DAVID
          Jesus, that was...

He can't find words to describe it. They push through the
double doors to...

INT. LENOX HILL HOSPITAL - CORRIDOR - SURGERY - DAY

Moreno holds a SEALED TEST TUBE filled with BLACK BLOODY
TISSUE. He hands it to David.

                    DR. MORENO
          Here's the tissue sample. I've
          arranged for a limo to take you to
          my lab. It will pick you up in a
          half-hour outside the Park Avenue
          entrance. You'll need to pay the
          driver yourself, in cash.

INT. LENOX HILL HOSPITAL - CASHIER WINDOW - DAY

David's in a LINE OF PATRONS; the test tube protrudes from
his jacket pocket. Behind the glass is Alia, the same dour
woman he had to deal with earlier. At last, it's his turn.
David produces the $100 BILL she gave him this morning.

                    DAVID
          Can I please get five twenties for
          this?

Alia eyes the bill suspiciously as he slides it through the
slit in the glass. She holds it up to her DESK LAMP,
examining it for signs of counterfeiting as MORE PEOPLE line
up behind David.

                    DAVID (cont'd)
          That's the bill you gave me this
          morning.

Alia turns it over, examining the back. Tilts it this way
and that under the light, scrutinizing the green ink for
evidence of forgery. David erupts.

                    DAVID (cont'd)
          JESUS CHRIST! MY MOTHER'S DYING OF
          A BRAIN TUMOR AND YOU THINK I'M
          TRYING TO PASS A COUNTERFEIT BILL?
          UNFUCKING BELIEVABLE!!!!!!!!!!

His volcanic outburst echos through the plaster-lined hall,
drawing stares from the people behind David, and even from
those at the far end of the corridor. Alia cuts her
performance short and deals FIVE $20 BILLS through the slit
in the glass.

EXT. LENOX HILL HOSPITAL - PARK AVENUE ENTRANCE - DAY

It's a side entrance. David stands on a small set of stairs
outside the door, with the tissue sample in his hand.
Suddenly, he starts crying. Violent sobs wrench their way up
through his guts and out his tight throat.

AN ELDERLY COUPLE approaches along the sidewalk. They stop,
deeply concerned.

                    WOMAN
          Are you all right?

David nods.

                    WOMAN (cont'd)
          What's wrong?

                    DAVID
          My mom...

David can't get more words out.

                    WOMAN
          Do you need help? Want us to call
          someone?

David shakes his head and waves the couple away.

                    DAVID
          I'm okay.

                    WOMAN
          You sure?

David nods and they reluctantly move on. He stands there
weeping. A BLACK TOWN CAR pulls to the curb. David races
down the steps as the CHAUFFEUR LOWERS THE FRONT PASSENGER
WINDOW.

                    CHAUFFEUR
          Are you Mr. Weddle?

David nods and hops in the back. The chauffeur eases the
town car into the TRAFFIC on Park Avenue.

INT. TOWN CAR/EXT. WHITE PLAINS - NEW YORK - DAY

The limo passes a sign for **WHITE PLAINS, POPULATION 49,526.**
It's a leafy upstate New York town.

David sits in the back seat, holding the TEST TUBE with a
piece of his mother's brain tumor.

                    DAVID
          My mom was born here in Westchester
          County.

                    CHAUFFEUR
          No kidding. Whereabouts?

                    DAVID
          Irvington.

                    CHAUFFEUR
          Oh yeah, just up the road on the
          Hudson River.

                    DAVID
          I was born there, too.

                    CHAUFFEUR
          Nice wholesome little town. Kind
          of a main street U.S.A.

                    DAVID
          Not so wholesome, if you heard my
          mom's stories about growing up
          there.

                    CHAUFFEUR
          Huh. Well, every place has got
          skeletons in its closets, I guess.

                    DAVID
          How much farther to the lab?

                    CHAUFFEUR
          A couple of miles.

David pulls a SLIP OF PAPER from his breast pocket.

                    DAVID
          Okay, Dr. Moreno said I should have
          you call the lab when we're a few
          minutes away, so they can prepare
          to receive the sample. You mind
          calling them?

The Chauffeur reaches down to the LARGE CAR PHONE beside his
seat.

                    CHAUFFEUR
          Not at all. What's the number?

                    DAVID
          Area code 914, 264-7675.

The chauffeur dials the number and holds the receiver to his
ear as he comes to a halt behind a TOYOTA COROLLA at a STOP
LIGHT.

                    CHAUFFEUR
          Yes, this is Five Star Limousine
          service. We will be delivering a
          tissue sample in about five
          minutes. It's from a patient
          named...

                    DAVID
          Gloria Weddle.

                    CHAUFFEUR
          Gloria Weddle... Great. See you
          soon...

While talking, the chauffeur absent-mindedly lifts his foot
off the brake and the car drifts up against the Toyota,
giving it a soft nudge. The chauffeur hangs up his phone.

                    CHAUFFEUR (cont'd)
          Shit.

                    DAVID
          Did you hit it?

                    CHAUFFEUR
          Just barely.

A WOMAN leaps out of the Toyota, grimacing and gripping the
back of her neck.

                    CHAUFFEUR (cont'd)
          Jesus Christ.

The chauffeur puts vehicle in park and gets out. David,
still gripping the test tube with his mother's tissue, lowers
the window so he can hear the conversation. The woman
hollers in outrage.

                    WOMAN
          What the hell? You ran into me!

                    CHAUFFEUR
          I apologize, Ma'am. I just took my
          foot off the brake for a moment.

                    WOMAN
          Took your foot off? You smashed
          into my car! I'm lucky I didn't go
          through the windshield!

                    CHAUFFEUR
          Ma'am, your airbag didn't even go
          off.

                    WOMAN
          Do you deny you rammed my car?

David sits there with a piece of him mom's brain tumor,
unable to believe this is really happening.

                    CHAUFFEUR
          Rammed seems like a bit of an
          exaggeration, don't you think? I
          mean, I don't even see a mark on
          your bumper.

                    WOMAN
          You snapped my neck! I heard the
          vertebrae crack... Oh... oh my...

She puts her hand on the car to steady herself.

                    WOMAN (cont'd)
          I feel light-headed. Got shooting
          pains all the way down my neck.

                    CHAUFFEUR
          Really?

                    WOMAN
          Yes, really. Now, what do you
          intend to do about it?

                    CHAUFFEUR
          Well, I guess there's nothing to
          do, but exchange insurance cards.

                    WOMAN
               (taken aback)
          What?

                    CHAUFFEUR
          Exchange insurance information, and
          get each other's license numbers.

                    WOMAN
          Why should I give you my insurance
          card? You hit me. I didn't hit
          you.

                    CHAUFFEUR
          It's the law, Ma'am. We exchange
          insurance info and let our
          companies sort it out.

                    WOMAN
          But then they might raise my
          premium. I mean, even if it's not
          my fault. They do that, you know.

                    CHAUFFEUR
          Ma'am, we have to report it --

                    WOMAN
          Couldn't we just settle this
          between the two of us?

                    CHAUFFEUR
          How do you propose to do that?

                    WOMAN
          Give me $500 and we go our separate
          ways. Leave the insurance
          companies out of it.

                    CHAUFFEUR
          I'm sorry, Ma'am, but my employer
          will not allow me to do that.

                    WOMAN
          Don't tell them.

                         CHAUFFEUR
              I have to. If I don't, I could
              lose my job.

                         WOMAN
              But if it's just between the two of
              us --

The chauffeur has fished his INSURANCE CARD from his WALLET.

                         CHAUFFEUR
              Here's my card. May I please have
              yours?

                         WOMAN
                    (blanches)
              You know what? My neck's feeling
              better. Let's just forget the
              whole thing.

OFF DAVID, clutching the test tube, staring numbly at the
woman as she climbs back into her car.

INT. GLORIA'S HOUSE - PALM DESERT - DAY

The house is empty and dim. MOVE ACROSS THE UNLIT WALLS,
past AN OIL PAINTING OF A COWBOY with a weathered stetson, a
walrus mustache, and, incongruously, a pair of kind and
forgiving eyes. PAST another PAINTING OF A CLOWN with a red
face and a wide greasepaint grin. PAST a big GOLD-FRAMED
PICTURE OF GLORIA'S PARENTS, gazing into the camera with
rigid, stoic eyes. And beside it, A PORTRAIT of her parents
with their THREE DAUGHTERS. The youngest -- Gloria, just
five years old -- sits on her mother's lap in a simple white
dress, blond hair trailing to her shoulders. MOVE IN ON
GLORIA'S IMAGE, on her eyes staring past camera with a
melancholy gaze, as if even at five she senses the many
disappointments and heartaches life will inflict on her.

MOVE PAST THE PICTURE TO THE FRONT DOOR AS THE LOCK RATTLES.
The door opens and David steps in, flipping on the lights as
he drags a WHEELED SUITCASE across the tiled entryway.
Gloria enters behind him. She's dressed immaculately in a
colorful sweater, slacks, and a cloche hat to hide the scar
on her temple.

                         DAVID
              Here we are, Mom. Home sweet home!

                         GLORIA
              Oh, thank goodness!

                    DAVID
          Feel good to be back?

                    GLORIA
          I should say so.

She picks up a PILE OF MAIL that was slipped through the slot
in the door, and heads to the ANSWERING MACHINE on a table
near the entryway.

                    DAVID
          I'll put your bag in the bedroom.

Gloria sees the MESSAGE LIGHT blinking on the machine.

                    GLORIA
          Thank you, honey.

David continues on to...

INT. GLORIA'S HOUSE - BEDROOM - DAY

David wheels the suitcase in and lifts it onto a CHEST at the
foot of the BED. From the other room comes a BEEP and then
the first message on the answering machine.

                    PEG (RECORDING)
               Hey Glo, it's Peggy. Hope you had
               a nice flight. Would you and David
               like to come over for dinner
               tonight?...

David's gaze drifts to a PICTURE hung on the wall in a gold
frame. It's of his mother (55) with JAMES WEDDLE (66), taken
on their last trip together to the South Pacific. They are
tanned and relaxed. Jim has his shirt off, his cheeks
stubbled with grey. Even then he exuded a rugged charisma.
Gloria grips his thick chin with her thumb and index finger,
her eyes bearing the dreamy expression of a young bride on
her honeymoon.

                    PEG (RECORDING) (cont'd)
               I'll make my world famous spaghetti
               and meatballs, with garlic bread.
               Give me a call when you get in.
               Oh, I'm so happy you're back!

David's eyes travel to another, smaller FRAMED PHOTO on the
BEDSIDE TABLE, taken seven years later at the Five Crowns
steakhouse, the site of so many family dinners in the past.
Jim now looks emaciated, depleted of energy, his eyes bearing
the haunted look of a dying man.

Beneath the image is a caption, written in Gloria's neat
handwriting: **July 17th, 1993. Our 38th Anniversary.**

From the other room comes another BEEP from an the answering
machine, announcing another message, and then the deep voice
of a man.

                    MAN (RECORDING)
          Where are you? I'm here all alone.
          Hoping to reach you. But you're
          out on the town, I suppose...

The hairs rise on the back of David's neck. He heads back
to...

INT. GLORIA'S HOUSE - LIVING ROOM - DAY

David finds his mother standing rigidly beside the answering
machine, tears in her eyes.

                    MAN (RECORDING)
          Well, I just wanted you to know I'm
          thinking about you. Missing you.
          But I guess you've forgotten all
          about me...

THE RECORDING ENDS.

                    GLORIA
          Did you hear that?

                    DAVID
          Yeah... it's weird to hear his
          voice, after all this time.

                    GLORIA
          He sent me a message!

                    DAVID
          Uh... hold on...

                    GLORIA
          He did! I can absolutely feel it.

                    DAVID
          It's an old message.

                    GLORIA
          From more than a year ago? It just
          happens to be on the tape and never
          got erased? Waiting for me to come
          home? No way. I never heard it
          before. It's new!

David walks over to the machine, pulls out the TAPE CASSETTE,
and examines it.

                    DAVID
          You must have missed it, somehow.
          And by a fluke it never got erased.

                    GLORIA
          I know you don't believe these
          things, but I do. I totally do.
          He's reaching out to me.

David sees how much she needs to believe this, so he doesn't
argue.

                    GLORIA (cont'd)
          I know it because I had a dream
          last night.

                    DAVID
          What kind of dream?

                    GLORIA
          An Angel came to me and said: "Yea,
          though you walk through the Valley
          of the Shadow of Death, you will
          fear no evil, for thou art with
          me."

                    DAVID
              (shifts uncomfortably)
          Huh... well...

                    GLORIA
          That's from the 23rd Psalm. It was
          the first verse from the Bible that
          my mother taught me. The first
          verse I memorized. Don't you see?
          It's a message. Like the one from
          your father on the machine.

                    DAVID
          And what's the message?

                    GLORIA
          It's going to be okay. I don't
          need to worry because God's
          watching over me.

David sees how she has grabbed onto this like a lifeline.
Rather than shoot it down, he decides to go with it.

                    DAVID
          That's wonderful, Mom.

                    GLORIA
          It brings me such comfort. I'm not
          afraid anymore. Because I've
          realized all this happened for a
          reason. That plane ride to New
          York triggered me so they were able
          to find the tumor and save my life.
          It's like being reborn. A whole
          new beginning. A new life. I'm so
          lucky. So, so lucky...

ON DAVID'S CONFLICTED FACE. He's unable to muster an
affirmation, and unwilling to shoot it down...

                                        FADE OUT.

          <u>END OF EPISODE</u>

Be A Clown

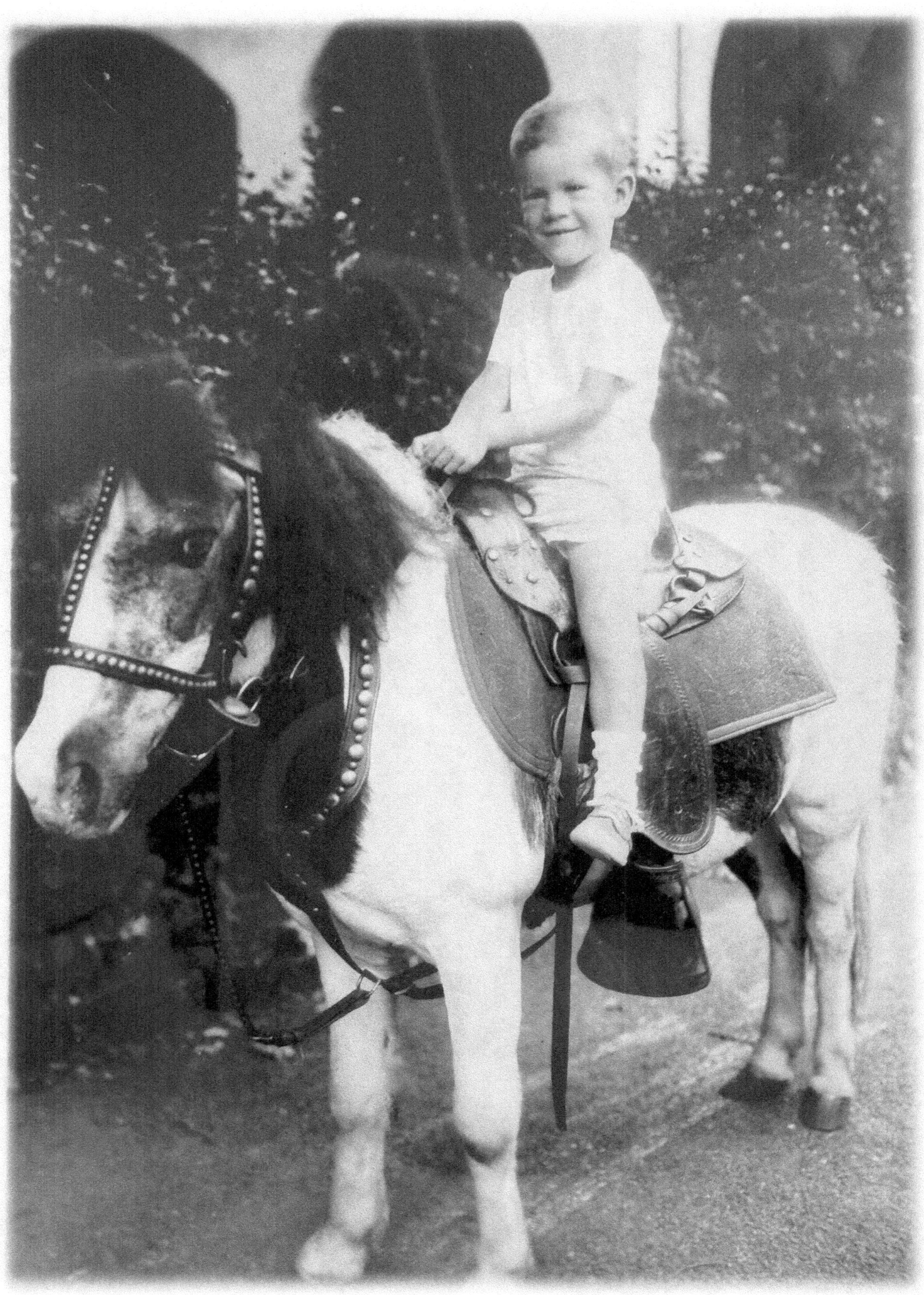

FADE IN:

EXT. CORONA DEL MAR - BACKYARD - DAY

An impossibly beautiful summer day in Southern California.
The sky brilliant blue, without a cloud on the horizon.
TANGERINE BUSHES weighed down with ripe fruit. MONARCH
BUTTERFLIES flitter among the blossoms. DAVID WEDDLE (39)
steps into frame, inhaling the citrus scented air. A DOG
BEGINS BARKING.

David turns to look deeper into the backyard. Beneath the
sprawling branches of a MASSIVE OAK TREE, a large gray
WEIMARANER barks at something on the other side of the fence.
He charges at the sound, bouncing off the ground as he
bellows. David regards him with wonder.

                    DAVID
          King... King, is that you?

King continues to bark at the perceived threat.

                    DAVID (cont'd)
          KING!

King turns, cocks his head and raises his silver ears, then
recognizes David and rushes toward him. Overjoyed, David
falls to one knee and throws open his arms.

                    DAVID (cont'd)
          King! Come here, boy!

King jumps into his arms, licking David frantically, emitting
small whines of happiness.

                    DAVID (cont'd)
          Oh my god, I thought you were...

A DOZEN TARNISHED DOG TAGS, from as many addresses, jangle on
King's LEATHER COLLAR.

                    DAVID (cont'd)
          I can't believe it... You've been
          in the backyard all this time? Oh,
          I've missed you so!

David pivots toward the patio's SLIDING GLASS DOORS that lead
into the house.

                    DAVID (cont'd)
          Mom! King's here! He's alive!

David rushes toward the doors.

                    DAVID (cont'd)
          He's been in the backyard all this
          time!

INT. WEDDLE HOUSE - LIVING ROOM - DAY

David enters to find GLORIA WEDDLE (33), young and as
beautiful as Grace Kelly, sitting on a FLOWER PRINT SOFA
beside TRACEY (5), her blond hair in a pixie cut.

                    DAVID
          Mom, Tracey, King's...

He notices their terrified expressions.

                    DAVID (cont'd)
          What are you guys doing?

                    TRACEY
          Waiting for Dad to come home.

                    GLORIA
          He'll be here any moment.

David sinks onto the sofa between them. Although he's an
adult, the news seems to shrink him until it looks as though
the couch may swallow him. His gaze follows theirs to...

THE FRONT DOOR. A TOWERING SLAB OF OAK. MONOLITHIC.
FOREBODING.

                    DAVID
          Is he in a good mood?

                    GLORIA
          I'm afraid not, children. In fact,
          your father's in a bad mood.

THE SLAB OF DOOR BEGINS TO TREMBLE, RATTLING ITS HINGES under
stress from a primeval force on the other side.

                    GLORIA (cont'd)
          A very, very bad mood.

                    DAVID
          I think I'll go to my room.

                    GLORIA
          Don't force him to come find you.
          It'll only make it worse.

THE DOOR RATTLES VIOLENTLY. THE WOOD BEGINS TO SPLINTER.

Gloria, David, and Tracey grip each other's hands

THE DOOR BLASTS OPEN WITH A TERRIBLE ROAR!

INT. DAVID'S TRAILER - LIVING ROOM - PARADISE COVE - DAY

David bolts upright and screams. He's on a FOLD-OUT SOFA BED
in his single-wide trailer.

                    GLORIA
          You okay, honey?

David turns toward his 63-year-old mother, who's making
breakfast in the small adjoining kitchen. Gloria's white
hair has grown over the DARK BLUE INCISION on her temple.
Her face is pale and has lost its fullness. A terrible
physical strain has drained her strength, but she still
manages a smile.

                    GLORIA (cont'd)
          What's wrong?

                    DAVID
          Nightmare.

                    GLORIA
          Come eat. You'll forget all about
          it.

David stumbles out of bed in a t-shirt and pajama bottoms.
Rubs his face, trying to wipe away the memory of his dream.

SUPER: **MAY, 1995**

IKEA BOOKSHELVES LINE ONE WALL, overflowing with chaotic
stacks of DUSTY VOLUMES by Steinbeck, Fitzgerald, Tolstoy,
Faulkner, Kesey, and tangles of movie books -- a weathered
history of silent movies, *THE PARADE'S GONE BY*, and multiple
editions about Buster Keaton, Charlie Chaplin, Laurel and
Hardy, and Jerry Lewis. A 30-inch MITSUBISHI TV sits on a
low table opposite the couch. A STEREO AND TURNTABLE rest
beside it.

Over the couch hang THREE PORTRAITS OF A WIZENED AND WEARY
BUSTER KEATON, taken when he was 70, by Roddy McDowell.

David shuffles into the kitchen to a BLOND WOOD TABLE with a
white enamel top, where his mother has placed a PLATE OF
SCRAMBLED EGGS, BACON, AN ENGLISH MUFFIN, and A GLASS OF
ORANGE JUICE.

                    DAVID
          This looks great, Mom. Thanks.

Gloria settles into the chair opposite him. She's uneasy,
embarrassed.

                    GLORIA
          I had a little problem.

                    DAVID
          What do you mean?

                    GLORIA
          I woke up and got to thinking about
          that funny movie you showed me last
          night.

                    DAVID
          Young Frankenstein.

                    GLORIA
          Yes! And it got me laughing.

                    DAVID
          Good. You gotta keep laughing.
          Keeps your spirits up, you know?

                    GLORIA
          Yes... Only I laughed so hard, I
          had a little accident.

                    DAVID
          What do you mean?

INT. DAVID'S TRAILER - BEDROOM - DAY

Gloria's open SUITCASE sits on a table. Some of her CLOTHES
and MAKEUP ITEMS rest on the dresser. She's been staying
here for some time. Gloria leads David into the room and
points to the bed. THE SHEETS AND MATTRESS PAD have been
balled into a jumble.

                    GLORIA
          I'm so sorry. It's only because I
          got to laughing so hard and
          couldn't stop.

David feels the sheets. THEY'RE SOAKED WITH URINE.

                    GLORIA (cont'd)
          I didn't mean to. It's just that I
          ...

                    DAVID
          It's okay, Mom. These things
          happen. I'll wash them. No big
          deal.

But as Gloria watches him pick up the bedding, she's consumed
with shame.

                    GLORIA
          It's only 'cause I got laughing so,
          thinking about --

                    DAVID
          I understand. Tell you what. Why
          don't you take a walk out to the
          bluff to your favorite bench. And
          look out at the ocean. That always
          makes you feel better, right?

                    GLORIA
               (brightens)
          Oh it does. It brings me... such
          peace. I can't even tell you.

                    DAVID
          Then go do that, and I'll take care
          of this and wash the dishes, okay?

                    GLORIA
               (smiles)
          Okay, honey.

EXT. DAVID'S MOBILE HOME - DAY

Gloria exits David's trailer and carefully makes her way down
the four steps to the driveway. She wears white linen
slacks, a colorful flower print blouse, a broad-brimmed straw
hat, and large sunglasses.

EXT. PARADISE COVE STREET - DAY

Gloria makes her way toward the edge of a bluff that
overlooks the brilliant blue ocean. She passes a gray-haired
MAN in his 60s, wearing plaid pants and a bright yellow
shirt. She beams excitedly.

                    GLORIA
          Jim! When did you get back?

The man's expression darkens and he veers around her.

seek mystery,
evoke mystery,
plant a garden
in which
strange plants grow
and mysteries bloom.

-Ken Kesey

                    GLORIA (cont'd)
          Jim? Where are you going?

                    MAN
          My name's not Jim.

                    GLORIA
          Since when?

He walks quickly away from her.

                    AUDREY
          Gloria?

Gloria pivots to find a thick, ruddy-cheeked Irish-American
woman, AUDREY (65), approaching. Gloria grins like a kid.

                    GLORIA
          Oh, hello nice lady, how are you?

Audrey takes Gloria's trembling hands.

                    AUDREY
          Out for a little walk?

                    GLORIA
          I should say so! To my bench.

                    AUDREY
          Well, it's a lovely day for it. I
          just saw a pod of dolphins out
          there. If you hurry, you might
          still see them.

                    GLORIA
          Oh, my lord, I love them so!

Gloria hurries onward, toward the bluff.

INT. DAVID'S TRAILER - OFFICE - DAY

The office is a small room that overlooks the street.
David's seated at a plain wooden desk that holds a KAYPRO
DUAL FLOPPY DISC DRIVE COMPUTER. On the wall beside him is a
huge PICTURE OF AUTHOR KEN KESEY standing before his
psychedelic school bus. Beneath the image is a quote from
Kesey: **"The answer is never the answer. What's really
interesting is the mystery. If you seek the mystery instead
of the answer, you'll always be seeking. I've never seen
anybody really find the answer -- They think they have, so
they stop thinking.**

But the job is to seek mystery, evoke mystery, plant a garden
in which strange plants grow and mysteries bloom. The need
for mystery is greater than the need for an answer."

David is on a WIRELESS PHONE.

                    DAVID
          It's just... the radiation
          treatments ended three weeks ago,
          but she seems to be getting worse.

                              INTERCUT WITH:

INT. TRACEY'S KITCHEN - DAY

TRACEY ladles STEAMED MILK into a CUP OF COFFEE. She looks
out at the LARGE SWIMMING POOL in her backyard.

                    TRACEY
          Dr. White told us that would
          happen.

                    DAVID
          Told us what would happen?

                    TRACEY
          The radiation continues to kill her
          brain tissue even after the
          treatments have stopped.

                    DAVID
          I don't remember hearing that.

                    TRACEY
          Well, that's what he said.

                    DAVID
          For how long? I mean, how much
          more damage will it do?

                    TRACEY
          Don't know. He was somewhat vague
          about that.

                    DAVID
          Of course, because if he told us
          the truth we never would've done
          the radiation and he wouldn't have
          been able to bill Mom's insurance
          for $250,000. All he cared about
          was --

                    TRACEY
          Okay, if you go on this rant again,
          I'll hang up.

EXT. PARADISE COVE BLUFF - DAY

Gloria arrives at her favorite BENCH, on the lip of the bluff
overlooking the shimmering expanse of the Pacific. She
settles down unsteadily, raises a trembling hand to adjust
her sun glasses, then sighs, letting her tension flow out
across the water.

                    GLORIA
          So... beautiful.

INT. DAVID'S TRAILER - OFFICE - DAY

David continues talking on the phone with Tracey.

                    DAVID
          Maybe we should have tried that
          experimental chemo that Moreno was
          pushing.

                                        INTERCUT WITH:

INT. TRACEY'S KITCHEN - DAY

Tracey gulps down the last of her latte.

                    TRACEY
          Have you forgotten what Dr. White
          said?

                    DAVID
          That it was highly toxic and might
          kill her.

                    TRACEY
          So why bring it up?

                    DAVID
          Because I can't help feeling White
          was just manipulating us.

                    TRACEY
               (losing patience)
          Jesus, come on, David.

always
Red Skelton

                    DAVID
          You really think it's so
          outlandish? He pushed radiation so
          he could make a quarter million off
          our Mom. He didn't give a shit if
          it was the right way to go, he just
          wanted the money, so he lied to us
          and we --

Tracey slams her phone down. END INTERCUT.

David hears a DIAL TONE, sets his phone in its cradle and
wishes he had restrained his temper. His eyes drift over to
a SMALL FRAMED PHOTO hanging beside his desk. It is of a
dapper television comedian, taken in the early 1960s, and
autographed in elegant penmanship: "Always, Red Skelton."
MOVE IN ON THE PICTURE.

EXT. CORONA DEL MAR ELEMENTARY SCHOOL - PLAYGROUND - DAY

Half of the playground is asphalt, with TETHER BALL POLES, a
BASKETBALL COURT, DODGE BALL CIRCLES, HOP SCOTCH GRIDS, and a
SET OF MONKEY BARS. The other half is a dirt expanse leading
to a BASEBALL BACKSTOP.

It is recess, and KIDS are playing all over the vast area.
MOVE TO EIGHT-YEAR-OLD DAVID WEDDLE -- skinny, physically
awkward, with bright red hair -- talking to another third
grader, JIM HILLIARD, who has dark hair and olive skin.

SUPER: **1964**

                    JIM HILLIARD
          How long did you live in
          Pennsylvania?

                    DAVID
          One year.

                    JIM HILLIARD
          Where'd you live before that?

                    DAVID
          Ohio.

                    JIM HILLIARD
          How long did you live there?

                    DAVID
          A year.

                    JIM HILLIARD
          And before that?

                    DAVID
          Irvington. That's in New York.

                    JIM HILLIARD
          Let me guess. You lived there a
          year.

                    DAVID
          Yeah.

                    JIM HILLIARD
          How come you move so much?

                    DAVID
          My Dad keeps getting better jobs.

                    JIM HILLIARD
          That's good.

                    DAVID
          Yeah. I like to keep moving.

                    JIM HILLIARD
          Why?

                    DAVID
          I've already had three best
          friends. Most kids only ever have
          one.

Another kid, DOUG DIETZ, hurries past them with a COUPLE MORE
BOYS.

                    DOUG
          Okay, we're ready, Jim. Let's go!

                    JIM HILLIARD
          Okay!

                    DAVID
             (to Jim)
          Where you going?

                    JIM HILLIARD
          To the fire engine. We're gonna
          pretend it's a space ship.

                    DAVID
          Like *Fireball XL-5*?

                    JIM HILLIARD
             (smiles)
          You like that show? It's my
          favorite!

                         DAVID
               Mine too.

From the way David smiles back it's clear he's hoping Jim
will become his new best friend.

                         JIM HILLIARD
               Then come on!

David follows Jim toward a corner of the playground where a
GROUP OF KIDS stand around a tarnished 1930s era FIRE ENGINE.
Its wheels have been removed and it sits on a GIANT BLACK
RUBBER PAD.

                         DAVID
               Where'd you guys get that fire
               truck, anyway?

                         JIM HILLIARD
               The fire department gave it to us,
               on account of it's so old. They
               thought we'd like to play on it.

                         DAVID
               Wow, that is so cool.

Jim stops and turns to David with a frown.

                         JIM HILLIARD
               We don't say "cool" here. It's
               corny and old fashioned.

                         DAVID
               Uh, okay. So what do you say?

                         JIM HILLIARD
               When we like something, we say it's
               "boss."

Jim leads him to the kids around the fire engine.

                         JIM HILLIARD (cont'd)
               Hey, guys. This is David. He's
               from Pennsylvania. He wants to
               play space ship with us. That
               okay?

                         DOUG
               Sure.

Another kid, MARK, grins warmly.

                         MARK
               Fine by me.

                    BRAD
          No way!

BRAD CASEY -- taller than the other kids, blond and blue-eyed
-- jumps down from the driver's seat of the fire engine,
landing firmly on his feet. The other boys fall instantly
quiet and tense up. Brad strides toward David.

                    BRAD (cont'd)
          We don't want no carrot tops on our
          ship.

He stabs a couple of thick fingers into David's skinny chest.

                    BRAD (cont'd)
          Get me, Red?

The other kids take their cue from Brad, friendly expressions
curdling into hostile grins.

                    DOUG
          Hey, look, even his face is turning
          red.

                    MARK
          Just like a tomato.

Brad jabs David's chest with his fingers -- harder this time.

                    BRAD
          You hear what I said, Red?

David nods.

                    BRAD (cont'd)
          Then start making tracks.

David looks to Jim for support, but Jim has turned away.
David pivots and walks quickly across the dusty field as the
kids behind him chant: "RED! RED! RED!" They explode with
derisive laughter.

EXT. WEDDLE HOUSE - FRONT YARD - DAY

It is the ranch style home from the opening dream sequence.
The colors are a little less vibrant, but it still looks
idyllic under the cloudless powder blue sky. BIRDS squawk
and chirp in an OLIVE TREE. BUTTERFLIES flitter about in the
TANGERINE BLOSSOMS and BOUGAINVILLEA BUSHES. A FLAG POLE
towers above the driveway, THE STARS AND STRIPES FLUTTERING
IN A LIGHT BREEZE. A huge craggy ROCK sits on the front
lawn. From the backyard comes the sound of KING BARKING.

INT. WEDDLE HOUSE - BATHROOM - DAY

David is alone in the bathroom with the door shut. He sits
before a SPACE HEATER INSET INTO THE WALL and holds TWO
PLASTIC ARMY MEN. David does the voice of the army man in
his left hand.

                    DAVID
          I'm going in.

He does the voice of the army man in his right hand.

                    DAVID (cont'd)
          Careful, Steve, the core could
          still be radioactive.

Does the voice of the army man in his left hand.

                    DAVID (cont'd)
          I know, Dallas, but I must
          deactivate it before it destroys
          the ship.

David carefully inserts the first army man through the grill
of the space heater, then switches it on. The metal coils
begin to glow. David does the voice of the army man in his
right hand.

                    DAVID (cont'd)
          Look out, Steve!

THE HOT YELLOW COILS BEGIN TO MELT THE ARMY MAN IN THE SPACE
HEATER. David does his voice.

                    DAVID (cont'd)
          AAAAIIIIEEEEE!

David watches with grim satisfaction as THE ARMY MAN BEGINS
TO BUBBLE.

                    DAVID (cont'd)
               (to himself)
          Boss...

The knob on the bathroom door jiggles. BANG! BANG! BANG!
Someone pounds on the door.

                    TRACEY (O.C.)
          David! Open up! I gotta tinkle!

In a sudden panic to conceal his crime, David flips off the
space heater.

                    TRACEY (O.C.) (cont'd)
           DAVID!   OPEN THE DOOR!

                    DAVID
           Give me a minute, will ya?

David flips on the CEILING FAN to suck up the fumes from the
burnt plastic.

                    TRACEY (O.C.)
           What're doing in there?

                    DAVID
           Pooping!   Use the other bathroom!

                    TRACEY (O.C.)
           I can't!   Mom's in there!

David uses a TOOTHBRUSH to scoot the scorched army man out of
the space heater.

                    TRACEY (O.C.) (cont'd)
           You're always pooping.   Give
           someone else a chance!

David throws the maimed army man in the toilet and flushes it
down.

                    TRACEY (O.C.) (cont'd)
           DAVID!   I'M GONNA HAVE AN ACCIDENT!

David whips the door open on...

INT. WEDDLE HOUSE - BATHROOM/HALLWAY - DAY

Tracey (5) wears a blond pixie cut, a flowered blouse, and
pink shorts. Her nose crinkles in disgust.

                    TRACEY
           Augghhh!   Your poopies stink worse
           than King's.

David slides past her into the hall. Tracey slams the
bathroom door.

INT. WEDDLE HOUSE - DEN - DAY

ON A 26-INCH G.E. COLOR TELEVISION. FIREBALL XL-5, a
miniature space ship on wires, fires up its engines, which
look suspiciously like a pair of SPARKLERS. SOUNDS OF
ROCKETS BLASTING reverberate in the set's solo speaker on the
right of the console.

The ship roars along a pair of rails that arc upward until it gains speed, soars free of Earth, and catapults to the stars.

                    DAVID
          Boss...

REVEAL David lying on the shag carpeted floor, enraptured.

                    GLORIA (O.C.)
          David! Dinner!

                    DAVID
          But Mom, *Fireball XL-5* is on!

                    GLORIA
          I said now! Your father just
          pulled into the driveway.

David casts a forlorn glance at the screen where A PAIR OF MARIONETTES -- blond, cleft-chinned COLONEL STEVE ZODIAC and a glowing transparent mechanical man, ROBERT THE ROBOT -- handle the craft's steering wheels.

                    STEVE (ON TV)
          I don't like the look of that
          planet, Robert. We better go down
          for a closer view.

                    ROBERT THE ROBOT (ON TV)
               (synthetic voice)
          Roger, Steve.

David hears the FRONT DOOR OPENING and quickly switches off the set. The picture collapses to a tiny blue dot and snuffs out altogether.

INT. WEDDLE HOUSE - DINING ROOM - DAY

CLOSE ON A ROAST AS A CARVING KNIFE slices off a juicy succulent piece.

                    JIM
          Gloria, you've outdone yourself
          once again.

REVEAL JAMES WEDDLE (44), a six-foot-three ex-marine with powerful hairy forearms, broad shoulders, a muscular chest, and the beginnings of a formidable pot belly. He's almost handsome enough to be a movie star -- except for his large gnarled nose, which has been broken several times.

Jim finishes cutting off the slice of beef, forks it onto a plate and hands it to a young and ravishing Gloria (33).

Gloria sets the plate down before TRACEY and spoons some
SPINACH and MASHED POTATOES onto it. She's pleased by Jim's
compliment.

                    GLORIA
          It's a new cut. The butcher calls
          it "watermelon roast." It was
          quite reasonably priced.

                    JIM
          Looks almost as delicious as you.

Gloria grins as she extends another plate and Jim places
another slice on it. There's a powerful sexual dynamic
between them.

                    GLORIA
          You sure about that? Maybe you
          should take a bite before you
          render a final judgement

Jim smiles, slaps his broad hand onto Gloria's ass and
squeezes hard. She emits a little yelp.

                    GLORIA (cont'd)
          Ouch. Jim, you hurt me.

But she's obviously titillated. They smile at each other for
a beat, both basking in the glow of their nuclear family.
Gloria sets the plate down before David. He eyes the meat
suspiciously, poking at it with his KNIFE and FORK. Gloria
frowns.

                    GLORIA (cont'd)
          There's not an ounce of fat on
          that, David.

But David has found a small blob. It may not be an ounce,
but it is too much for him to bear. He initiates surgical
procedures to remove it.

                    GLORIA (cont'd)
          Oh, for Pete's sake. Your sister
          eats all her fat.

Tracey senses an advantage over her brother and presses it.

                    TRACEY
          I love fat, Mommy. Can I have some
          more?

                    DAVID
          It makes me gag.

                    GLORIA
          Stop being so dramatic. For the
          life of me, I don't know how you
          ended up such a picky eater.

Jim -- who is now seated, along with Gloria -- spoons spinach
and mashed potatoes onto his plate beside his two slices of
roast. He notes David's morose expression and feels some
sympathy.

                    JIM
          Fat's an acquired taste. Give him
          time.

                    GLORIA
          He ends up giving half his meat to
          the dog.

Jim notices King sitting patiently beside David, licking his
moist lips.

                    JIM
          No wonder King's so fond of you.
          You're his biggest benefactor.

David eyes the piece of meat on his fork, examining it from
all angles to make sure a stealthy piece of fat isn't hiding
somewhere.

                    JIM (cont'd)
          So, David, how did you like your
          first day at the new school?

                    DAVID
          I didn't.

Gloria and Jim exchange a worried glance.

                    JIM
          How come?

                    DAVID
          The other kids.

                    JIM
          What about them?

                    DAVID
          They call me "Red."

Gloria winces, as if personally experiencing her son's
humiliation.

                    GLORIA
          Oh, honey, I'm sorry. It's 'cause
          you're new.

                    DAVID
          No. It's because I have this
          stupid red hair. I hate it.

                    JIM
          David, look at me.

David apprehensively meets his father's eyes.

                    JIM (cont'd)
          Do you know that one of the most
          famous comedians in the world is a
          man named Red Skelton?

David forgets his fat phobia and listens intently.

                    JIM (cont'd)
          In fact, Red Skelton is a great
          artist. A pantomimist admired the
          world over. So when those kids
          call you Red, you say to them,
          "Thank you for the compliment.
          It's an honor to share the
          spotlight with the great Red
          Skelton."

David stares back at his father, slowly absorbing the
implications.

INT. WEDDLE HOUSE - DEN - NIGHT

CLOSE ON THE G.E. COLOR TV as A FLORID GRAPHIC fills the
screen featuring RED SKELTON in the guises of his many zany
characters -- the punch drunk boxer, Cauliflower McPug;
Southern con artist, San Fernando Red; and hobo, Freddie the
Freeloader, in circus clown makeup. A MUSICAL FANFARE WORTHY
OF A BIGTOP CIRCUS.

                    ANNOUNCER (ON TV)
          And now, live from Hollywood, it's
          The Red Skelton Hour! With Red's
          special guests Vincent Price and
          Carol Lawrence, the Redette
          Dancers, and David Rose and his
          orchestra!

REVEAL DAVID lying on his belly in his cowboy pajamas, chin
propped up by the palms of his hands as he drinks in every
nuance.

                    ANNOUNCER (ON TV) (cont'd)
               And now, here's the star of our
               show... Red Skelton!

ON THE TV: A TELEVISION STAGE. THE RAINBOW CURTAIN PARTS.
Tall and lanky RED SKELTON (50) strides forward to THUNDEROUS
APPLAUSE. He wears a black tuxedo, his long glistening red
hair combed straight back. Red grins with impish delight and
claps along with the audience, like a child delighted with
the approval of the adults around him.

IN THE DEN: David smiles, liking him immediately.

ON THE TV: The applause dies. Skelton addresses the crowd.

                    RED SKELTON (ON TV)
               Good evening, ladies and gentlemen.
               I feel good tonight! I really feel
               good! A funny thing happened
               outside the theater tonight, just
               as I arrived. Someone shouted,
               "Hey, Red Skelton's in the crowd!"
               And the people went wild. You
               never saw such pandemonium. I was
               so embarrassed... I was almost
               ashamed I shouted it.

IN THE DEN: David laughs, wiggling closer to the screen so he
won't miss a single detail.

ON THE TV: Red pulls out a LARGE COMB.

                    RED SKELTON (ON TV)   (cont'd)
               Pardon me while I fix my hair.

He meticulously runs the comb through his shiny locks,
combing every strand back to gleaming perfection.

                    RED SKELTON (ON TV) (cont'd)
               That's better.

He slips his comb into his breast pocket, then sneezes,
jerking his head forward and whipping his long hair over his
face in a chaotic tangle.

IN THE DEN: David howls with laughter, pounding his fist into
the shag carpet and writhing in comedic ecstasy.

ON TV: Red Skelton turns toward the wing of the stage.

                    RED SKELTON (ON TV) (cont'd)
               Hey, can I please have my hat?

A BIG FELT FEDORA flies out of the wing. Skelton reaches for
it, but pretends to miss it. The hat falls to the floor.

IN THE DEN: David laughs, eyes shining with affection.

ON TV: Skelton picks up the hat, dusts it off, and looks into
the wing at the unseen stage hand.

                    RED SKELTON (ON TV) (cont'd)
          You're new here, ain't ya?

Skelton turns back to the audience.

                    RED SKELTON (cont'd)
          Hey, did you ever notice how
          dramatic movie stars get whenever
          they get to do a dying scene? You
          can tell they're thinking: "This is
          it! I'll finally get my chance to
          win an Oscar!" So they overact,
          chewing the scenery like it's made
          of peppermint candy. Here, I'll
          show you what I mean. First,
          there's the gangster picture, where
          the star always has to die for his
          crimes in the final reel. And, oh
          brother, does he die!

IN THE DEN: MOVE IN on David's glistening eyes as he absorbs
the action on the screen, every synapse of his young mind
firing as he begins to sense the possibilities...

INT. WEDDLE HOUSE - ENTRYWAY - NIGHT

ON THE FRONT DOOR. A LARGE SLAB OF OAK, like the one in
David's nightmare, but this is smaller, scaled to human
dimensions. THE DOORBELL RINGS.

                    GLORIA
          Coming!

Gloria approaches the door in a long white dress with a
single strand of pearls around her neck, hair coiffed in an
elegant bouffant. She opens the door to greet TOM "FITZ"
Fitzpatrick and his wife, DARLENE. Tom (40) wears horn-
rimmed glasses, a gray sports jacket, his hair slicked into
place by generous portions of Vitalis. Darlene wears a black
cocktail dress with a fur wrap, her bouffant sprayed to
static perfection. They smile stiffly, their manner self-
conscious.

                    GLORIA (cont'd)
          Well, hello, hello! Welcome to our
          humble abode!

Jim appears behind her wearing checkered slacks, a bright
yellow shirt, and a gregarious grin. David and Tracey enter
behind him, dressed up for the guests, excited and curious.

                    JIM
          Fitz, you magnificent bastard!

Jim's bombastic manner assaults the couple's formal exterior.
He pumps Fitz's hand furiously.

                    JIM (cont'd)
          Look at you, all slicked up like
          Adolphe Menu with a hair lip. And
          Darlene, you look like a young Cyd
          Charisse tonight.

                    DARLENE
             (blushes)
          Oh, Jim, stop it.

                    JIM
          It's the truth. Better keep a
          close eye on her, Fitz, or I'll
          snatch her away from you.
             (to Darlene)
          Here, let me take your wrap, you
          won't be needing that tonight.

Jim takes her fur wrap and her purse and hands them to David.

                    JIM (cont'd)
          David, take her things and put them
          in our room on the bed.

                    DAVID
          Yes, sir.

As David moves off to the hall, Jim claps Fitz on the
shoulder.

                    JIM
          What you need, my friend, is a face
          tightener.

                    FITZ
          Lead the way.

                    JIM
          Step over to my alter and we shall
          ingest the sacrament.

INT. WEDDLE HOUSE - MASTER BEDROOM - NIGHT

David hustles in and places the fur and purse on his parents'
KING SIZED BED. The room is tastefully decorated in pastel
tones.   AN OIL PAINTING OF THE GREAT CIRCUS CLOWN EMMETT
KELLY hangs the wall. THE DOORBELL RINGS AGAIN. Excited,
David rushes back out to...

INT. WEDDLE HOUSE - ENTRYWAY/LIVING ROOM - NIGHT

David appears as his mother greets another couple at the
door.

His father has moved to a SWEDISH FOLD-OUT BAR in the living
room. It has elegantly polished wood doors, a black slate
top, and is filled with a vast array of booze -- JOHNNY
WALKER SCOTCH, JACK DANIELS WHISKEY, STOLICHNAYA VODKA,
DRAMBUIE, and an assortment of TEQUILAS, COGNACS, BRANDIES,
and SAKE. Jim makes drinks for Fitz and Darlene as he
recounts a recent adventure. David is captivated by the
passion in his father's voice.

                    JIM
          Oh, god were we stoned. You coulda
          used our blood for embalming fluid.
          Ken says, "Let's see what this baby
          can do." So I swerve off the road
          right onto the 18th fairway and
          floor it.

                    DARLENE
               (laughs)
          Jesus, Jim, you could've hit
          somebody.

                    JIM
          At three in the morning? Not a
          soul out there. But tell you what
          was there. Pine trees.

                    FITZ
               (laughs)
          Oh no.

                    JIM
          Oh yes. So this tree jumps right
          in front of my car. I swerve to
          avoid it, but the sucker was too
          fast for me.

                    FITZ
          Pine trees are like that. Much
          quicker than oaks.

                    DARLENE
               (titters)
          Don't tell me you --

                    JIM
          Sideswiped it. Took the entire
          wood panel off the station wagon.

                    DARLENE
          Did you hurt yourself?

                    JIM
          You kidding? Ken and I were so
          vulcanized we just bounced around
          like a couple of rubber balls.

Fitz and Darlene laugh as they accept their drinks. Fitz
takes a sip. The skin on his face pulls tight around the
contours of his skull.

                    FITZ
          Jesus, Jim, that ate the enamel off
          my teeth! What'd you put in this?

                    JIM
          Just a dollop of aviation fuel with
          a splash of soda. You're flying
          the friendly skies tonight!

                    GLORIA
          David, come here, please.

David scurries to the ENTRYWAY, where Gloria has greeted HERB
PINTARD (45) and his wife, LOUISE (40). Herb has a flattop
haircut, a plaid jacket, and grey slacks. Louise wears a
flower print dress and a gold necklace with a jeweled
pendant. Gloria has already taken her coat and purse.

                    GLORIA (cont'd)
          David, please take Mrs. Pintard's
          things to our bedroom.

David takes the coat and purse past the living room where his
father has turned toward the new guests. David continues
down the hall.

                    JIM
          Herb, you old reprobate! You look
          like a Gladstone bag without a
          handle. Louise, darling, get your
          lovely dimpled ass over here!

INT. WEDDLE HOUSE - MASTER BEDROOM - NIGHT

A SERIES OF JUMP CUTS as David unloads another COAT AND
PURSE, and another onto the bed. RAUCOUS LAUGHTER
reverberates from the living room.

INT. WEDDLE HOUSE - LIVING ROOM - NIGHT

David cautiously makes his way from the hall to the mouth of
the living room, where the adults sit in a semicircle on a
FLOWER PRINT COUCH and some STRIPED VELOUR CHAIRS. They
include Fitz and Darlene, Herb and Louise, PEG SHAW (45),
BILL (39) and LAVONNE GARNER (42). Jim sits in a LARGE
OVERSTUFFED CHAIR, holding court while Gloria moves silently
about, emptying ASH TRAYS and refreshing PLATTERS OF SALAMI,
CHEESE, and TRISCUITS.

                    JIM
          Oh, my mother was tough. Rocky
          Marciano wouldn't have lasted one
          round against her. She woulda
          pounded him into stew meat.

Everyone laughs except Gloria, who continues her tasks with
solemn inward eyes.

                    JIM (cont'd)
          My favorite position as a kid, was
          this --

Jim falls into a crouch, holding his arms up to protect his
head.

Everyone laughs except Gloria.

David moves cautiously to his father's side.

                    JIM (cont'd)
          That woman was obsessed with
          cleanliness. She'd scrub the paint
          right off the walls. Literally
          scrubbed it down to the plaster!
          Covered all the furniture in our
          parlor with white sheets. And put
          a cloth runner across the rug.
          Whenever we walked through the
          parlor we had to stay on that
          runner.

                    HERB
               (laughs)
          My Mom and Dad did the same thing.

                    JIM
          And God help us if we strayed from
          the runner. Went to school many a
          time with a black eye or
          cauliflower ear. And then the
          bathroom. We weren't allowed to
          take a shower 'cause we'd get water
          spots on the tile. Had to take
          baths, and be careful not to
          splash.

                    LOUISE
          What happened if you stained the
          tile?

                    JIM
          Oh brother. Remember this one
          time, she came at me with a mop
          handle. I bobbed and weaved like
          Floyd Patterson. She missed, hit
          the tile, and vibrated like a
          cartoon character.

                    PEG SHAW
               (laughs heartily)
          Wish I coulda seen the expression
          on her face.

                    JIM
          No, you don't! See, she cracked a
          tile with that mop handle.

                    FITZ
          Uh-oh...

                    JIM
          Uh-oh is right. She went crazy as
          turpentined cat. Whirls, chases me
          out the bathroom and down the hall
          to the back porch. As I fly out
          the door, she swings again, misses
          me and hits the door frame, lands
          flat on her back, and I get away
          clean down the alley.

The others laugh and applaud -- all except Gloria.

                    JIM (cont'd)
          Well, I missed dinner that night.

                    LAVONNE
          She sent you to bed without it?

                    JIM
          Hell no! I didn't dare set foot in
          that apartment until she went to
          sleep. Stood in the alley,
          shivering, waiting for the light in
          her bedroom window to go out.

                    LOUISE
          Interesting parenting techniques.
          I wonder what Dr. Spock would say
          about that.

                    BILL
          He'd have to admit, she was larger
          than life.

                    GLORIA
          So is King Kong.

Everyone turns to look at her. Jim's gaze is sharply
pointed. Gloria shrugs uncomfortably.

                    GLORIA (cont'd)
          She's still alive. And she's a
          real charmer.

Gloria disappears with an HORS D'OEUVRE TRAY into the
kitchen. Jim gazes after her and is about to say something
when David nudges him.

                    DAVID
               (softly)
          Dad.

Jim swivels his eyes to his son.

                    JIM
          Yeah, David.

                    DAVID
          Can I do my dying act?

                    JIM
               (perplexed)
          Your what?

                    DAVID
          I have an act where I die. Can I
          do it for everyone?

                    JIM
          Now?

David nods. Jim turns to the guests, who are engaged in
small talk.

                    JIM (cont'd)
          Listen up, everyone.

The others fall silent and turn to him. Peg continues
talking with Herb.

                    JIM (cont'd)
          You too, Peggy.

They all look at Jim.

                    JIM (cont'd)
          David would like to do his dying
          act for us.

There are titters of amusement. David freezes, suddenly
anxious.

                    JIM (cont'd)
          Well, what are you waiting for?
          You've got our undivided attention.

David swallows dryly then launches into it.

                    DAVID
          Did you ever notice how dramatic
          movie stars get when they do a
          dying scene? They overact like
          crazy. I'll show you what I mean.
          First, there's the gangster
          picture, where the star gets
          machine gunned. It goes something
          like this...

David falls into a crouch, gripping an imaginary pistol and
speaking like a cartoon version of Edward G. Robinson.

                    DAVID (cont'd)
          You want me coppers? Come and get
          me!

David pantomimes shooting his pistol, making gunshot noises.

                    DAVID (cont'd)
          Come get some, coppers! Come and --

Suddenly, David makes machine gun sounds. He jerks violently
about the room as imaginary bullets pierce his body, then
staggers in a caricature of a death dance. The partygoers
erupt with laughter.

Loudest of all is Jim, bellowing above the others, inspiring
David to go further as he spins and careens. A final volley
of imaginary machine gun bullets sends him flying. He falls
on his back on the shag carpet, twitching and gasping and
finally lying still.

The guests burst into applause. David leaps to his feet and
bows, experiencing a flash flood of adrenaline. Jim steps
over to his son, wiping tears from his eyes.

                    JIM
          What a pratfall! Worthy of Buster
          Keaton himself.

                    DAVID
          Who?

                    JIM
          I'll tell you later. That was
          beautiful, David.

David beams, basking in the warm glow of his father's
approval. He glances at his mother, in the doorway to the
kitchen. She smiles then turns away, stepping through the
door to prepare the dinner.

INT. WEDDLE HOUSE - DAVID'S ROOM - NIGHT

ON AN ELECTRIC WESTCLOX on the bedside table. It reads ONE
AM. David lies asleep. A MODEL OF A FIREBALL XL-5 SPACESHIP
dangles from the ceiling. A CORK BOARD ON HIS CLOSET DOOR
features pictures of GEMINI SPACECRAFT, and AN AUTOGRAPHED
PICTURE OF ROCKY MARCIANO posing in his trunks and boxing
gloves, with the inscription: *To Dave. Your Pal, Rocky!*

Also on the bedside table is AN ARRAY OF PLASTIC ROMAN
SOLDIERS, ordered from a comic book. THEY BEGIN TO VIBRATE
AND FALL OVER because of the SOUND emanating from the living
room. HERB ALPERT'S TIJUANA BRASS blasts *THE LONELY BULL.*

David tosses and turns. Pulls the pillow over his head to
try to blot out the sound. Suddenly, the stereo falls
silent. David relaxes. Finally, he hopes, the ordeal has
ended. But no, the stereo resumes, cranked even louder as
the percussive beat of THE DRUMS OF BORA BORA rocks the
house, punctuated by the guttural cries of Polynesian drum
masters. And louder still, the Dionysian shouts from his
father.

                    JIM (O.C.)
          Come on, Herb! Your turn! Get up
          and shake that thing. You may
          never pass this way again!

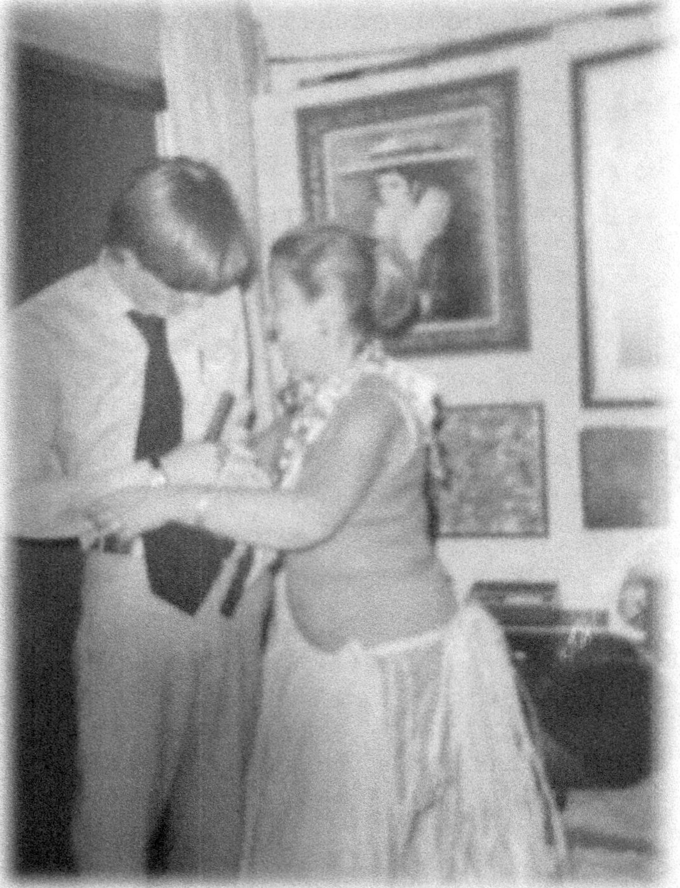

MEXICO

DRUMS OF BORA BORA
THE EXCITING DRUMMERS OF BORA BORA • WORLD FAMOUS TAHITIAN PERCUSSIONISTS AND THEIR EXCITING ISLAND RHYTHMS
and Songs of Tahiti
A BLEND OF THE OLD CHANTS, BALLADS AND SOUTH PACIFIC JAZZ FEATURING NATIVE DRUMS, NOSE FLUTE, GUITARS AND CLARINET
LP TT-1600
RECORDED IN
WIDE RANGE
HI-FI
IN TAHITI
BY GARZON GUILBERT

David gives up all efforts to sleep. Drawn by his father's
ecstatic cries, he slips out of bed and steps to his bedroom
door, opening it a crack.

                    JIM (cont'd)
          Wait! Hold on! Let me get my
          hats!

David watches through the door crack as his father rushes
into the hallway and yanks open a storage cabinet stacked
with every imaginable chapeau -- STETSONS, MEXICAN SOMBREROS,
BULLFIGHTER CAPS, JET FIGHTER HELMETS, BERETS, FEDORAS,
VIKING HELMETS, LONDON BOBBY HELMETS, FUR-LINED HUNTING CAPS,
and on and on. Jim fills both arms with them and rushes back
to the living room.

David eases his door wider, gets down on his belly and snakes
along the hallway with the stealth of French Resistance
fighter to the entrance of...

INT. WEDDLE HOUSE - LIVING ROOM - NIGHT

The Fisher Stereo, ensconced in a walnut cabinet, spins an LP
that rocks the room with pagan sounds of the South Pacific.
The partygoers have been transformed by the hats Jim plopped
on their heads. Darlene has become a French cabaret singer;
Herb, a Viking Warrior; Louise, a London bobby; Bill, a
Mexican bandit; Lavonne, a lady fighter pilot; Fitz, a
bullfighter.

In the center of the room, Peg Shaw wears a grass skirt,
undulating provocatively before each of the men. Jim grabs
Fitz's arm and yanks him to his feet, shoving him toward
Peg's shimmying hips.

                    JIM
          Come, Fitz! Let's see some moves!
          Show her what you've got!

Fitz wiggles and jerks his thick body, seeking oneness with
the tempo of primitive Polynesia.

DAVID, on his belly in the hall, drinks it all in with huge
hungry eyes -- spellbound by the way his father has
transformed their prosaic suburban home into a realm of
wonder.

EXT. WEDDLE HOUSE - DAY

Another idyllic Southern California day, identical to the
last one.

                    GLORIA (PRE-LAP)
             All right, Jim. Time to get up.

INT. WEDDLE HOUSE - MASTER BEDROOM - DAY

Jim lies in bed, semiconscious in the tangled sheets. An
amused Gloria, David, and Tracey stand beside him, dressed
for day.

                    GLORIA
             Let's go. I'm going to start
             breakfast.

Jim rolls onto his back, moaning, playing up his hangover.
Tracey shakes his arm.

                    TRACEY
             Come on, Daddy. Mommy's gonna make
             pancakes.

Jim moans melodramatically, his voice thick and nasal.

                    JIM
             Never again.

Gloria and the kids laugh. This is a beloved ritual.

                    DAVID
             Dad, we're starving.

                    JIM
             I mean it. This is the last time.
             Oh, feel like the Russian army
             marched across my tongue in their
             stockinged feet.

The others laugh affectionately.

INT. WEDDLE HOUSE - MASTER BATHROOM - DAY

There are two porcelain sinks set in a white formica counter.
Jim stands before the left one in checkered boxer shorts,
face covered in SHAVING CREAM. He picks up a DOUBLE-EDGED
RAZOR.

David appears in the doorway.

                    DAVID
             Can I shave with you?

                    JIM
             Sure. Hold on.

Jim opens the medicine cabinet, takes out ANOTHER DOUBLE-
EDGED RAZOR. Unscrews the handle so the blade compartment
opens. Removes the BLADE, screws the compartment closed
again, and hands it to his son.

          JIM (cont'd)
     There you go, Chief. Here, use
     this stool.

Jim slides a STEP STOOL up to the sink. David stands on it.
His father sprays shaving cream onto his broad calloused palm
then carefully applies it to David's face.

          JIM (cont'd)
     Okay. All set.

Jim begins to shave. David watches him and carefully
duplicates his movements, scraping cream from his face and
swishing it off in the sink full of warm water.

          JIM (cont'd)
     Hey, I got something I wanna watch
     with you today.

          DAVID
     What's that?

          JIM
     A Buster Keaton movie. Found it in
     the *TV Guide.*

David remembers his father mentioning Keaton last night.

          DAVID
     So who is this Keaton guy, anyway?

          JIM
     Why, only the greatest clown of all
     time.

          DAVID
     Better than Red Skelton?

          JIM
     Oh yeah. In fact, he taught
     Skelton everything he knows.

          DAVID
     What makes him so great?

          JIM
     Well, for one thing, he took
     amazing pratfalls.
          (MORE)

                    JIM (cont'd)
Stunts that no one -- not Charlie
Chaplin, or Harold Lloyd, or Laurel
and Hardy -- would ever dare try.
He'd fly off the tops of buildings,
moving trains, and cars. Hit the
ground so hard you'd think he would
never get up again. They called
him The Great Stone Face.

                    DAVID
How come?

                    JIM
Because no matter how crazy the
action got, no matter how
outlandish, he never smiled. Just
remained stoic and determined to
endure whatever misfortunes life
threw at him. Never tried too hard
for a laugh by mugging it up. And
he was the ultimate perfectionist.

                    DAVID
How do you know that?

                    JIM
Well, one time, years ago, I saw
him do a routine live on stage.
Believe it or not, Buster Keaton
came to my home town, McKeesport,
Pennsylvania, to perform at the
Memorial Theater in 1926. And my
father took me to see him.

                    DAVID
And he was great?

                    JIM
The greatest pantomimist I've ever
seen. He took a fall into the
orchestra pit. Jesus, you woulda
thought he broke his neck. The
audience howled like a pack of
rabid hyenas. But Keaton wasn't
satisfied. We were sitting in the
front row. And as he climbed out
of the pit I heard Keaton mutter to
himself, "Well, that stunk."

                    DAVID
But I thought you said he was
great.

                    JIM
          He was! He was fantastic! Laughed
          so hard I almost wet my pants.
          But, see, it didn't matter that the
          audience loved it. Keaton wasn't
          satisfied, because he knew he
          coulda done better.

David scrapes more foam from his cheek as he absorbs the
implications.

INT. WEDDLE HOUSE - DEN - DAY

ON THE G.E. TELEVISION is a black and white BUSTER KEATON
COMEDY, *COPS*, ACCOMPANIED BY A JAZZ SCORE.

David and Jim are on a CHECKERED COUCH, watching together.

ON TV: A wide boulevard. Deserted. Not a moving vehicle or
living thing in sight. Suddenly, at the far end of it, a
tiny figure rounds a corner and runs full tilt toward camera.
As he draws closer, his features become more distinct: a
porkpie hat, oversized slap shoes, a vest and a clip-on tie.
Why is he running, this solitary figure, down a vast corridor
of street in this ghost city? Then, the answer: around the
corner behind him comes a stampede of policemen. Hundreds of
cops, flooding the boulevard with black uniforms, all of them
after this one man, Buster Keaton.

IN THE DEN: Jim roars with laughter. David's shoulders pump
up and down, his open mouth emitting a high pitched scream of
hilarity.

ON TV: The chase continues through the brick and concrete
labyrinth of an early 20th Century city.

Keaton flees down a narrow alley with the cops right behind
him, their faces gripped with homicidal rage. Buster dashes
from the alley to a street suddenly thick with traffic.
Stops and turns to face the cops who are closing fast.
Sticks his arm out as a car passes and grabs the door handle.
The car whisks him off his feet and away from the clutches of
the police.

IN THE DEN: David gasps in wonder.

                    DAVID
          Oh my god! How'd he do that?

                    JIM
          Only one way he could, by doing it
          for real.
                    (MORE)

                    JIM (cont'd)
          You see how that car swept his feet
          out from under him? Means the car
          had to be going fast.

David's eyes are wide, drinking in every nuance of the film.

ON TV: The car rounds a corner and slows. Keaton jumps off,
landing right between two cops. They swing their billy clubs
at him but miss, hit each other over the head instead, and
collapse on the sidewalk, unconscious.

IN THE DEN: Jim releases a great howl of laughter, like a
hurricane, a true force of nature, primal, impossible to
resist. David is swept away by it. He laughs so hard his
cheeks cramp, tears fill his eyes, and his face turns bright
red.

ON TV: Keaton dashes down another alley, the cops right
behind him. A tall ladder leans against a high wood fence.
Buster sprints up it. As he reaches the middle, the ladder
tilts like a teeter-totter that will enable him to climb down
the opposite side of the fence. But one of the cops leaps as
the end of the ladder rises and catches hold of it. Buster
climbs to the ladder's other end, pitting his weight against
the cop's. Several more police arrive and join the first
cop. They pull down collectively and Buster's end of the
ladder springs skyward, catapulting him over the heads of the
cops to the opposite side of the street.

IN THE DEN: Jim screams so loud the whole house seems to
vibrate. David falls to the floor in comic ecstasy and
crawls away, muttering in a strangled voice...

                    DAVID
          Can't breathe!... I need to...
          Can't take it...

Jim continues to howl with unhinged laughter, a cry that
seems to reach all the way to heavens.

INT. WEDDLE HOUSE - ENTRYWAY/KITCHEN - DAY

ON THE OAK FRONT DOOR. David enters with a CANVAS BACKPACK
FULL OF SCHOOL BOOKS slung across his shoulders. Gloria's in
the kitchen, preparing a CHICKEN for dinner.

                    DAVID
          Hi, Mom.

                    GLORIA
          Hello, honey. How was school?

KEVIN
BROWNLOW
THE PARADE'S
GONE BY...
A vivid, nostalgic,
immediate portrait
of an art in the
making

                    DAVID
          Fine.

David stops short when he finds a THICK HARDBACK BOOK on the
ENTRYWAY TABLE. He steps closer to examine it. The SILVER
COVER features SEPIA IMAGES of a silent movie crew. Men in
fedoras and peaked caps, ties, jackets, and vests, grouped
around two cinematographers with hand-cranked cameras. The
title: ***The Parade's Gone by... A vivid, nostalgic, immediate
portrait of an art in the making. By Kevin Brownlow.***

                    DAVID (cont'd)
          What's this?

                    GLORIA
          What's what?...
               (looks over)
          Oh, something your father picked
          up, God knows where.

Fascinated, David opens the cover to the flyleaf. It
features a photo of a silent movie company assembled around
an array of cameras. David turns to the table of contents,
perusing it until he comes upon a chapter on Buster Keaton.
He turns to page 473 and finds an image of Keaton perched on
the bow of a ship called *The Navigator*. Buster wears a
sailor's outfit and a melancholic deadpan expression.

David picks up the book and wanders off to...

INT. WEDDLE HOUSE - HALLWAY - DAY

David heads down the hall, reading the book.

                    GLORIA
          You going to do your homework?

                    DAVID
          Yeah...

He enters his room and shuts the door behind him.

INT. WEDDLE HOUSE - LIVING ROOM - NIGHT

Another dinner party. Fitz and Darlene are seated on the
flower print sofa, along with Herb and Louise, Peg Shaw, a
new couple, FRED and ROBIN SWENSON (40's), and Jim and
Gloria.

David addresses his audience.

                    DAVID
          Okay, this is my impression of a
          small scrawny boxer who has to
          fight a slugger twice his size.
          Dad, could you sound the opening
          bell?

                    JIM
          Okay, fellas, I want a nice clean
          fight.

Jim picks up his COCKTAIL GLASS and hits it with a CHEESE
KNIFE. PING!

David dances forward, bobbing and weaving, his legs moving
like an eccentric tap dancer, thumbing his nose with small
snorting sounds.

The crowd laughs.

Finally, David swings a roundhouse punch at his much larger
invisible opponent. His fist stops abruptly, as if hitting a
concrete wall, and his body vibrates like a tuning fork. He
does a dance of agony, cradling his bruised fist.

The audience rewards him with a hearty laugh.

David tries to recover and starts to swing again, but before
he can connect his jaw is pummeled by a series of invisible
lightning punches, head bobbling rapidly, like a battered
punching bag.

The crowd howls with hilarity.

A final imaginary punch sends David airborne. His legs fly
upward, parallel with his torso, and he seems to hang in
midair for a moment before crashing down on the shag carpet.

The guests explode with laughter and wild applause.

David lies there soaking it all in, enraptured. A shadow
falls over him. His father's big hand descends, gripping
David's palm and gently hoisting him to his feet. Jim's eyes
shine with pride.

                    JIM (cont'd)
          Jesus! What a fall! Didn't think
          you'd ever get up!

OFF DAVID, close to tears as he basks in his father's
approval.

INT. WEDDLE HOUSE - DAVID'S ROOM - NIGHT

THE WESTCLOX, reads 12:03 a.m. MOVE FROM THE BEDSIDE TABLE
TO DAVID, propped up by PILLOWS, reading a new book, *KEATON,
BY RUDI BLESH*. The cover features Buster wearing his
signature porkpie hat, clip-on tie, and a melancholic
expression.

FROM THE LIVING ROOM comes the sound of COUNT BASIE'S BIG
BAND SWING and the RAUCOUS CRIES AND LAUGHTER OF DRUNKEN
ADULTS.

A LARGE POSTER OF KEATON now covers the cork board. He's
leaning against a wooden boat called *The Love Nest*, his eyes
downcast.

The door opens. Light from the hall silhouettes Gloria, her
hair slightly disarrayed, voice a bit blurred.

                    GLORIA
          What're you doing up?

                    DAVID
          Reading.

                    GLORIA
          It's late. You need to go to
          sleep.

David's brow tightens. He nods to the cacophony in the
living room.

                    DAVID
          You said you'd keep the noise down
          this time.

                    GLORIA
          I tried... But you know your
          father.

David's stare makes her uncomfortable.

                    GLORIA (cont'd)
          To bed. Now.

David sighs. Deposits the book on the table and snakes
beneath the covers.

                    DAVID
          Please ask him to turn it down.

Gloria turns off the light and shuts the door. David lies
there, hoping his mother will come through for him.

Count Basie stops. Conversation in the living room falls to
murmurs. David begins to relax when...

THE DRUMS OF BORA BORA blast down the hall, punctuated by his
father's Dionysian cries.

                    JIM (O.C.)
          Move it, Peggy! Oh yeah! Like a
          paint shaker! Fred, get up there!
          Let's see some moves! You may
          never pass this way again!

David sighs and yanks the pillow over his head.

INT. LIVING ROOM - DAY

SUNLIGHT streams through the open sliding glass door to the
back yard. Flies buzz about lazily in the rays. Beneath
them, every square inch of the coffee table is covered by
BOOZE BOTTLES, COCKTAIL GLASSES, and OVERFLOWING ASH TRAYS.

David appears in his cowboy pajamas, scratching his butt as
he yawns away the cobwebs. He approaches the table,
examining the various glasses, many of them puddled with
amber and clear liquids. PUCKERED OLIVES float in some,
blackened CIGARETTE BUTTS in others.

He finds one with an inch of unpolluted liquid. Raises it to
his nose and sniffs, nostrils twitching from the strange but
enticing fumes. He takes a sip. His face puckers and his
body shivers as the alcohol works its way down.

                    TRACEY
          What are you doing?

Tracey has suddenly appeared at the other end of the table.

                    DAVID
          Nothing.

                    TRACEY
             (advancing)
          What's it taste like?

                    DAVID
          Tingly.

                    TRACEY
          Can I try?

                    DAVID
          No.

                    TRACEY
          Why not?

                    DAVID
          'Cause you're only five.

                    TRACEY
          If you don't let me, I'll tell on
          you.

Blackmailed, David shrugs and hands it to her.

                    DAVID
          Take a nice big gulp. So you get
          the full flavor.

Tracey does, and turns pale, gagging. David laughs.

A loud, low BARK. King has entered from the yard with a
TENNIS BALL in his mouth. He sets it down at David's feet,
barks again, stares intently at the ball, then at David,
inviting him to throw it. David tosses it into the dark hall
where it can be heard BOUNCING OFF THE WALLS. King barks
excitedly and pursues it down the corridor.   A few moments
later he reappears without the ball, barking at David.

                    DAVID (cont'd)
               (impatient)
          You lost it? How?

King barks shrilly.

                    DAVID (cont'd)
          Okay...

David starts into...

INT. WEDDLE HOUSE - HALLWAY/LIVING ROOM - DAY

David heads down the dark passage, searching for the ball.
King follows, barking all the way.

IN THE LIVING ROOM, Tracey tries another sip of the drink and
shivers.

IN THE HALL, David finds the ball, resting in a deep shadow
next to the closed door to his parents' bedroom.

                    DAVID
          Here it is, lamebrain.

David picks it up. King barks frantically, bouncing up and
down on his paws. David throws the ball back into the living
room. THE SOUND OF CRASHING GLASSWARE.

                    TRACEY
          David! I'm gonna tell!

Before David can reply, the door to the master bedroom flies
open. Jim towers over the boy in his checkered boxers, eyes
fissured by engorged blood vessels, chin tight with rage.

                    JIM
          DO YOU KNOW WHAT TIME IT IS?

David is too stunned to respond.

IN THE LIVING ROOM, Tracey dives behind the couch, out of
sight.

                    JIM (cont'd)
          WELL, DO YA? PEOPLE ARE TRYING TO
          SLEEP! DID YOU STOP TO THINK ABOUT
          THAT?

Jim grabs his son's arm and yanks him into...

INT. WEDDLE HOUSE - MASTER BEDROOM - DAY

Jim slams the door shut. Gloria stands in her light blue
nightgown, brow furrowed with concern.

                    JIM
          I asked you a question! Do you
          know what time it is?

David, shivering with terror, shakes his head. Jim thrusts
his head close to David's face. The pores of his father's
skin are as big as moon craters. His scar-ravaged nose
presses closer; eyes flat, staring at David as if he doesn't
know him.

                    JIM (cont'd)
          Course not. You know why? Because
          you didn't think!

Jim takes the palm of his hand and smashes it against his own
temple again and again, with tremendous force.

                    JIM (cont'd)
          THINK! THINK! THINK!

                    GLORIA
                 (tentative)
          Jim...

The tip of Jim's flat pale tongue curls under itself and his
uneven yellow teeth bite down on it. Now David knows he's
going to get hit. His father rips the pants of David's
cowboy pajamas down with such force he tears some of the
stitching loose. He slaps David's white fanny over and over
with his broad calloused palm.

                    GLORIA (cont'd)
          Please, Jim... Jim...

Jim hits David another time and much to David's horror his
shrunken penis spits forth a STREAM OF URINE. It flies over
his father's leg and clings to the hairs of his calf in large
golden droplets. This only feeds Jim's fury.

                    JIM
          Look at that! LOOK AT IT!

Jim hits David, again and again.

                    GLORIA
                 (voice breaking)
          Okay, Jim! That's enough!

Jim lets go of his son. Red marks rib David's arm where his
father held him. David wails uncontrollably.

                    JIM
          Pull your pants up and stop crying.

David awkwardly yanks the pants of his cowboy pajamas up over
his bright red fanny, still sobbing.

                    JIM (cont'd)
          I said stop crying!

David tries to swallow his sobs, but they keep clawing their
way up his throat, one after another.

                    JIM (cont'd)
          I said stop it! Or I'll give you
          something more to cry about.

                    DAVID
                 (gasping)
          I... I... I'm trying...

A tormented Gloria watches her son fight desperately to
control his rebellious body. MATCH TO:

EXT. PARADISE COVE - BLUFF - DAY

Gloria's eyes stare out at the blue ocean that seems to
stretch into eternity, her face knotted with memories that
even the tumor inside her brain won't allow her to forget.

She decides it is time to walk back to the trailer. Rises to
her feet and turns, but almost loses her balance. Gloria
grabs hold of the bench to steady herself, hyperventilating
as the ground seems to surge beneath her feet.

INT. DAVID'S TRAILER - OFFICE - DAY

David dials his WIRELESS PHONE. On the wall behind him is a
FRAMED PICTURE OF BUSTER KEATON in his bungalow at MGM
Studios. Keaton's face is half in shadow, his gaze filled
with despair. The other end of the phone line RINGS AND
RINGS. Finally...

                                        INTERCUT WITH:

INT. KEN KESEY'S FARM HOUSE - OREGON - DAY

FAYE KESEY, 59, answers a PHONE ATTACHED to a wall near the
front door of a converted barn. The walls behind her are
painted in eye-popping primary colors. The floor is covered
by an incandescent, psychedelic ZODIAC. She's in jeans and a
TIE-DYED BLOUSE -- an attractive aging hippy who has the
austere manner of a Kansas farm wife.

                    FAYE KESEY
          Hello?

                    DAVID
               (nervous)
          Hello, Faye. It's David Weddle.

                    FAYE KESEY
          Oh, hello. What can I do for you?

                    DAVID
          I was hoping to speak with Ken.
          About the reading he's doing down
          here in L.A. at the end of the
          month.

                    FAYE KESEY
          Hold on.

Faye turns and calls into the vast living room.

                         FAYE KESEY (cont'd)
               Ken. It's David Weddle.

A heavy grunt. KEN KESEY (59) comes around the corner. Bald
except for the grey curls boiling around the edges of his
massive Buddha-like head, he's barrel chested with broad
shoulders and long powerful arms and hands. But age has
rusted his joints and he moves slowly to the phone. [Sharp-
eyed viewers may notice this is the same man standing next to
the psychedelic school bus in the framed poster on David's
wall, with the quote about the need for mystery.]

                         KEN KESEY
               Hey, David. What's up?

                         DAVID
               I spoke to my editor at *L.A.
               Weekly*. He agreed to let me write
               a piece about the reading you're
               doing at the Los Angeles Public
               Library.

                         KEN KESEY
               The 30th, at noon. I'll see you
               there.

Kesey begins to hang up.

                         DAVID
               Uh, Ken, hold on! I was hoping to
               meet up with you before the
               reading. To talk about your book.

                         KEN KESEY
               Okay. I'm staying at the Biltmore.
               Swing by around nine that morning.

                         DAVID
               Great. See you then.

David hangs up -- thrilled he has nailed down this important
interview.

EXT. PARADISE COVE STREET - DAY

Gloria walks unsteadily toward David's trailer at the far end
of the street. Up ahead, she spots a white-haired MAN (60)
walking with his attractive DAUGHTER (30). Gloria's brow
furrows. Her eyes shine with a sharp jab of pain.

                         GLORIA
               Jim?

The couple turn to see Gloria striding unsteadily toward
them.

                    GLORIA (cont'd)
          Who is she?

Alarmed by this strange unhinged lady, father and daughter
walk swiftly away.

Gloria picks up speed, fighting to maintain her balance.

                    GLORIA (cont'd)
          Jim! You think I don't know? JIM!
          YOU COME BACK HERE!

INT. DAVID'S TRAILER - OFFICE - DAY

David's on the phone with his editor, RICK SCHULTZ.

                    DAVID
          Ken Kesey committed. I am set to
          interview him on the 30th.

                    RICK (ON THE PHONE)
          Awesome! You are the man. We'll
          send a photographer to the reading.
          I'm going to need a quick turn
          around on this one, buddy.

                    DAVID
          Give me a deadline.

                    RICK (ON THE PHONE)
          The 3rd. Can you do it?

                    DAVID
          No problem.

                    RICK (ON THE PHONE)
          Seriously? We need to get you a
          cape. You're a super hero. Can
          you call me afterward, let me know
          how the interview went?

                    DAVID
          You bet. Thanks, Rick. I'll get
          you a great story. Promise.

As David hangs up, the front door opens.

                    DAVID (cont'd)
          Mom?

                    GLORIA
          Hi!

                    DAVID
          How was your walk?

                    GLORIA
          Wonderful!

Gloria appears in the his office doorway. Her straw hat and
sunglasses are gone. A THICK STREAK OF RED-BLACK BLOOD
trails down the side of her face from a CUT ON HER FOREHEAD.
She smiles, oblivious to it.

                    GLORIA (cont'd)
          I get such a sense of peace --

Horrified, David leaps to his feet.

                    DAVID
          Mom! What happened to your head?

                    GLORIA
          What do you mean?

                    DAVID
          You're bleeding!

She touches the side of her face. Her hand comes away
covered in blood. Gloria stares at it in wonder.

                    DAVID (cont'd)
          Did you hit something? Fall?

                    GLORIA
          I fell. Walking back. Couldn't
          get up. So I laid there for a
          while.

                    DAVID
          In the middle of the street?

                    GLORIA
          Yes.

                    DAVID
          For how long?

                    GLORIA
          I don't know.

                    DAVID
          How did you get up?

                    GLORIA
          I don't know.

INT. DAVID'S TRAILER - KITCHEN/LIVING ROOM - DAY

CLOSE ON THE SINK FAUCET as David runs a TOWEL under a stream
of warm water.

He hurries over to his mother, who sits on the couch without
expression. He presses the towel gently to her forehead.
Gloria whimpers.

                    DAVID
          I know it hurts, but I've got to
          clean it.

David pulls the towel away to examine the cut.

                    DAVID (cont'd)
          You're going to need some stitches.

                    GLORIA
          Will I be okay?

                    DAVID
          Yes. But we have to get you to a
          hospital.

David cleans the cut some more. Gloria cries like a small
child.

                    DAVID (cont'd)
          I'm being as gentle as I can. But
          I gotta clean it, so hold still.

As he works, David is stricken by the realization that their
living conditions have become untenable.

EXT. PACIFIC COAST HIGHWAY/INT. HONDA ACCORD - DAY

David drives his mother down the highway, fighting the urge
to floor it. Gloria sits beside him, holding a folded TOWEL
to her temple. BLOOD HAS BEGUN TO SEEP THROUGH IT.

                    GLORIA
          Where are we going?

                    DAVID
          To the hospital.

                    GLORIA
          Why?

                    DAVID
               (exasperated sigh)
          To get your cut stitched up.
               (glances at her)
          Mom, hold the towel tight, put
          pressure on it, or you're gonna
          bleed all over the car.

Gloria presses it tighter.

                    GLORIA
          I don't want to go to the hospital.

                    DAVID
          Too bad. You're going.

                    GLORIA
          I want to go home.

                    DAVID
          After we get you stitched up.
          We'll go back to my place and I'll
          make you a nice --

                    GLORIA
          Don't want to go to your place. I
          want to go <u>home</u>.

                    DAVID
          You can't.

                    GLORIA
          Why not?

                    DAVID
          Mom, we talked about this.

                    GLORIA
          No, we didn't.

                    DAVID
               (rising irritation)
          Yes, we did.

                    GLORIA
          Why can't I go home?

                    DAVID
          Because you can't take care of
          yourself.

                    GLORIA
          I can too.

                    DAVID
          Really?

David jerks the rear view mirror over to display Gloria's
reflection.

                    DAVID (cont'd)
          Take a look at yourself.

Gloria drops her eyes.

                    DAVID (cont'd)
          Look!... Do you see yourself? You
          can't go home. Ever. Understand?
          It's too dangerous... Besides, we
          have to sell your house.

                    GLORIA
             (horrified)
          What on earth are you talking
          about?

David tightens his grip on the steering wheel, his knuckles
whiten.

                    DAVID
          We talked about this.

                    GLORIA
          Stop saying that! We did not!

                    DAVID
          Okay, we didn't.

They ride in silence for a moment. David hopes she will drop
it.

                    GLORIA
          Why are you selling my house?

                    DAVID
          To pay your medical bills.

                    GLORIA
          Bills? What bills?

                    DAVID
          For the radiation, and the chemo
          and...

David's already decided she's going to need to be put in a
facility, but he can't bring himself to say it.

                    DAVID (cont'd)
          ...everything else we might need to
          do.

                    GLORIA
          Like what?

                    DAVID
          Let's talk about it later, okay?
          After we get this taken care of.

Gloria's mouth puckers with quiet rage.

                    GLORIA
          Boy, you are really something. I'm
          just glad your father isn't alive
          to see this.

                    DAVID
          See what?

                    GLORIA
          Selling my house out from under me.
          Stealing from me. Of all the low
          down --

David finally blows, losing all ability to contain his anger.

                    DAVID
          Stealing? You think I'm stealing
          from you?

                    GLORIA
          You just admitted it.

                    DAVID
          Let me tell you something, okay? I
          have put my entire fucking life on
          hold to take care of you! I hardly
          get to see Risa anymore! Probably
          can kiss that relationship goodbye.
          Barely have time to write, to earn
          enough to hang onto my trailer.
          AND YOU ACCUSE ME OF STEALING FROM
          YOU? JESUS FUCKING CHRIST
          ALMIGHTY!

Gloria shrinks down in her seat and begins to cry. The
strangled, high pitched sobs of a small child.

                    DAVID (cont'd)
          STOP IT!

She continues crying.

                    DAVID (cont'd)
          STOP CRYING! RIGHT NOW! YOU HEAR
          ME?

Gloria's sobs subside into small whimpers. She sniffles.
They ride in silence as David tries to slow his breathing and
regain control of himself.

                    GLORIA
          David...

                    DAVID
          What?

                    GLORIA
          I'm sorry... My mind... this
          thing... I'm not thinking
          straight... I'm sorry I said those
          things...

David melts, tears of remorse in his eyes. He gently touches
her shoulder.

                    DAVID
          It's okay, Mom.

                    GLORIA
          I'm sorry.

                    DAVID
          I'm sorry, too, okay? I shouldn't
          have yelled like that. You have
          every right to be angry. I'm
          angry, too -- that this has
          happened to you. It's a rotten
          stinking deal. I get it. And I'm
          not upset anymore, okay?

                    GLORIA
          I didn't mean to --

                    DAVID
          I know. Let's just forget it,
          okay?

                    GLORIA
          Okay.

They fall into silence, the two of them staring at the road
ahead as they drive into an uncertain future.

                    <u>END OF EPISODE TWO</u>

EPISODE THREE

Ragtime

FADE IN:

EXT. ENCHANTED HILLS RETIREMENT HOME - DAY

A modest, but well maintained assisted living facility
located in the San Fernando Valley city of Encino. It is
surrounded by SMALL SHOPPING MALLS and RETAIL STORES.

INT. ENCHANTED HILLS RETIREMENT HOME - HALLWAY - DAY

A STAINLESS STEEL ELEVATOR DOOR opens. David leads a
reluctant Gloria into the bland beige hallway, past a GENERIC
WATERCOLOR OF A SEASCAPE in a frame from T.J. Maxx. Gloria's
in a colorful blouse and white linen pants. A FRESH BLUE
SCAR from her recent fall adorns her forehead, above the
SURGICAL SCAR on her temple.

                    DAVID
          You'll have plenty of people to
          look after you, you'll make lots of
          new friends, and there's a nurse on
          duty 24 hours a day. Let me show
          you your room.

David steps up to a door. UNLOCKS IT with a KEY. Then takes
her hand and coaxes her toward the open door.

                    DAVID (cont'd)
          Come on. You're going to like it.
          Promise...

INT. ENCHANTED HILLS RETIREMENT HOME - GLORIA'S ROOM - DAY

It's a bright, pleasant room. The furnishings are early
Holiday Inn. There's a private BATHROOM and a CLOSET with
SLIDING MIRRORED DOORS.

                    DAVID
          See, isn't this nice?

Gloria's mouth remains puckered. David runs his hand over a
TASTEFUL DOWN QUILT on the bed.

                    DAVID (cont'd)
          I brought your comforter, from
          home, remember?

Gloria makes a small cooing noise and runs an appreciative
hand over the soft fabric.

                    DAVID (cont'd)
          And look what we have here.

David opens the closet. It is full of GLORIA'S CLOTHES.
HIGH END SNEAKERS line the floor, in white, tan and gold.

Gloria emits a small "oooh" as she runs her hand over the
garments, remembering them from her past life.

                    DAVID (cont'd)
          And look what I hung here.

David gestures to a wall where the GOLD FRAME PICTURE OF HER
MOTHER, FATHER, AND SISTERS hangs. Gloria cries out in glee.
She walks up to the picture, her nose just inches away from
it, and stares into her parents' eyes.

                    GLORIA
          Oh, my favorite. I've missed them
          so.

David relaxes a little. Maybe this will be okay after all.

INT. ENCHANTED HILLS RETIREMENT HOME - DINING ROOM - DAY

The ELEVATOR DOOR opens. David leads Gloria out and to the
precipice of the dining hall. FIFTY ELDERLY PEOPLE sit at
GLASS-TOPPED TABLES. FROSTED LIGHT FIXTURES dangle overhead.
An abundance of PLASTIC FERNS adds atmosphere. WAITERS AND
WAITRESSES hustle plates of TUNA SALAD and QUICHE across the
bright floral patterned carpet to the waiting patrons. Some
residents engage in small talk, others remain glumly silent
as they shovel food into their mouths. The nearest table has
only two occupants and a pair of empty seats. David leads
Gloria toward it, but she suddenly digs her heels in, her
grip tightening around her son's hand.

                    GLORIA
          No.

                    DAVID
          There's nothing to be afraid of.
          These are nice people.

                    GLORIA
          But my mind. I can't... When I
          talk...

                    DAVID
          It's going to be all right, Mom.
          Don't worry. I'm right here with
          you. Come on, let's sit down and
          have some lunch.

David steps up to the table. Seated there are SOPHIE (80),
in a bright green dress with a rhinestone broach, and ADOLPH
(90), with sagging jowls and a plaid jacket.

                    DAVID (cont'd)
          Excuse me, are these seats taken?

                    SOPHIE
               (smiles)
          No. By all means, join us.

David ushers his mother into a chair.

                    DAVID
          I'm David Weddle. This is my
          mother, Gloria. It's her first day
          here.

                    SOPHIE
          Welcome. My name's Sophie.

She offers Gloria her hand. Gloria shakes it.

                    GLORIA
          I should say. The hamburger is
          very American.

                    DAVID
          She has a brain tumor, so she has
          trouble choosing the correct words.

                    SOPHIE
               (to Gloria)
          Don't you worry, hon. There are
          people here who are a lot nuttier
          than you, *believe me*.

Gloria spots the BASKET OF ROLLS in the center of the table.
She grabs one and begins to slather on some BUTTER. David
looks at Adolph, who has not glanced up from his TOMATO SOUP.

                    DAVID
          And you are, sir?

                    ADOLPH
          Adolph.

He slurps another spoonful of soup.

                    SOPHIE
               (to David)
          These waiters can be a little
          scatter-brained.
               (MORE)

                    SOPHIE (cont'd)
          But don't you worry, I'll make sure
          your mom gets plenty to eat.

A waiter attempts to walk past their table. Sophie hoists
her COFFEE CUP and glares at him.

                    SOPHIE (cont'd)
          Hey, you! I asked for decaf.

                    WAITER
          That is decaf, ma'am.

                    SOPHIE
               (erupts)
          LIKE HELL IT IS! I CAN TASTE THE
          CAFFEIN! YOU THINK I WAS BORN
          YESTERDAY? BRING ME SOME GODDAMNED
          DECAF RIGHT NOW, YOU SON-OF-A-
          BITCH, OR I WILL HAVE YOU FIRED SO
          FAST YOUR HEAD'LL SPIN!

The waiter bites back his irritation and picks up Sophie's
cup.

                    WAITER
          Right away, ma'am.

                    SOPHIE
          And bring my friend Gloria some
          soup. Try to make it back here
          this month, okay?

                    WAITER
          Yes, ma'am.

Sophie turns back to Gloria and smiles warmly, as if the
outburst never happened.

                    SOPHIE
          You'll like it here, dear. We all
          get along. It's like one big
          family.

Gloria looks up and smiles, a DAB OF BUTTER clinging to her
lips.

                    GLORIA
          Don't I know it! It's very, very
          mayonnaise. But what are you going
          to do?

David slips away from the table and approaches GAIL ARICO
(45), the facility's manager, who stands at the entrance,
with a NAME TAG on her blouse.

                    GAIL
          Hello there, Mr. Weddle. I see
          your mother's already made some
          friends.

                    DAVID
          She has. I have to go home to do
          some work. After she finishes
          eating, can someone make sure she
          takes her medication and escort her
          back to her room?

                    GAIL
          I'll do it myself. Don't worry
          about a thing.

                    DAVID
          Thank you, so much.

David walks back to the table, steeling himself. Gloria's
bent over a BOWL OF TOMATO SOUP, slurping it up eagerly. He
touches her shoulder.

                    DAVID (cont'd)
          Mom, I have to go now. I'll be
          back tomorrow.

A look of bewilderment and alarm grips Gloria's face.

                    GLORIA
          You mean you're leaving?

                    DAVID
          Yes. I have to go work.

                    GLORIA
          Oh, I don't believe this!

                    DAVID
          Come on, now. Don't make this hard
          on me. I'll be back tomorrow
          night. Risa and I will take you
          out to dinner and we'll have a
          wonderful time, okay?

Gloria stares into her soup, shrugging her shoulders with
resignation and disgust.

                    GLORIA
          If you say so.

                    DAVID
          You're going to like it here once
          you get used to it.

142

Gloria stares listlessly at her spoon. David bends down and
kisses her on the forehead.

                    SOPHIE
          Don't worry. I'll take care of
          her.

David nods and turns, walking quickly to the elevator, tears
falling from his eyes.

INT. ENCHANTED HILLS RETIREMENT HOME - NURSE'S OFFICE - DAY

ON A PILL CASE. It's divided into clear plastic boxes, one
for each day of the month. The boxes are loaded with MULTI-
COLORED PILLS. The box for today is open and has only two
pills left. The NURSE removes one and hands it to Gloria,
who holds a PAPER WATER CUP.

                    MAGGIE
          And here's another...

Gloria swallows the pill, wincing as it works its way down
her throat.

                    NURSE
          Very good. And one more.

The nurse hands the pill to Gloria.

                    GLORIA
          Oh for Pete's sake. I don't
          believe this.

                    NURSE
          Last one. I promise.

Gloria downs it. Gail Arico appears in the doorway.

                    GAIL
          Is she finished?

                    NURSE
          Swallowed all her pills, like a
          good girl.

                    GAIL
          Come on, Gloria, I'll take you to
          your room.

                    GLORIA
          I'm tired.

                    GAIL
          I know you are, dear. It's been a
          stressful day. Come with me.

INT.   ENCHANTED HILLS RETIREMENT HOME - RECEPTION - DAY

Gail leads the way toward the elevator. WALLY (80), a dapper
man with a CANE and OVERSIZED GLASSES, watches Gloria with
keen interest. The RECEPTIONIST puts a call on hold and
looks up from her TELEPHONE.

                    RECEPTIONIST
          Mrs. Arico, I've got Mr. Delvalle
          on line one.

                    GAIL
          Tell him I'll call him back in a
          few minutes.

                    RECEPTIONIST
          Okay, but he's pretty upset.
          Insists he needs to speak with you
          immediately.

                    GAIL
               (exasperated)
          Well, he'll just have to wait until
          I get Gloria to her room.

Wally rises to his feet.

                    WALLY
          I can take her, Gail.

Gail welcomes the offer to remove one item from her
overloaded schedule.

                    GAIL
          You sure, Wally?

                    WALLY
          Got nothing better to do. Might as
          well make myself useful.

                    GAIL
          Okay. Room 305. The key is on
          that bracelet on Gloria's wrist.

INT. THIRD FLOOR HALLWAY - DAY

The ELEVATOR DOORS OPEN. Wally exits, using his cane for
balance. He looks back at Gloria, who's still standing in
the elevator.

                    WALLY
          This is your floor. Don't you want
          to go to your room?

                    GLORIA
          I want to go home.

                    WALLY
          This is your home. Remember?
             (she doesn't move)
          Wouldn't you like to lie down?
          Rest a while?

                    GLORIA
          To be sure.

                    WALLY
          Then come on.

He gestures for her step out of the elevator and she finally
does. Wally leads her down the hall.

                    WALLY (cont'd)
          I hope you don't mind me making a
          frank observation. You are a very
          vital, attractive woman.

                    GLORIA
          To be sure. After all, the
          hamburger is very American.

                    WALLY
             (smiles)
          You have a unique sense of humor.

                    GLORIA
          Ragtime.

                    WALLY
          Ragtime?

                    GLORIA
          That's what I speak.

                    WALLY
          You can speak any language you
          like, far as I'm concerned.

They arrive at Gloria's room.

                    WALLY (cont'd)
          Here we are. This is your room.
          Remember?

                    GLORIA
          Oh, yes.

Gloria takes the key attached to her COILED EXPANDABLE RUBBER
BRACELET, slips it into the lock. Wally steps closer.

                    WALLY
          You want me to help you?

                    GLORIA
          No.

She opens the door.

                    WALLY
          Aren't you going to invite me in?

                    GLORIA
          No.

Wally gently takes hold of her arm.

                    WALLY
          Listen, I'm a very sensitive
          person, okay? And I feel a
          chemistry.

                    GLORIA
          Chemistry?

                    WALLY
          Between you and me. Do you deny
          it, Gloria?

Gloria tries to free her arm. He grips it tighter.

                    GLORIA
          Let go.

                    WALLY
             (rising passion)
          Jesus, you smell good. So
          beautiful...

Wally tries to kiss her. Gloria struggles, averting her
face.

                    GLORIA
          Stop it! Jim! Help!

                    WALLY
          My name's Wally, remember? Please,
          just let me --

He presses his lips to her face. Gloria shoves him and Wally
topples to the floor, dropping his cane. He lies on his
back, staring up at the FOAM PANELED CEILING, his breath
labored. Gloria feels remorse.

                    GLORIA
          Are you okay?

Wally starts to cry. Sobbing uncontrollably.

                    GLORIA (cont'd)
          Did I hurt you?

Wally continues to bawl, like a young boy.

                    GLORIA (cont'd)
          What's wrong?

                    WALLY
          I'm sorry... My wife died... three
          years ago... So lonely. I'm so,
          so...

He grips his stomach as his body spasms with grief.

                    WALLY (cont'd)
          Don't know what to do... What do I
          do?

                    GLORIA
          I'm married. I have to go now.

She steps into her room and slams the door.

INT. ENCHANTED HILLS RETIREMENT HOME - GLORIA'S ROOM - DAY

Gloria sits on her bed, struggling to calm herself. Her eyes
drift up to...

A FRAMED BLACK AND WHITE PHOTO OF A 23-YEAR-OLD GLORIA IN AN
AMERICAN AIRLINES STEWARDESS UNIFORM. It's a glamor shot
worthy of a Hollywood studio. Gloria has one silk clad leg
propped up on a chair to raise the hemline of her dress as
she smiles seductively over her shoulder at the camera.

ON THE BED, a faint smile rises on older Gloria's mouth as
long dead memories surface.

MOVE IN ON THE PHOTO. MATCH IT TO:

INT. AMERICAN AIRLINES STEWARDESS ACADEMY - DAY

THE SCENE IS IN COLOR. Gloria smiles at a PHOTOGRAPHER. A
FLASH IGNITES.

                    PHOTOGRAPHER
          Got it! Beautiful!

Gloria steps down from the chair and proceeds across the
LARGE STAGE, passing a line of 100 NEWLY MINTED STEWARDESSES.
She arrives at a PODIUM where an AMERICAN AIRLINES EXECUTIVE
stands with a RIBBON-TIED DIPLOMA.

SUPER: **NEW YORK, 1954**

                    EXECUTIVE
          Gloria Byrne, this diploma
          stipulates that you have completed
          your course work and have graduated
          from the American Airlines
          Stewardess Academy.

He hands the DIPLOMA to Gloria.

                    EXECUTIVE (cont'd)
          Welcome to the American Airlines
          family.

REVEAL AN AUDITORIUM full of RELATIVES AND FRIENDS of the new
STEWARDESSES.

                    EXECUTIVE (cont'd)
          Miss Sally Holloway, please step
          forward to have your photo taken
          and to receive your diploma.

IN THE BACK OF THE AUDITORIUM, Gloria's father, NICHOLAS
BYRNE (54), watches proudly in the three-piece suit he wears
to church on Sundays. Though his hair is shot through with
gray, he's still devastatingly handsome. Next to Nick are
his three beautiful daughters, ELEANOR (29), MURIEL (26), and
SHEILA (21) -- all in their church dresses. Eleanor and
Muriel wear wedding rings. Sheila, still unmarried, is swept
away by the splendor of the moment.

                    SHEILA
          Aren't you proud of her, Daddy?

Eleanor already wears the embittered demeanor of an older
woman disappointed by life.

                    ELEANOR
          What's there to be proud of? Men
          treat these stewardesses like
          prostitutes.

                    SHEILA
          How dare you call Glo a prostitute!

                    ELEANOR
          I didn't. I said men treat them
          like that. If Glo's not careful --

                    MURIEL
          Glo's always careful.

                    ELEANOR
          Don't see why she couldn't take
          that job with Mutual of Omaha and
          stay in Irvington, where she
          belongs.

                    SHEILA
          That's the whole point. She
          doesn't want to stay in Irvington.

                    ELEANOR
          Why? What's wrong with Irvington?

                    NICK
          Enough.

He says it with quiet authority. His daughters immediately
stop bickering.

                    SHEILA
          Sorry, Daddy.

Eleanor has a lot more she'd like to say, but even she
doesn't dare defy her father.

ON STAGE, the new stewardesses smile out at the audience.
The executive booms from the podium...

                    EXECUTIVE
          Ladies and Gentleman, allow me to
          present the class of 1954!

The audience rises to their feet in a standing ovation. Many
have tears in their eyes.

MOMENTS LATER, Gloria rushes to her family at the back of the
hall. Sheila hustles forward to hug her.

                    SHEILA
          Oh, Glo, we're so proud.

Nick embraces his daughter, his eyes moist and voice choked
with emotion. He speaks with an Irish brogue.

                    NICK
          That we are, girl.

Muriel embraces Gloria, then Eleanor -- ad-libbing
congratulations.

                    GLORIA
          I wish Mom were here.

                    NICK
          She _is_.

                    GLORIA
          I know. I know. Still...

She begins to break down.

                    ELEANOR
          Get hold of yourself.

                    MURIEL
          This is a happy occasion.

                    GLORIA
              (forces a smile)
          Guess what, Daddy. I can get you
          passes. You can fly anywhere in
          the world. For free.

                    NICK
          There's nowhere I want to go.

                    GLORIA
          How about Ireland? You haven't
          been home in what, 30 years?

                    NICK
          Thirty-three.

                    MURIEL
          But who's counting?

Nick sees his daughters all grinning at him.

                    NICK
          All right, sure. I'd like to go
          back one day. But if I do, it'll
          be on ship, not an aeroplane.

                    SHEILA
          But Daddy, don't you want to
          experience it?

                    NICK
          Experience what?

                    SHEILA
          Flying! Soaring through the
          clouds, looking down at the Earth
          from 13,000 feet.

                    GLORIA
          Twenty-one thousand. The new DC-7
          reaches an altitude of 21,000 feet.
          And with the four new double
          cyclone engines, it cruises at 410
          miles per hour.

                    MURIEL
          How about that, Dad? Wouldn't you
          like to try it, just once?

                    NICK
               (shrugs)
          I wouldn't mind it.

Gloria's frustrated by her father's provincial attitude. Her
sisters find it endearing.

                    SHEILA
          Well, I wanna try it. Oh, Glo, I'm
          so excited for you. Zipping across
          the sky from coast to coast,
          looking down on all the big cities,
          it's going to be so, so...

                    MURIEL
          Glamorous.

EXT. LAGUARDIA AIRPORT - DAY

Dressed in sleek navy blue American airlines uniforms and
caps, Gloria and Sally Holloway carry their FLIGHT BAGS
across the tarmac toward a DC-7, it's long cylindrical
aluminum exterior glistening in the sun, four massive double
prop cyclone engines poised for action.

                    SALLY
          Still can't believe it, Glc. We're
          gonna fly across the United States
          in that beauty.

                    GLORIA
               (grinning)
          Move over Buck Rodgers. There are
          a couple of new girls in town!

Gloria and Sally laugh as they head up the MOBILE STAIRCASE
that leads to the open door to the aircraft.

EXT. SKY - DC-7 - DAY

The airship's propellers ROAR as they claw their way across a
NASTY STORM SYSTEM. RAIN PELTS the aluminum skin.
LIGHTENING flashes in the distance as unstable air currents
violently jostle the plane. A CHIME RINGS

                    JERRY COREY (PRE-LAP)
          Ladies and gentlemen, we're
          encountering some turbulence.
          Please return your seats to the
          upright position and fasten your
          seatbelts.

INT. DC-7 - PASSENGER CABIN - DAY

Gloria and Sally move down the red carpeted aisle with
SERVICE CARTS, collecting DRINK GLASSES, DINNER PLATES, and
SILVERWARE from the 100 PASSENGERS in wide luxuriously padded
aqua-colored seats -- the men in jackets and ties, the women
in formal dresses.

The cabin jerks and jolts like a bucking bronco, spilling
drinks and plates. Some passengers grip the leather arm
rests with white knuckles, others puke into AIRSICKNESS BAGS.
Some peel back the gold curtains to peer out the windows,
fascinated by the LIGHTENING.

Gloria takes a drink from a NERVOUS WOMAN.

                    WOMAN
          Is this normal?

Gloria bestows a confident smile.

                    GLORIA
          When we fly through a storm, yes.
          I've been through this many times.
               (MORE)

                    GLORIA (cont'd)
          Captain Corey is one of our best
          pilots. He's never had a mishap.

The woman nods, marginally reassured.

Gloria approaches a MAN bathed in cold sweat, nervously
sucking on a CIGARETTE.

                    GLORIA (cont'd)
          I'm sorry, sir. But you need to
          put that cigarette out.

                    MAN
          Why?

Gloria points to the ILLUMINATED NO SMOKING SIGN.

                    GLORIA
          The captain has put on the no
          smoking sign.

                    MAN
          All these fabrics are fireproof.
          Why you being such a drama queen?

                    GLORIA
               (firm)
          I'm not going to debate the issue.
          Put it out. Now.

The man angrily stubs the cigarette out in his ash tray.

                    MAN
          You are one stone cold ball buster.
          I'm going to write the president of
          American Airlines and tell him --

THE PLANE HITS A MASSIVE AIR POCKET, dropping violently.
Drinks, dinnerware, and barf bags fly into the aisle, LUGGAGE
topples from the open storage racks onto the heads of
passengers. Gloria's catapulted upward, head smashing on a
rack.

EXT. LAGUARDIA AIRPORT - DAY

The DC-7 roars out of the sky in PELTING RAIN, hits the slick
runway, bounces, skids, then stabilizes.

                    JERRY COREY (ON THE P.A.)
          Ladies and Gentlemen, we have
          touched down at LaGuardia Airport.
          The local time is 4:30.
                    (MORE)

                    JERRY COREY (ON THE P.A.) (cont'd)
          Our total flight time from Los
          Angeles was 13 hours and 27
          minutes, which puts us a just an
          hour and a half behind schedule.

INT. DC-7 - PASSENGER CABIN - DAY

Gloria and Sally stand at the open door that leads to the
exterior stairs. Gloria's hat is dented from her collision
with the luggage rack. The wilted passengers -- spattered
with food, coffee, booze, and barf -- file past them with
1000-yard stares.

                    GLORIA
               (pleasant smile)
          Thank you for flying with American
          Airlines. We hope to see you
          again...

When the last passengers have departed, Gloria turns to...

THE COCKPIT, festooned with a plethora of GAUGES, DIALS and
SWITCHES. The wrung out CO-PILOT and NAVIGATOR step past
her. JERRY COREY (40) stands wearily in his rumpled pilot
uniform, stretching his aching back. He picks up a
HALLIBURTON ALUMINUM BRIEFCASE.

                    GLORIA (cont'd)
          Jerry...

                    JERRY COREY
               (genial smile)
          Hey, Glo. How's that pretty little
          noggin of yours?

                    GLORIA
          Ringing like a tuning fork, but
          I'll be okay. Could I grab a ride
          into Manhattan with you?

                    JERRY COREY
          Sure, darling. Meet me in the
          Admiral's Club. Need a drink after
          riding that bitch.

                    GLORIA
          Thanks a million. Be there as soon
          as I finish cleaning up here.

Jerry heads out. Gloria turns to regard THE CABIN. Sally
moves down the aisle with a cart, collecting DEBRIS.

It looks as though a hurricane hit it -- food, coffee, booze, and barf sprayed everywhere, along with CRUMPLED CIGARETTE PACKAGES AND BUTTS, TISSUES, NAPKINS, AND GUM WRAPPERS. Gloria sighs wearily, then joins Sally.

INT. AMERICAN AIRLINES ADMIRAL'S CLUB - DAY

The airline industry's prototype of a lounge for first class passengers is truly luxurious. Oak paneled walls, deep nylon carpet, art deco tables and chairs where formally attired PATRONS are served by WAITRESSES in blue American Airlines uniforms. Gloria enters, casting her eyes about for Jerry. The HOSTESS, at a gleaming reception desk, notices her.

                    HOSTESS
          Hey, Gloria. Looking for someone?

                    GLORIA
          Jerry Corey. I was supposed to
          meet him here.

                    HOSTESS
               (looking around)
          Saw him a little while ago.

                    GLORIA
          Thanks.

Gloria heads over to the BAR, stocked with an impressive ARRAY OF POLISHED LIQUOR BOTTLES. A PAIR OF BARTENDERS, in white jackets and ties, service a DOZEN CUSTOMERS.

                    GLORIA (cont'd)
               (to a bartender)
          Bob, have you seen Jerry Corey?

                    BOB
          Left a couple of minutes ago with
          Arlene Spielman.

                    GLORIA
          Oh, for Pete's sake! He was
          supposed to give me a ride into the
          city. Can't believe he did that.

The bartenders exchange a smirk. They refrain from sharing their unseemly observations with Gloria.

                    GLORIA (cont'd)
          Well, I guess I'll have to take a --

                    JIM
          Excuse me, young lady...

Gloria turns to look into the penetrating blue eyes of JAMES
WEDDLE (34). He's tall and lean, with broad shoulders and a
muscular physique. His broken nose adds a rugged edge to his
movie star looks. Jim wears a tailored three-piece Brooks
Brothers suit, polished Oxfords, and holds a LEATHER
BRIEFCASE. Just behind him stands WOODY EISENHARDT (35) --
similarly attired, medium height and stocky, his iconoclastic
smile warped by the CUBAN CIGAR jammed into the right corner
of his mouth.

                    JIM (cont'd)
          Couldn't help overhearing your
          dilemma. We're going into
          Manhattan. We'd be happy to give
          you a ride.

Jim's gaze cuts right into Gloria. She feels flushed,
strangely excited. Still, she's not about to accept a ride
from a stranger.

                    GLORIA
          Thank you. That's very kind. But
          I don't want to inconvenience you.

                    JIM
          It's not an inconvenience. I'm the
          regional manager for BPS Paint.
          Our corporate showroom is on East
          38th Street.

He hands her an EMBOSSED BUSINESS CARD.

                    JIM (cont'd)
          Where do you live?

                    GLORIA
          Stanhope Hotel, 995 5th Avenue.

                    JIM
          We'd be happy to drop you off,
          wouldn't we, Woody?

                    WOODY
          But of course. No trouble at all.

Off Gloria, considering the offer and titillated by the heat
of Jim's electric blue eyes.

INT. MERCEDES/EXT. WILLIAMSBURG BRIDGE - MANHATTAN - DAY

Woody drives, Jim sits in the front passenger seat, Gloria in
the back. The Mercedes is five years old, the leather
upholstery worn.

6

Outside, the SKYLINE OF 1954 MANHATTAN reaches toward the
clouds, the Empire State and Chrysler Buildings the most
prominent. Below, sunlight glitters on the brown water of
the East River.

                    JIM
               (singing)
          When the blue of the night, meets
          the gold of the day, someone waits
          for me...

He nudges Woody.

                    JIM (cont'd)
          Well, it worked.

Woody emits a conspiratorial chuckle. Gloria's mouth
tightens.

                    GLORIA
          What worked?

                    JIM
               (to Woody)
          Should we tell her?

                    WOODY
          Why not?

                    GLORIA
          Tell me what?

Jim hefts his leather satchel.

                    JIM
          These briefcases are full of rocks.
          We rented our suits and had those
          business cards printed so we could
          pick up girls.

Jim leans across the seat and presents an UNFILTERED
CIGARETTE to Gloria.

                    JIM (cont'd)
          Want a reefer?

                    GLORIA
          I already smoked one.

Jim's surprised by this response, but he goes with it.

                    JIM
          When?

                    GLORIA
          In the cockpit, with the pilot.
          Just before the we took off. You
          don't think I'd fly straight, do
          you?

Jim scrutinizes her. Like a Gladstone bag without a handle,
he can't quite get a grip on her. And he likes that.

                    JIM
          You're good.

                    GLORIA
          Glad I meet with your approval.

They have driven off the bridge into lower Manhattan.

                    GLORIA (cont'd)
          Let me out here. I'll take a cab
          the rest of the way.

                    JIM
             (sincere)
          Hold on now. Don't get mad. We
          were just having a little fun.
          Talking ragtime.

                    GLORIA
          Ragtime?

                    JIM
          You know, ad-libbing whatever crazy
          nonsense we can come up with. Life
          is bleak enough already. If you
          can't find a way to laugh at it,
          you're finished.

                    GLORIA
             (studies him)
          Do you really work for a paint
          company?

Jim elbows Woody and smiles.

                    JIM
          Hit it.

Jim and Woody break out in song.

                    JIM AND WOODY
          BPS is best for me! Try it out and
          you will see! Best paint that's
          sold.
                    (MORE)

160

                    JIM AND WOODY (cont'd)
          Put it on the walls and on the
          ceeeiilling, and you will have that
          fresh as springtime feeeellllinng!
          BPS is best for me, try it out and
          you will see! Best Paint that's
          soooooolllld!

Jim looks back at Gloria's unsmiling face.

                    JIM
          You don't believe us?

                    GLORIA
          Because you sang a jingle you heard
          on the radio?

                    JIM
          Oooh, you're tough. Very well.
          Take a look inside my briefcase.

He unsnaps the satchel. It's filled with DOCUMENTS ADORNED
WITH BPS LOGOS.

                    JIM (cont'd)
          See, not a rock to be found.

He hands her a memo made out to JAMES WEDDLE, SALES MANAGER,
EASTERN DIVISION.

                    WOODY
          Here we are.

They pull up to a BPS PAINT showroom. CUSTOMERS mill about
in the brightly lit interior, perusing huge DISPLAYS OF PAINT
CHIPS, and PYRAMIDS OF BPS PAINT CANS. They are waited on by
BPS PAINT SALESMEN in spotless white BPS aprons and ball
caps.

                    WOODY (cont'd)
          The flagship.
               (to Jim)
          Permission to disembark, Admiral.

                    JIM
          Permission granted, Ensign.

Woody salutes, exits the car, and heads into the showroom.
Jim looks at Gloria.

                    JIM (cont'd)
          We gotta check on a few things.
          You can catch a cab on the corner
          there. Or if you want to wait,
          we'll take you to your apartment.

Gloria's no longer angry. There's something different about
this man. She's never encountered anyone quite like him.

                    GLORIA
          I'll come in for a few minutes.
          Thinking of painting my apartment.

EXT. EAST 38TH STREET - DAY

Gloria and Jim exit the cab and head for the showroom.

                    JIM
          Pick out any color your want. I'll
          give it to you, free of charge.

                    GLORIA
          You don't have to do that.

Jim opens the showroom door and beckons her in.

                    JIM
          It's the least I can do after
          acting like such a cad. Were you
          looking for fun and frivolity, or
          something more reserved?

                    GLORIA
          I... uh... What do you mean?

                    JIM
          The color. We have 1080 to choose
          from.

                    GLORIA
          Uh, reserved, I guess.

INT. BPS PAINT SHOWROOM - DAY

Jim and Gloria enter.

                    JIM
          Then I suggest something in the
          blue family.

The showroom manager, DON WICHMAN (30), rushes over, nervous
and deferential.

                    DON
          Mr. Weddle, I'm sorry, didn't know
          you were coming in today.

                    JIM
          Just stopped by to see the monthly
          sales figures.

                    DON
          Yes, sir. They came in over the
          telex about an hour ago.

                    JIM
               (to Gloria)
          Our blues are right over there.
          You'll find an ample selection.

He points to a LARGE PAINT CHIP DISPLAY, then hurries off.

LATER: ON A PAINT CHIP DISPLAY OF VARIOUS SHADES OF BLUE.
REVEAL GLORIA, scrutinizing two of the lighter shades. Jim
appears behind her.

                    JIM (cont'd)
          See anything you like?

                    GLORIA
          Well, I'm thinking about this
          Robin's Egg Blue. But I'm afraid
          it might be too dark.

                    JIM
               (points)
          You could go with Montana Sky.

                    GLORIA
          But it's a shade too light.

                    JIM
          Not a problem. Come with me.

He leads her to a big RAINBOW DISPLAY at the back of the
store. Beneath it is a gleaming MACHINE festooned with a
complicated array of dials and switches.

                    JIM (cont'd)
          Our new Mytron Full Color System
          can whip up any shade of blue you
          can imagine, and a few you never
          dared dream of.

He scrutinizes the controls.

                    JIM (cont'd)
          Okay, something between Robin's Egg
          and Montana Sky.

Jim adjusts some calibrated dials then hits a button. The
machine WHIRRS AND HUMS, LIGHTS FLASHING. A SPIGOT VIBRATES
then ejaculates a DOLLOP OF LIGHT BLUE PAINT.

                    JIM (cont'd)
          What do you think?

Gloria tries to imagine it on her apartment walls.

                    GLORIA
          Maybe a tad lighter.

                    JIM
          A tad lighter. Okay, the tad dial
          is right here.

He makes an adjustment and hits a button. The Mytron whirrs
and hums again.

                    JIM (cont'd)
          All of our low luster super satin
          finish latexes have beautiful
          flowing and leveling because of our
          unique blends of flexo-alkyne
          resins.

                    GLORIA
               (no idea what that means)
          I would hope so.

The machine spits out another BLOB OF BLUE PAINT, this one a
tad lighter.

                    GLORIA (cont'd)
               (smiles)
          Perfect.

                    JIM
          Okay, I'll mix up several gallons.
          Have it ready tomorrow.

                    GLORIA
          Hold on. Gotta find a painter
          first.

                    JIM
          No, you don't. I'll put my best
          man on the job.

INT. GLORIA'S APARTMENT - DAY

ON A ROLLER SLATHERING BLUE PAINT across a section of wall.

                    GLORIA
          It's too dark.

REVEAL JIM in a t-shirt and jeans, painting her STUDIO
APARTMENT. DROP CLOTHS enshroud the FURNITURE and hardwood
floors. Gloria casts a critical eye on his efforts.

                    JIM
          It'll lighten when it dries.

                    GLORIA
          You sure?

                    JIM
          Positive. Tested it yesterday on a
          piece of drywall at the store.

Gloria's impressed by his thoroughness.

LATER: ON A SECTION OF TRIM as a BRUSH delicately dabs some
paint on it. REVEAL JIM completing his job. The entire
apartment has now been painted. Gloria's inspecting a
section that has dried.

                    GLORIA
          You're right. It has lightened.
          This looks fantastic.

                    JIM
          If you have any doubts, the
          slightest misgivings, just say the
          word and I'll strip it down and
          start over.

                    GLORIA
          That won't be necessary.

                    JIM
          Okay then. I guess we're done.

Jim begins to meticulously clean his BRUSHES in a BUCKET of
PAINT THINNER, and another BUCKET OF WARM WATER. Gloria
hands him a STEAMING MUG.

                    GLORIA
          Here's your coffee.

                    JIM
          Thanks.

He takes a big gulp.

                    JIM (cont'd)
          So, how long have you worked for
          American Airlines?

                    GLORIA
          I don't.
               (off his look)
          I just put that uniform on to lure
          unsuspecting men to my apartment so
          I can poison their coffee. You
          wouldn't happen to know where I
          could get deal on some quick lime,
          would you?

                    JIM
               (grins)
          Let me make some calls.

Gloria picks up her PHONE and holds it out to him.

                    GLORIA
          Can you do it quickly? Before you
          become unavailable for further
          consultations?

Jim is really beginning to like her.

                    JIM
          Can I take you out to dinner?

                    GLORIA
          No.

                    JIM
          Why not?

                    GLORIA
          This was supposed to be penance for
          your vile behavior. Not a ploy to
          get into my pants.

                    JIM
          I don't want to get into them.

                    GLORIA
               (surprised)
          Why not?

                    JIM
          Because you are a real lady. Knew
          that the moment I met you.

Gloria blushes. Jim sees he still has a chance.

                    JIM (cont'd)
          Okay, if you won't have dinner with
          me tonight, will you at least think
          about doing so in the future?

                    GLORIA
          Maybe.

                    JIM
          When will you think about it?

                    GLORIA
          I'm thinking about it now. That's
          a start.

OFF JIM, missing her terribly before he's even stepped out
the door.

INT. GLORIA'S APARTMENT - ANOTHER DAY

ON A BLACK DIAL PHONE on a TABLE. A LOUD METALLIC RING. Mid-
morning light streams through the Venetian blinds. Gloria
picks up the receiver.

                    GLORIA
          Hello?

                                        INTERCUT WITH:

INT. JIM'S APARTMENT - DAY

A FRAMED POSTER OF W.C. FIELDS playing poker adorns the wall.
On the coffee table: A SMALL OAK WHISKEY CASK with a tiny
brass spigot -- the kind that were popular at the turn of the
20th Century. Jim's voice is strong and confident, but his
left hand betrays nervousness as he winds the phone cord
around his thick index finger.

                    JIM
          How's my paint job holding up?

                    GLORIA
          No fading, peeling, or blistering.
          Of course, it's only been four
          days.

                    JIM
          So, you've been counting the days
          since you saw me.

                    GLORIA
          No. I'm counting the days until
          the paint's 30-day warranty
          expires. In case I need to ask for
          a refund. Thanks for checking in.
          I gotta --

                    JIM
          Hold on. How'd you like to see the
          revival of *Carousel* at the City
          Centre?

                    GLORIA
          I would love to.

                    JIM
          Great!

                    GLORIA
          If I hadn't already seen it.

She hangs up.

INT. LITTLE ITALY - ITALIAN RESTAURANT - NIGHT

Red checkered table cloths. Candles in wine bottles serve as
centerpieces. More straw covered wine bottles dangle from
the ceiling. JERRY WARRINER (30) -- a Long Island insurance
agent wearing a J.C. Penny sports jacket and a pencil thin
tie -- regales Gloria with the intricacies of the insurance
industry.

                    WARRINER
          ...in fact, annuities are among our
          most popular policies. Now, you
          may ask yourself, "Jerry, what the
          heck is an annuity anyway?" Well,
          Gloria, I'll tell you. An annuity
          is a financial product that allows
          you to lock in a guaranteed monthly
          income for your golden years.

Gloria fights to keep her eyes open.

INT. GLORIA'S APARTMENT - DAY

The black dial phone RINGS. Gloria picks it up.

                    GLORIA
          Hello?

                                        INTERCUT WITH:

INT. JIM'S APARTMENT - DAY

Jim winds the phone cord around his finger.

                    JIM
          Hey, it's me.

                    GLORIA
          Thanks for checking in. The paint
          still looks good.

                    JIM
          Want to go see *Pajama Game*?

                    GLORIA
          I already have.

                    JIM
          How about *The Rainmaker*?

                    GLORIA
          Loved it. But not in the mood to
          see it again.

                    JIM
          Jesus. Is there a Broadway play
          you haven't seen?

                    GLORIA
          Guess you'll just have to figure
          that out.

Gloria hangs up.

INT. FRENCH RESTAURANT - NIGHT

Gloria raises a GLASS OF RED WINE. RICHARD, a mortgage
broker in a pinstriped suit, holds up his hand.

                    RICHARD
          Hold it! Before you taste it, roll
          it around in your glass, inhale the
          bouquet, and tell me what you
          smell.

Gloria does.

                    GLORIA
          Uh... wine.

Richard bestows a condescending smile.

                    RICHARD
          To be sure, that's all the layman
          smells. But a pair of highly
          trained nostrils can detect a
          complex medley of influences.

He inhales deeply from his glass.

                    RICHARD (cont'd)
          For instance, I'm picking up a
          distinct floral aroma, as well as
          the scent of cherries, currants and
          spices, hints of potassium,
          calcium, and oak from the casks in
          which this vintage was fermented in
          the sun-kissed wine country of
          Burgundy...

Gloria loses patience and swallows her glass in one gulp.
Richard frowns with profound disappointment.

                    RICHARD (cont'd)
          Well, that's a shame. You just
          squandered an opportunity for an
          intimate relationship with the
          grape.

                    GLORIA
          I'm not interested in having an
          intimate relationship with a grape.

Richard is shocked and outraged.

INT. GLORIA'S APARTMENT - DAY

Gloria's on the phone with...

                                        INTERCUT WITH:

INT. JIM'S APARTMENT - DAY

Jim wraps the phone cord around his finger. It's bunched
into a tangled series of knots.

                    JIM
          Okay, I've got two tickets for the
          Saturday night performance of *The
          Caine Mutiny Court-Martial* at the
          Plymouth Theatre.

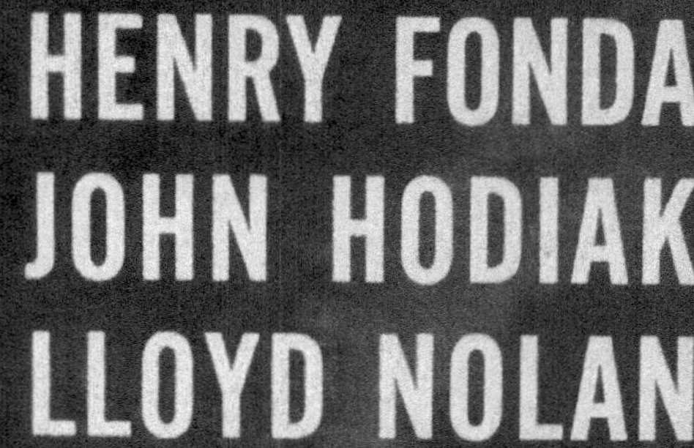

NOW...A Stage Sensation!
Paul Gregory
presents
— IN PERSON —
HENRY FONDA
JOHN HODIAK
LLOYD NOLAN
and Company of 15
in
Herman Wouk's
"The CAINE MUTINY Courtmartial"
Directed by Dick Powell
A PAUL GREGORY-CHARLES LAUGHTON PRODUCTION
PLYMOUTH THEATRE
236 W. 45th ST., NEW YORK 36, N. Y.
OPENING WED. EVE. JAN. 20
MAIL ORDERS NOW!
See other side for mail order coupon

                    GLORIA
          Is that the one that stars Henry
          Fonda?

                    JIM
          The very same.

                    GLORIA
          What're the seats?

                    JIM
          Fourth row, center.

                    GLORIA
          Deal.

INT. PLYMOUTH THEATRE - NIGHT

A grand proscenium frames the stage. Ornate crystal
chandeliers dangle over the audience. Jim and Gloria sit
fourth row center -- he in a Brooks Brothers suit, she in a
simple black dress with a string of artificial pearls and
matching earrings.

ON STAGE, a climactic confrontation takes place in a HOTEL
BALLROOM. A drunk and angry Navy defense attorney, HENRY
FONDA, confronts the FORMER OFFICERS of the U.S.S. Caine.

                    FONDA
          See, Mr. Keefer, while I was
          studying law and you were writing
          your short stories for national
          magazines, and little Willie here
          was on the playing fields of
          Princeton, why, all that time men
          like Captain Queeg, the ones we
          call regular Navy, they were
          standing guard on this fat stupid
          country of ours...

IN THE AUDIENCE, Jim crosses his legs, fighting to control a
rising agitation.

                    JIM
               (through his teeth)
          Damn right...

Gloria glances over, worried by his reaction.

ON STAGE, Fonda has raised his CHAMPAGNE GLASS to the most
dapper of the Caine's former officers, Lieutenant Thomas
Keefer, played by ROBERT GIST.

                         FONDA
               Here's to the guy who started the
               whole idea that Queeg was a
               dangerous paranoiac -- who argued
               you into it for a year and a half;
               who invented the nickname "Old
               Yellowstain."

Fonda lifts his champagne glass until it is level with Gist's
nose.

                         FONDA (cont'd)
               Here's to you. You bowled a
               perfect score. You went after
               Queeg and got him. You kept your
               own skirts all white and starchy.
               You'll publish your novel proving
               the Navy stinks and you'll make a
               million dollars and marry Heddy
               Lamar...

IN THE FOURTH ROW, Jim leans forward, eyes hungry, mouth
salivating for what he senses is imminent.

                         FONDA (cont'd)
               Here's to you, and here's to your
               book.

Fonda flings his champagne onto Gist's face.

IN THE FOURTH ROW, Jim mutters so low Gloria barely hears it.

                         JIM
               Beautiful.

TIME CUT: ON STAGE Fonda, JOHN HODIAK, Robert Gist, and LLOYD
NOLAN face the audience, join hands, and bow.

IN THE AUDIENCE, Jim is the first to jump to his feet, big
hands beating out thunderclaps, and whistling, his moist eyes
burning. Gloria follows suit, and soon the entire audience
rises, rewarding the actors with a passionate ovation.

EXT. PLYMOUTH THEATRE - WEST 45TH STREET - NIGHT

Gloria and Jim file out of the theatre with the rest of the
audience. They head toward Broadway, Jim withdrawn,
wrestling with a tumult of emotions. The crowd around them
thins.

                    GLORIA
          Wow, that was really something.
               (off his silence)
          You okay?

                    JIM
          Yeah... It's just, I had to deal
          with a lot of those assholes.

                    GLORIA
          What assholes?

                    JIM
          College boys. Ivy Leaguers.
          Joined the service in droves after
          Pearl Harbor. Thought their shit
          didn't stink.

                    GLORIA
          You were in the Navy?

                    JIM
          Marines. Joined in '38.

                    GLORIA
          That early? How come?

                    JIM
          Oh, I was a pretty rough kid. Got
          into trouble, so a judge gave me a
          choice. The marines, or juvenile
          hall.

Gloria's surprised. It doesn't fit with her image of him as
a dynamic and successful sales manager.

                    JIM (cont'd)
          My mother said, "President
          Roosevelt will never allow us to
          get involved in that war in
          Europe." I said, "I got news for
          you, Mom. We're already in it."

                    GLORIA
          What do you mean?

                    JIM
          Found myself on a destroyer in the
          North Atlantic in 1941. We were
          helping the British hunt the
          Bismarck. One night, this German U-
          Boat hits us with a spotlight,
          screaming Prussian over a
          loudspeaker.
                    (MORE)

                    JIM (cont'd)
          They knew what we were doing. See,
          we were in the fight before any of
          those college boys enlisted.
          Before the Japs bombed Pearl,
          nobody gave a shit about the war or
          the soldiers already fighting it.
          In fact, restaurants used to post
          signs in their windows: "No
          servicemen allowed." But the day
          after Pearl Harbor it all changed.
          Literally overnight. By then I was
          stationed at the Philadelphia Navy
          Yard. I'm walking down the street,
          go to light a cigarette and drop my
          lighter. Three civilians dove to
          pick it up for me. "Here you go,
          soldier!" I looked at 'em and
          said, "Not one of you sons-of-
          bitches woulda picked that up
          yesterday." Within six months the
          college boys joined us as freshly
          minted lieutenants. Didn't know
          shit from Shinola, but didn't
          prevent them from strutting around,
          barking orders at us. Those
          bastards got a lotta people killed.

                    GLORIA
          So you saw combat.
               (off his nod)
          Where?

                    JIM
          Guadalcanal. Peleliu. Okinawa.
          Lotta other places.

His eyes turn inward, jaw clenching. Gloria feels extremely
uncomfortable, uncertain what to say.

Suddenly, Jim comes to a halt, his eyes brightening with
childlike wonder.

                    JIM (cont'd)
          Here it is. Wanted to show you
          this.

They've come to a stop before THE PALACE THEATRE on Broadway.
The marquee declares the headliners: *In Person Judy Garland,
and Alan King.*

                    JIM (cont'd)
          The Palace. First opened in 1913.
          Can you imagine?
               (MORE)

45

                    JIM (cont'd)
          Used to be the premiere vaudeville
          theatre in the country. The
          pinnacle of American show business.
          Ed Wynn played here, Sara
          Bernhardt, Fanny Brice, The Three
          Keatons...

Gloria's relieved his dark mood has passed.

                    GLORIA
          Must have been something to see.

The doors open and PATRONS file out.

                    JIM
          You've never been inside?
               (she shakes her head)
          Come on!

He takes her hand. She hesitates.

                    GLORIA
          But we don't have tickets.

                    JIM
          So what? The show's over. They
          won't care.

Jim leads her past the stained glass and bronze framed doors
into...

INT. PALACE THEATRE - LOBBY - NIGHT

The ceiling soars 40 feet above them. The walls are yellow
Carrara marble. Gloria's awestruck.

                    GLORIA
          Oh my Lord!

                    JIM
          You ain't seen nothing yet. Come
          on.

                    GLORIA
          You sure it's okay?

                    JIM
          'Course.

He leads her into...

INT. PALACE THEATRE - AUDITORIUM - DAY

Eighteen hundred seats, two balconies, and 20 private boxes
laid out in tiers. A 14-foot-wide chandelier dangles above
them, beyond it a dome of molded concrete adorned with
hundreds of ornate rosettes. A massive proscenium with
scrolls and floral patterns. The French decor is Ivory-
Bronze, accented with liberal helpings of gold leaf. Jim is
as excited as a kid on Christmas morning.

                    JIM
          What do you think?

                    GLORIA
          It's... unbelievable... Like a
          cathedral.

                    JIM
          A cathedral of the American
          theatre.
               (points to the stage)
          Just think. Will Rogers stood
          there. And Al Jolson, Leon Errol,
          Ethel Barrymore and... so many
          others.

                    GLORIA
          It's the most beautiful thing I've
          ever seen.

EXT. BROADWAY - NIGHT

Jim and Gloria move down the street together, still glowing
from their experience in The Palace.

                    GLORIA
          How do you know so much about show
          business?

                    JIM
          My old man. He used to take me to
          the Memorial Theater in McKeesport.

                    GLORIA
          Where's that?

                    JIM
          Pennsylvania. Steel mill town just
          outside of Pittsburgh. That's
          where I grew up. We saw Harry
          Langdon at the Memorial.

                    GLORIA
          Who's he?

                    JIM
          A baby faced clown. Silent movie
          comedian. He came to McKeesport to
          do a live show. Afterward, we went
          to see him back stage, and... it
          was the damndest thing. Langdon
          wouldn't talk. He was still in his
          clown makeup, so he spoke only in
          pantomime. But you could
          understand everything, just through
          his gestures.
               (lost in the memory)
          It was... extraordinary... Still
          can't believe that really happened.

                    GLORIA
          Was your father in show business?

                    JIM
          No, he was a dentist. But he loved
          vaudeville. Knew all the comics'
          routines by heart. Could do any
          kind of accent -- German, Irish,
          Yiddish. Did all kinds of crazy
          characters. Loved to talk ragtime.

                    GLORIA
          So that's where you learned it...
          Is he...

                    JIM
          Dead... Died when I was 12. But
          not a day or an hour goes by that I
          don't think about him.

Gloria's affected by his intensity. It stirs memories of her
own.

EXT. P.J. CLARKE'S SALOON - 3RD AVENUE - NIGHT

A 19th Century brick edifice with a wood framed entrance.
Jim and Gloria approach it...

                    JIM
          Can't believe you've never been to
          P.J. Clarke's

                    GLORIA
          Heard about it. Was always
          curious...

                    JIM
          Best saloon in Manhattan, dates
          back to before the turn of the
          century. All the reporters in town
          hang out here, along with actors
          and producers from Broadway, TV,
          movers and shakers of all shapes
          and sizes.

Jim pushes through the doors.

INT. P.J. CLARK'S SALOON - NIGHT

The bar is packed. CIGARETTE SMOKE hangs in a thick fog
bank, making Gloria's eyes water. TWO BARTENDERS contend
with the jostling CUSTOMERS shouting drink orders. Jim leads
Gloria by the hand toward the closest mixologist -- RAFFERTY
(50), a leathery old Irishman with a busted purple nose that
contrasts with his gleaming white coat and black tie.

                    JIM
          Hey, Rafferty, whatdaya hear,
          whatdaya say?

                    RAFFERTY
          Hey Jimbo. You want your usual?
               (off Jim's nod)
          And for the lady?

Jim looks at Gloria.

                    GLORIA
          What's your usual?

                    JIM
          Martini, extra dry.

                    GLORIA
          I'll have the same.

                    JIM
               (to Rafferty)
          We'll be at a table in the back
          room.

INT. P.J. CLARK'S SALOON - BACK ROOM - NIGHT

Jim and Gloria sit at a table with a pair of EMPTY MARTINI
GLASSES. A WAITER, in a white apron and black tie, sets TWO
MASSIVE BACON CHEESEBURGERS before them, with PILES OF FRENCH
FRIES.

                    WAITER
          Two Cadillac Cheeseburgers with all
          the fixings.

Jim eyes a GROUP OF MEN who move past their table. He leans
forward to whisper excitedly.

                    JIM
          You see who that was? Sid Caesar,
          with his writing staff. They come
          in here all the time. Saw Nat King
          Cole here once. Heard him say to
          the waiter --

Jim notices Gloria staring at her cheeseburger.

                    JIM (cont'd)
          Something wrong?

She looks up with a stricken expression.

                    GLORIA
          My mother died when I was eighteen.
             (off his look)
          You talked about your Dad. I know
          how it feels.

                    JIM
          That was only, what, five years
          ago? Still pretty fresh.

                    GLORIA
          The worst part was... We had a
          fight the morning that she died. I
          was working on Wall Street at the
          time, as a secretary for a stock
          broker. Felt I was all grown up,
          too grown up to be taking orders
          from her anymore. She tried to
          reprimand me for staying out late,
          and it got... pretty nasty... My
          father found her that afternoon on
          the kitchen floor. Cold to the
          touch... She'd had a massive
          stroke... I feel so...

Tears spill from Gloria's eyes. She's unable to go on. Jim
takes her hand and holds it tight. She looks down at his
huge fingers enveloping hers, comforted by his incredible
strength.

INT. COMMUTER TRAIN/EXT. HUDSON RIVER - DAY

Gloria and Jim sit beside a window as the train makes its way
north. The river's bright blue water glistens in the
sunlight.

                    JIM
          You're so lucky.

                    GLORIA
          Why's that?

                    JIM
          To have grown up here. In one of
          these sleepy little storybook towns
          on the Hudson. It's like that
          Thornton Wilder play, *Our Town.*

                    GLORIA
               (amused)
          You think so? Look out the window.

He sees nothing. Throws her a quizzical glance.

                    GLORIA (cont'd)
          Keep watching. It's coming up.

                    JIM
          What is?

                    GLORIA
          You'll see, just past this next
          grove of trees.

The train clears the trees and Jim's eyes widen when he
sees...

OUTSIDE THE WINDOW, A LINE OF MEN standing on the river bank,
facing the train, zippers open, erect cocks in their hands as
they furiously jack off for the passengers.

                    JIM
          Holy shit! How'd you know they'd
          be there?

                    GLORIA
          Because they always are.

                    JIM
          Why?

                    GLORIA
          You're the show business expert.
          You tell me.

                    JIM
          (shakes his head)
     Wonder what Thornton Wilder would
     think.

They begin to laugh. Unable to stop, they lean against each
other.

EXT. IRVINGTON, NEW YORK - RAILROAD STATION - DAY

Gloria and Jim step off the TRAIN outside the quaint, steep-
roofed station, along with a DOZEN COMMUTERS returning from
Manhattan. Gloria scans the PEOPLE waiting to greet their
loved ones and spots Nick Byrne at the far end of the
platform.

                    GLORIA
     There he is.

She anxiously leads Jim toward her father, who wears a plaid
short-sleeved shirt, khaki pants, and work boots. Gloria
hugs Nick a little too tightly, out of nervousness.

                    GLORIA (cont'd)
     Hello, Daddy.

She turns and gestures to Jim.

                    GLORIA (cont'd)
     This is Jim Weddle.

Nick warmly takes Jim's hand.

                    JIM
     Mr. Byrne. An honor to meet you,
     sir.

                    NICK
     The honor is mine. From what Glo
     has told me, you must be a fine
     man.

                    JIM
     I could say the same about you,
     sir.

EXT. PLAYFAIR ESTATE/INT. NICK'S AUTOMOBILE - DAY

Nick's gray VOLKSWAGEN BEETLE pulls up to an enormous wrought
iron GATE.

High on a grass hill behind it sits a gray stone ENGLISH
STYLE COUNTRY ESTATE HOUSE, it's slate roof sprouting
multiple gables. A UNIFORMED GUARD opens the gate and waves
Nick's car through.

                    NICK
          Here we are. Home sweet home.

But instead of driving up the great CURVED DRIVEWAY to the
main house, Nick turns right and comes to a stop before a
small TUDOR CARETAKER'S HOUSE. They climb out. Gloria
covers her embarrassment with a self-conscious smile.

                    GLORIA
          This is where me and my sisters
          grew up.

Jim's fascinated and, to Gloria's surprise, impressed.

                    JIM
          It feels so... warm.

An IRISH COLLIE, chained outside of a DOG HOUSE, barks
excitedly.

                    NICK
          Quiet boy. It's not the first
          visitor you've seen.
               (to Jim)
          That's Joey. He's just a bunch of
          hide wrapped around an appetite.

Jim chuckles appreciatively.

INT. CARETAKER'S HOUSE - KITCHEN - DAY

They enter a modest kitchen with a WOOD AND COAL BURNING
STOVE. A PILE OF COAL IS STACKED BESIDE IT. BRASS POTS HANG
FROM AN OVERHEAD RACK. A PINE HUTCH DISPLAYS FLORAL
PATTERNED PLATES. Nick pulls a LINEN NAPKIN from a TRAY,
revealing a FRESHLY BAKED PIE.

                    NICK
          Do you fancy rhubarb pie, Jim?

                    JIM
               (lying)
          I do indeed.

                    NICK
          Help yourself. Would you like a
          spot of tea?

                    JIM
          That would be nice.

Nick feels the top of the stove and frowns. He opens the
oven door and sees it's dark inside.

                    NICK
          Ah, fire's gone out. I'll get some
          more wood. Be right back.

Nick steps out the door.

                    GLORIA
               (embarrassed)
          I've been begging him to get a gas
          stove, but he won't do it.

                    JIM
          So, you were born here.

                    GLORIA
               (nods)
          In my parents' bedroom.

                    JIM
          Can I see it?

INT. CARETAKER'S HOUSE - NICK'S BEDROOM - DAY

Gloria leads him in. There's a DOUBLE BED with a WORN QUILT.
A SILVER CROSS on the plaster wall. And a SILVER FRAMED
PICTURE OF GLORIA'S MOTHER, ANNA, on a PINE DRESSER. She's a
round-faced woman with gray hair and a gentle smile.

                    JIM
          Your mother?

Gloria nods. He picks up the picture to look at it more
carefully. Then sets it down again, his eyes drifting to the
bed.

                    JIM (cont'd)
          So right there.

Gloria nods, self-conscious.

                    GLORIA
          It's not much to look at, but --

                    JIM
          Hell, you shoulda seen the
          apartment I was born in. This is a
          palace compared to that.

186

Gloria's relieved.

EXT. PLAYFAIR ESTATE - DAY

Nick leads them through a GROVE OF FRUIT TREES. Joey
follows, excitedly sniffing about for rabbits.

                    NICK
          I planted these cherry trees here.
          As you can see, they're just
          beginning to bloom.

Jim examines the WHITE BLOSSOMS.

                    NICK (cont'd)
          And those apple trees there, and
          the peach just beyond.

A SAVAGE ROAR ruptures the tranquility.

                    JIM
          Jesus! What the hell is that?

They come to the top of a rise. ANIMAL CAGES are visible in
the distance.

                    NICK
          That's Caesar. The lion.

                    JIM
          Lion? What kind of lion?

                    NICK
          African. Mr. Playfair collects
          exotic animals.

                    GLORIA
          Daddy feeds them.

                    JIM
          You're kidding.

                    NICK
          I wish I was. That big cat bit the
          tip of me finger off. See?

Nick holds up his right index finger. The first digit is
missing. Before Jim can react, a series of LOUD HOOTS
reverberates from another cage. A SILVERBACK MOUNTAIN
GORILLA can be seen rattling the iron bars of his enclosure.

                    JIM
          Is... that a...

ZU5399

                    NICK
          Gorilla. Don't get too close. He
          likes to toss his dirty business at
          you. Got quite a sense of humor,
          that one.

They descend the hill onto a vast EMERALD LAWN with a view of
the Hudson.

                    JIM
          How often do you have to mow this?

                    NICK
          Never.

                    JIM
          Never? Then how do you --

                    NICK
          I'll show you.
               (to his dog)
          Joey, go get 'em!

Joey's ears pick up, his eyes snap into focus, and he runs
down the hill toward a depression near some distant OAK
TREES. Jim waits, mystified. Nick whistles sharply.

INARTICULATE CRIES ECHO FROM THE TREES. Suddenly, a HERD OF
WHITE SHEEP comes galloping into view. Nick uses a series of
whistles and hand gestures to command Joey, who brings them
to his master, zig-zagging, nipping at the baaing herbivores
with incredible speed and skill.

                    JIM
          That's amazing. Did you teach him
          to do that?

                    NICK
          Well, it wasn't Mr. Playfair, I can
          assure you.

The herd comes to a halt before them.

                    NICK (cont'd)
          They keep the grass shorn better
          than any mower, and fertilize it in
          the bargain.

Nick gestures and Joey lies on the grass, engorged tongue
spraying fine droplets of saliva. Nick squints at a large
sheep standing apart from the herd.

                    NICK (cont'd)
          Don't like the look of that one.
          Jim, would ya do me a favor? I've
          a bit of a bad back. Pick up that
          sheep for me.

                    JIM
          You want me to...

                    NICK
               (annoyed)
          Pick it up! Should be simple
          enough for a strapping young man
          like yourself.

                    JIM
          Uh, okay.

He tentatively walks over to the animal. It stares
impassively at him through vertically slit pupils. Jim's
uncertain about how to best proceed.

                    JIM (cont'd)
          I've never, how do I...

                    NICK
          Haven't got all day, man. Just do
          it!

Jim shrugs then bends over and wraps his long arms around the
torso of the sheep. The animal goes wild, bucking and
kicking like a bronco and sending Jim flat on his ass. He
slides a good three feet on the wet grass. As he shakes off
his shock, he hears...

Nick and Gloria doubled over, laughing.

                    NICK (cont'd)
          That's not how you pick up a sheep.

Nick walks over to the animal, grabs the wool of its neck in
his strong hand, lifts it, and sets it down on its butt.
Legs dangling in the air, the sheep becomes instantly docile.

                    NICK (cont'd)
          That's how you pick up a sheep.

                    JIM
          Duly noted.

ON A GLIMMERING POND WITH DUCK AND GEESE paddling about.

                    JIM (cont'd)
               (enraptured)
          It's like something out of a
          storybook.

Jim, Gloria, and her father stand at the water's edge.

                    NICK
          I pick me self fresh duck eggs
          every morning for breakfast.

Jim looks back at the now distant manor house.

                    JIM
          Hard to believe one man owns all
          this.

                    NICK
          He doesn't.

                    JIM
          What do you mean? I thought --

                    NICK
          Oh sure, he has a piece of paper
          that says he owns it. And maybe he
          pulls it out every now and again so
          he can show it to folks and puff
          out his chest a bit. But he no
          more owns this land than I do. We
          just take care of it for a while.
          Look after it until the next fellow
          comes along. There's only one real
          owner.

Nick points to the sky. Jim smiles.

                    JIM
          That's good... Very good.

Gloria's eyes glow. She's brought other men here who wanted
to argue the fine points of real estate law with her father.
Jim is the first one to understand.

INT. COMMUTER TRAIN/EXT. IRVINGTON STATION - DAY

Gloria and Jim sit together, waving at Nick on the platform
as the train pulls away.

                    GLORIA
          The lion didn't bite off the tip of
          Daddy's finger.
                    (MORE)

                    GLORIA (cont'd)
          He lost it in Ireland. Before I
          was born.

                    JIM
          How?

                    GLORIA
          We have no idea. He told each of
          my sisters a different story.

                    JIM
          So he speaks ragtime, too.

                    GLORIA
          Fluently.

They share a smile.

                    JIM
          I tell ya, he is really something.
          So pure, you know? Doesn't want
          much. Doesn't need it. Has a
          sense of his place in this world.
          His purpose. Not many people can
          claim that.

Gloria begins to cry. Jim's caught off guard.

                    JIM (cont'd)
          What'd I say? Did I --

                    GLORIA
          No. What you said was beautiful.

Jim hands her a LINEN HANDKERCHIEF from his breast pocket.

                    JIM
          Then what's wrong?

This is something she has never told anyone.

                    GLORIA
          Growing up, I was so ashamed of
          him. Because he was just a poor
          Irish farmer. A gardener, pulling
          weeds on a rich man's estate.

                    JIM
          He's more than that. Much more.

                    GLORIA
          I know that now... Should've
          always known it. I think... I
          think he sensed I was...

Gloria sobs harder; she's kept this locked inside for so
long. Jim takes the handkerchief clutched in her hand and
gently wipes away her tears.

                    JIM
          Hey... Hey, it's okay. Believe me,
          I know about shame.

Gloria looks into his blue eyes, wondering what he means.

EXT. PENNSYLVANIA COUNTRYSIDE/INT. MERCEDES - DAY

Jim drives through the rolling green hills of Pennsylvania,
Gloria beside him gazing out the open window, enjoying the
grass-scented air. They pass RED BARNS EMBLAZONED WITH ADS
FOR BULL DURHAM TOBACCO, COWS grazing in fields, groves of
large OAK TREES, picturesque STREAMS AND LAKES.

                    GLORIA
          So beautiful. Like upstate New
          York.

                    JIM
          Here's the turn-off.

They approach a sign for HIGHWAY 148 to MCKEESPORT,
PENNSYLVANIA. The car descends into a large RIVER VALLEY.
An ORANGE-BROWN HAZE soon envelops them, shrouding the sun.

                    GLORIA
          What's this smoke?

                    JIM
          It's from the mill.

As they continue their descent the GRASS ON THE HILLS turns
brown, then gray, then disappears altogether. The trees are
dead -- skeletal black branches reach toward the brown sky,
as if trying to claw their way through the soot.

Then below them, on the bank of the MONONGAHELA RIVER, the
STEEL MILL comes into view. A vast rust colored
conglomeration of enormous metal sheds, railroad tracks
crowded with freight cars loaded with steel pipe, coal, coke
and slag. And towering over the heaving metal labyrinth,
BLAST FURNACES -- rows of huge metal chimneys spewing orange-
black smoke into the sky; BESSEMER CONVERTERS spouting flames
as brilliant and hot as the sun. Gloria's both horrified and
awestruck.

                    GLORIA
          My Lord!

                    JIM
          Picturesque, isn't it? That's the
          National Tube Works. Any steel
          pipe you see anywhere in the United
          States, from flag poles to bridge
          railings -- all of it's made here.
          The mill stretches for the entire
          length of the town.

                    GLORIA
          Can't believe you grew up here.

                    JIM
          Joined the Marines to get the hell
          out. Guadalcanal was a garden of
          Eden compared to this place.

EXT. MCKEESPORT - LOCUST STREET - DAY

Jim and Gloria are on foot now, walking through a thriving,
grimy retail district. They pass THE STONE FRONT CAFE, a
large restaurant filled with STEEL WORKERS and MERCHANTS;
its windows coated with a thin layer of soot that obscures
the patrons' features.

                    JIM
          Grew up with my mother and brother
          in a little two bedroom apartment
          on Union Avenue.

                    GLORIA
          Where's that?

Jim gestures to a tall BLUFF overlooking the town, crammed
with LARGE HOMES and APARTMENT BUILDINGS.

                    JIM
          Up on that hill there. Anyway,
          when I started going to school, in
          first grade, that's when it hit me.
          All the other kids had fathers. So
          I asked my mother. "How come I
          don't have a dad?" She said, "You
          have one. He's a dentist. He has
          an office downtown. You can go see
          him anytime you want." She gave me
          the address and...

They arrive at a FOUR-STORY OFFICE BUILDING. The stone
exterior has been blackened by decades of soot laden air.

                    JIM (cont'd)
          That's the first time I came here.

The glass door to the building has been propped open with a
CINDER BLOCK. A PAIR OF WORKMEN trudge out, carrying a SLAB
OF STAINED WHITE MARBLE. The sight disturbs Jim.

                    JIM (cont'd)
          Something's going on...

He steps in the door to...

INT. LOCUST STREET OFFICE BUILDING - LOBBY - DAY

WORKMEN are busy removing SLABS OF MARBLE from the lobby's
walls, revealing the gray concrete behind them. POWER TOOLS
WHINE, men curse, and a FINE SPRAY OF DUST floats in the air.

Gloria has reluctantly followed Jim inside. He taps the
FOREMAN on the shoulder.

                    JIM
          What're you guys doing?

                    FOREMAN
          Getting ready to tear this place
          down. We're taking all the marble.
          These old buildings are filled with
          it. Worth a fortune.

                    JIM
               (bewildered)
          Why you demolishing it?

                    FOREMAN
          Redevelopment. City wants to put a
          a shopping mall here.

The news stings, but Jim struggles to hide it.

                    JIM
          Mind if we go upstairs?

                    FOREMAN
          Nothing up there. All the tenants
          moved out.

                    JIM
          That's okay. Just want to see my
          father's old office -- take one
          last look before it's gone.

                    FOREMAN
          Sure. Go ahead.

INT. LOCUST STREET OFFICE BUILDING - 3RD FLOOR HALLWAY - DAY

Jim leads Gloria down the marble-lined corridor, past old
wood doors with peeling varnish -- the brass knobs and
deadbolts have been removed.

                    JIM
          Was nervous as hell, first time I
          walked down this hall. What if he
          didn't want to see me? What if he
          yelled at me to go away and never
          come back?

                    GLORIA
          Why would you think he'd do that?

                    JIM
          He never made an effort to come see
          me. Didn't seem interested. Later
          I realized that was 'cause of my
          mother. He just couldn't deal with
          her.

Jim comes to a stop before a door. The brass numbers have
been removed, but they left a shadow on the cracked aging
wood: 305.

                    JIM (cont'd)
               (hushed reverence)
          This is it.

He pushes the door open; its hinges groan in protest.

INT. OFFICE - DAY

A yawning void. No furniture, no decor on the water damaged
walls. The hardwood floors splintered and stained. Jim
walks to the center, his mind reeling. Gloria steps in
behind him.

                    JIM
          Guess this is the last time I'll
          see it. Funny. Thought it would
          always be here... Never occurred
          to me that... First time I came, it
          was a thriving dentist office.
          Walked in, told the receptionist my
          name and said I wanted to see my
          father. He came right out.

Jim looks about, trying to spot a recognizable artifact. Is
there anything left to prove his father once lived?

196

                    GLORIA
          What was he like?

Jim's eyes snap back into focus.

                    JIM
          Most fascinating man I ever met.

Jim walks to the window, which looks out on the giant mill
spewing ash and fire. METALLIC BOOMS OF COLLIDING STEEL PIPE
echo across the town. Jim's eyes become dreamy, transported
to another time.

                    JIM (cont'd)
          He could see beyond this stinking
          rusted tin can of a town. He
          traveled. He and some of his pals
          took a train trip to California
          once. To go deep sea fishing off
          Catalina Island. Can you imagine?
          In the 1920's no one traveled
          beyond the towns they lived in. It
          was like going to Tahiti or
          something. He told me about all
          the movie stars he met. Buster
          Keaton, Charlie Chaplin, Stan
          Laurel...

Jim smiles at the memory. Gloria just listens, aware of
something terribly sad beneath his nostalgia.

                    JIM (cont'd)
          And all the time I knew him, in the
          entire six years, he never once
          laid a hand on me.

Jim says this as if it is remarkable. Extraordinary. He
wanders over to a far corner.

                    JIM (cont'd)
          Toward the end, he fell ill and his
          dental practice went to hell. Lost
          all his patients. He slept right
          here on a little cot. Wasted away
          until he weighed no more than 90
          pounds.

                    GLORIA
          What was wrong with him?

                    JIM
             (evasive)
          Don't know. No one ever told me.
          I think maybe...

                    GLORIA
          Maybe what?

                    JIM
          He died of a broken heart.

                    GLORIA
          Because of the split with your
          mother?

                    JIM
          No, it was bigger than that. See
          he was so bright, graduated Phi
          Beta Kappa from the University of
          Pittsburgh. But that worked
          against him.

                    GLORIA
          What do you mean?

                    JIM
          I think some people are too smart
          for this world. They, they can't
          cope. They see too much. Know too
          much. It works on their mind and
          they have trouble accepting
          things...

Jim squats down before a stain on the splintered floor.

                    JIM (cont'd)
          I wonder if he made this. Maybe he
          spilled something. Maybe this is
          his.
                    (looks up at her)
          When it was time for me to go, he
          always gave me a quarter. "Here, I
          got something for you," he'd say
          with a wink, and he'd press a
          quarter into my hand.

                    GLORIA
          And your brother?

Jim's expression hardens, his eyes narrowing.

                    JIM
          What about him?

                    GLORIA
          Did he come here, too?

                    JIM
          Never.

                    GLORIA
          Why not?

                    JIM
          He hated my father. Said he was a
          no good drunk who ran out on us.
          Left my mother to fend for herself.

Off Gloria, struggling to reconcile those two points of view.

EXT. GRANDVIEW CEMETERY/INT. MERCEDES - DAY

Jim drives into the hills above the mill town. The brown
haze hangs low overhead. The weather has turned cold and
there's a WIND. He hangs a right past the CONCRETE SIGN FOR
GRANDVIEW CEMETERY. Heads up an ASPHALT PATH, passing
headstones. Pulls to a stop before the FOURTH PINE TREE on
the left.

                    JIM
          This is it.

He steps out. Gloria follows. A cold blast of wind ripples
through the branches of the leafless trees, CRACKING the
joints of the skeletal fingers clutching at the low hanging
sky.

Jim walks to the fourth tree and stops, resting his big hand
against its gray bark. Looks up to the crest of the slope at
a BLACKENED STONE CROSS. Rests his back against the tree
trunk, facing the cross, and takes four measured steps
forward. They are the short strides of a little boy. Jim
stops, looking at the stone cross then back at the tree.
Carefully turns 90 degrees and counts off more half-steps.

Gloria realizes she is witnessing a ritual that no one has
seen before, a ritual he has chosen to reveal to her.

He stops just short of the crest of hill, looking down at
something in the grass.

                    JIM (cont'd)
          Here it is! I found it!

Gloria starts up the hill, DEAD BRANCHES AND LEAVES crunching
underfoot. She passes headstones from the early 1900s
bearing inscriptions -- "Cherished Wife," "Faithful Husband,"
"Beloved Sister." People remembered by people who are
themselves no longer remembered.

As she ascends, the dates on the tombstones move into the
1920s then 30s. Gloria comes to a halt beside him and looks
down at the weedy brown grass.

Grandview
Cemetery
Established 1902

                    JIM (cont'd)
          There. That's the one.

At first she sees nothing, but then a GUST OF WIND sends a
patch of leaves airborne and she spots it...

A SMALL MUDDY BLACKENED STONE MARKER cn the ground, bearing
only a number: 262. And all at once she realizes.

                    GLORIA
          That's your father.
               (off his nod)
          How can you be sure?

                    JIM
          Because I've been coming here since
          I was 12.

Jim kneels to wipe the sludge from the marker. Some comes
away easily, but some of the grime is too deeply embedded in
the stone.

                    JIM (cont'd)
          The night he died, my mother took
          us to see him at McKeesport
          Hospital.

                    GLORIA
          You and your brother?

                    JIM
               (nods)
          The old man was wasted away.
          Almost nothing left, but those blue
          eyes, burning so bright I could
          hardly stand to look into them. He
          fumbled around on the little tray
          beside his bed, looking for
          something, but he couldn't find it.
          Finally he falls back on the
          pillow, exhausted, and says, "I'm
          sorry, Jimmy. I had a quarter here
          somewhere, but I can't find it
          now." Can you imagine?
          Apologizing to me.

                    GLORIA
          And your brother? Did he say
          anything to him?

                    JIM
          He told Bill he loved him. But
          Bill just stood there, like a
          manikin. Didn't say a word.
               (MORE)

                    JIM (cont'd)
          We left after a few minutes. He
          was too weak to say more. Then,
          about 20 minutes after we got back
          to the apartment, the phone rings.
          My mother answers it. Speaks a few
          words then hangs up. Turns to me
          and says, "Your father's dead."

Gloria's eyes well up.

                    JIM (cont'd)
          I burst out crying and bam! My
          brother smacks me across the face
          and yells, "Don't you dare! Don't
          you ever cry for him in this
          house!"

Gloria takes Jim's hand. He pulls her close as he begins to
cry. The small strangled sobs of a young boy.

                    JIM (cont'd)
          They didn't even put a headstone on
          it. That's how little they thought
          of him

                    GLORIA
          Why don't you do it?

                    JIM
          Because...

                    GLORIA
          Because why?

                    JIM
          'Cause I want my brother to do it
          with me. Pay for half.

                    GLORIA
          You think he'll agree to that?

                    JIM
          He hasn't yet.... But he will.
          He's got to...
               (wipes his tears)
          My old man told a lot of crazy far-
          fetched stories, but there was one.
          One I'll always remember.

                    GLORIA
          What's that?

                    JIM
          About the birds that fly backwards.

                    GLORIA
          The... what?

                    JIM
          The birds that fly backwards. He
          said, "Watch for them every winter,
          Jimmy. You'll see whole flocks of
          them flying north. You know why
          they fly backwards?"

Jim looks at her with strange urgency.

                    JIM (cont'd)
          "Because in order for them to know
          where they're going, they need to
          see where they've been."

Gloria meets the intensity of his gaze.

                    GLORIA
          Wish I could have met him. Known
          him. Like you did.

Jim pulls her to him and they kiss passionately on the hill
of a denuded graveyard, under a brown poisoned sky.

EXT. VERSAILLES AVENUE/INT. MERCEDES - DAY

Jim drives down the hill past once grand now decaying
VICTORIAN HOMES.

                    GLORIA
          So what about your Mom?

                    JIM
          What about her?

                    GLORIA
          Where does she live now?

                    JIM
          Here. She never left this place.
          My brother, too. He takes care of
          her.

                    GLORIA
          Where in town?

Jim pulls to the curb in front of a modest BRICK DUPLEX. He
points to the apartment on the corner.

                    JIM
          There. That's where I grew up.

                    GLORIA
          Are we going in to see her?

                    JIM
          No.

Jim slips the car into gear and executes a U-turn.

                    GLORIA
          Jim, she's your mother. I want
          to...

                    JIM
          Trust me, you don't.

                    GLORIA
          Yes, I do.

                    JIM
          Another time.

                    GLORIA
          You mean we came all this way and
          you're not even going to...

                    JIM
          Gloria, drop it. Okay?

Gloria falls silent as the car pulls away. Then she
notices...

THE LIVING ROOM WINDOW OF THE APARTMENT. A curtain parts.
In the dark void of the interior, she spots A BEEHIVE OF RED
HAIR and the glint of SILVER WINGTIP EYEGLASSES. Bumps rise
on the back of Gloria's neck. Something about that presence,
there in the darkness, causes her to cease her protest.

INT. ST. BARNABAS CHURCH - IRVINGTON NY - DAY

ON GLORIA'S SLENDER FINGER as Jim slips a GOLD BAND up it,
snug against a DIAMOND ENGAGEMENT RING.

                    PRIEST
          I now pronounce you man and wife.
          You may kiss the bride.

REVEAL GLORIA AND JIM standing before the ALTAR and the
PRIEST. Jim wears a black tux, Gloria a billowing white gown
and sheer flowing veil. Jim gingerly lifts her veil and they
kiss deeply. The priest gently touches their shoulders,
indicating they should turn and face...

THE PEOPLE IN THE PEWS.

                    PRIEST (cont'd)
          Ladies and Gentlemen, I now present
          to you Mr. and Mrs. James Weddle.

The crowd leaps to its feet, applauding. Nick, Eleanor,
Muriel, and Sheila are in the first pew, wearing their best
Sunday clothes. Nick has tears in his eyes. So do Muriel
and Sheila. Eleanor is more reserved.

EXT. ST. BARNABAS CHURCH - IRVINGTON NY - DAY

Jim and Gloria rush down the front steps as people pelt them
with RICE. They head for a polished black CADILLAC festooned
with CREPE PAPER, STRINGS OF TIN CANS, AND SOAPED MESSAGES
ABOUT ENJOYING THEIR HONEYMOON.

Nick stands with his daughters at the top of the steps as the
couple climb into the car.

                    ELEANOR
          I give it a year, tops.

                    SHEILA
          Can't you just be happy for her?

                    ELEANOR
          For marrying a first class bastard?

                    MURIEL
          Why in God's name would you call
          him that?

                    ELEANOR
          Take a good look. It's written all
          over him.

                    NICK
               (to Eleanor)
          Hush! This is Glo's day. Don't
          ruin it.

Eleanor falls silent, filled with foreboding as she waves to
her sister. Gloria looks out of the Cadillac's window,
beaming as she waves back. The car begins to move, carrying
her away from her family and toward her new life with James
Weddle.

EXT. DC-7 - ACAPULCO - DAY

The four-propeller airliner descends toward a postcard
perfect tropical bay.

FISHING AND DAY BOATS bob in the glistening water. HOTELS
are perched on bluffs overlooking white sand beaches.

                    GLORIA (O.C.)
          So beautiful.

INT. DC-7 - PASSENGER CABIN - DAY

Gloria and Jim peer out the curtained windows, excited as a
couple of kids.

                    GLORIA
          It's like something out of a movie.

                    JIM
          Reminds me of the South Pacific.

A STEWARDESS takes the DAIQUIRI GLASSES from their tray
tables.

                    STEWARDESS
          Please fasten your seatbelts and
          secure your trays. We'll be
          landing soon.

They comply. Jim reaches his hand out to Gloria. She takes
it and they look deeply into each other's eyes.

INT. ACAPULCO HONEYMOON SUITE - SUNSET

ON GLORIA'S BACK as she stands on the balcony, looking out at
the bay. The ENLARGED ORANGE SUN bobs on the golden water,
sinking slowly into it. She wears a bright flower print
dress that reaches to her thighs.

                    JIM (O.C.)
          Gloria.

She continues to stare at the water.

                    JIM (cont'd)
               (gently insistent)
          Gloria.

She turns to see her husband -- wearing navy shorts and a
Hawaiian shirt -- handing CASH to a red-jacketed ROOM SERVICE
WAITER.

                    GLORIA
          Sorry. Was just looking at the
          ocean. It gives me such a sense of
          peace.

The waiter departs, leaving behind a CART with A BOTTLE OF
CHAMPAGNE AND GLASSES.

                         GLORIA (cont'd)
               What's this?

                         JIM
               Management sent us a complimentary
               bottle of champaign. You want
               some?

                         GLORIA
               After all those drinks at dinner?

                         JIM
               We'll save it for later, then.

He sits on the HUGE KING-SIZED BED. Begins unbuttoning his
shirt.

Gloria realizes the moment of consummation is upon her.
Suddenly uneasy, she steps to the champagne bottle. Reads
the CARD sent with it.

                         GLORIA
               What a lovely sentiment. By the
               way, I signed us up for water
               skiing tomorrow.

He doesn't answer. She turns. His shirt is now off,
revealing his lean muscular torso.

                         JIM
               Nervous?

                         GLORIA
               About water skiing? Oh, I don't
               know. I think I'll be able to --

                         JIM
               No. About this.

He places his hand on the bed. Gloria blushes, suddenly
fascinated by the label on the champagne.

                         GLORIA
               A little, I guess...

                         JIM
               You don't need to be.

                         GLORIA
               Muriel says it hurts the first
               time.

                    JIM
          A little. Just for a moment. Then
          it's quite nice.

Gloria looks up with a smile.

                    GLORIA
          Oh, you know all about it, do you?

Now Jim blushes. Shifts uncomfortably.

                    JIM
          I'm only saying --

                    GLORIA
          That you've deflowered a multitude
          of virgins -- and know all the ins
          and outs, so to speak?

                    JIM
          Okay, hold on, don't know what you
          think you know about me --

                    GLORIA
          I know whenever I'm at your
          apartment the phone rings and rings
          and yet you never pick it up. Why
          is that, Jim?

                    JIM
               (laughs, busted)
          Those are just friends.

                    GLORIA
          Friends who taught you all about
          women's bodies?

Jim gets up and walks toward her.

                    JIM
          Maybe. But they're not in the same
          class as you. Not even close.
          You're the one, Gloria.

                    GLORIA
          The one? What does that mean?

                    JIM
          The one I want to spend the rest of
          my life with. The one I want to
          wake up with every morning.

                    GLORIA
          Even when I'm old and gray with my
          teeth and hair falling out, my mind
          gone...

He places his huge hands on her shoulders, his blue eyes
boring deep into hers.

                    JIM
          Hell yes. I go bonkers for a dame
          wearing a diaper and a drool cup.
          Really stokes my furnace.

                    GLORIA
          Is that a fact?

                    JIM
          Yes, it is, Mrs. Weddle.

He kisses her. Still apprehensive, she breaks it off.

                    GLORIA
          I'm gonna take a shower.

Jim watches her walk to the bathroom, contemplating her
anxiety.

INT. ACAPULCO HONEYMOON SUITE - BATHROOM - EVENING

Gloria sticks her hand into the shower to test the warmth of
the water. Satisfied, she slips out of her white TERRYCLOTH
ROBE and into the marble-lined chamber.

Runs the water through her hair, hoping the warm rivulets
will wash away her fear.

Suddenly, the door opens and Jim steps in, stark naked.

                    GLORIA
                 (startled)
          What are you --

He laughs, pulling her into his arms, nuzzling her neck.
Gloria feels his incredible strength and her fear begins to
subside. His mouth meets hers. She kisses him tentatively,
then with rising passion.

His mouth moves down to her breasts.

Gloria tilts her head back. The spray bounces off her
forehead and hair. She moans softly.

His mouth comes back to hers. She kisses him wildly.

Jim grabs her legs and hoists them up around his waist.

The shower pounds her face.

                    GLORIA (cont'd)
          Oh....

He thrusts. She cries out. Then he moves more slowly.
Languidly. The pain subsides and she begins to move with
him, finding her rhythm.

Her left hand digs into his broad shoulder.

Her right hand rakes the back of his head.

CLOSE ON GLORIA'S FACE, her eyes glassy.

                    GLORIA (cont'd)
          Oh, Jim... Jim!

INT. ENCHANTED HILLS RETIREMENT HOME - GLORIA'S ROOM - DAY

Forty years later, Gloria sits on her bed, staring up at the
photo of her and Jim on their last trip together to the South
Pacific. Both of them gray and wrinkled, but their eyes
aglow like the young lovers they had once been so very long
ago.

Gloria's eyes roil with conflicting emotions -- tenderness,
rage, heartache, horror, and... love.

                                        FADE OUT.

          <u>END OF EPISODE THREE</u>

EPISODE FOUR

Semper Fi

INT. BILTMORE HOTEL ROOM - LOS ANGELES - DAY

SUPER: **1995**

MOVE ACROSS THE TOP OF A DRESSER past a battered HALLIBURTON
BRIEFCASE. Its aluminum skin has been painted with WILD DAY-
GLOW RAINBOW SWIRLS THAT FORM A CONSTELLATION OF MANDALAS.
The broken hinges have been buttressed with aging DUCT TAPE.
Next to it lies a LOS ANGELES PUBLIC LIBRARY FLYER with Ken
Kesey's picture on it and a headline: KEN KESEY, AUTHOR OF
ONE FLEW OVER THE CUCKOO'S NEST, READS FROM HIS NEW NOVEL,
LAST GO ROUND.

KEEP MOVING TO FIND KEN KESEY (60) standing before a FULL
LENGTH MIRROR as he slowly pulls on the elements of his
costume. He's a big man with a huge boulder-sized bald head
fringed with gray hair, thick powerful shoulders, arms and
hands that contrast sharply with his vulnerable blue eyes and
soft voice. Kesey's already wearing a pair of black cowboy
boots and black slacks. Now he pulls an American flag blouse
over his undershirt, followed by a a string tie held together
by a silver medallion, and a brown riverboat gambler's hat
with a snakeskin band.

                    KESEY
          So what have you been up to lately,
          David?

REVEAL DAVID WEDDLE (39) sitting on a nearby couch with a
LEGAL PAD, a PEN, and a PORTABLE TAPE RECORDER that's slowly
turning.

                    DAVID
          Working.

                    KESEY
          I can see that. What else?

                    DAVID
          Well... been taking care of my
          mother. She has a malignant brain
          tumor.

Kesey pauses to look at David, noting the strain on his face.
The crevices in his broad forehead deepen.

                    KESEY
          I'm sorry to hear that.

                    DAVID
          Thanks... I had to put her into an
          assisted living facility. She
          wasn't happy about it. It's been a
          bit... overwhelming.

Kesey resumes dressing, but watches David in the mirror.

                    KESEY
          Yeah, taking care of someone when
          they get into that state can become
          a full time job, even after you put
          them into a home. My mother took
          care of my grandmother for ten
          years. Now that she's gone, my mom
          doesn't know what to do with
          herself.

                    DAVID
          It's impacting my ability to work.
          I have other books I want to write,
          but... Can't seem to get it
          together.

                    KESEY
          Maybe you're not meant to right
          now.

                    DAVID
          What do you mean?

                    KESEY
          In 1969 the Beatles hired me to
          work for Apple Records. So I moved
          my family to London. My father was
          dying at the time and he asked me
          to send my oldest daughter home
          early so he could spend a few days
          with her. I figured she had three
          weeks more to finish out the school
          year and that it could wait. Well,
          he died before he could see her
          again.
                    (turns to look at David)
          When I play with my grandkids now
          and think what it would be like not
          have the chance to say goodbye to
          them... That's a very big regret.
          Our work's important, but the
          people we love are more important.

OFF DAVID, taking this in.

INT. LOS ANGELES PUBLIC LIBRARY - DAY

A CLOCK ON THE WALL READS 2:33. MOVE DOWN FROM IT AND ALONG
A LINE OF EXCITED FANS holding COPIES OF KEN KESEY'S NOVELS --
*One Flew Over the Cuckoo's Nest, Sometimes a Great Notion,
Demon Box*, and *Last Go Round*.

They are tweedy academics, aging hippies in tie-dyed regalia,
and young Deadheads in Rastafarian braids.

ARRIVE AT KESEY, seated at a DESK, signing books with an
array of COLORED PENCILS, and embellishing each signature
with DIFFERENT COLORED STAMPS of HOLY FOOLS, MANDALAS, and
GRATEFUL DEAD SKULLS AND DANCING BEARS. INK PADS are laid
out beside the stamps; more ART SUPPLIES are in the
Halliburton briefcase, lying open on the desk.

REVEAL David standing nearby, his TAPE RECORDER documenting
every moment.

Kesey signs a HARDBACK EDITION OF *SOMETIMES A GREAT NOTION*
for a wide-eyed YOUNG WOMAN with blond and purple hair. He's
in mid-conversation with her.

> KESEY
> We're fighting a battle to save the
> world, whether it wants to be saved
> or not. We've got to stand up and
> holler, "Christ yes we're
> liberals!" It takes a whole lot
> more brains, and it takes a whole
> lot more common guts to be a
> liberal. We've got to get off each
> other's cases and begin to reach
> out there and strengthen the other
> person. Because we've got a world
> to save.

He hands the book to her. She clutches it to her breast,
ecstatic.

> YOUNG WOMAN
> Thank you, Mr. Kesey!

She pivots and walks away as the next person steps up to
Kesey to have a book signed.

David follows the young woman as she heads toward the exit.

> DAVID
> Hi, my name is David Weddle. I'm
> writing an article for *L.A. Weekly.*
> Is that your favorite Kesey book?

> YOUNG WOMAN
> *Sometimes a Great Notion* is my
> favorite book, period! That man's
> work has meant so much to me.

TIME CUT: THE WALL CLOCK READS 4:58. MOVE DOWN to where
Kesey is signing a POSTER FOR THE *TRIPS FESTIVAL* IN 1966,
featuring a disorienting swirling vortex. It belongs to a
YOUNG MAN with DREADLOCKS AND HOLE-RIDDLED JEANS, holding a
SKATEBOARD under one arm. Kesey pauses to admire the
battered image on the poster.

                    KESEY
          That was a great time. Hot stuff.
          I feel fortunate to have been a
          part of it.

                    YOUNG MAN
          Thank you, man!

The young man turns and heads for the exit. David approaches
him with his tape recorder.

                    DAVID
          David Weddle, *L.A. Weekly.* Which
          of his books have you read?

                    YOUNG MAN
          I haven't actually read any of
          them. I saw the movie, *One Flew
          Over the Cuckoo's Nest.* See, I'm a
          Deadhead, and I heard it all
          started with him. That's why I
          came.

BACK AT THE DESK, Kesey is talking with a conservatively
dressed ENGLISH PROFESSOR. Ken fingers the lapel of his
American Flag blouse.

                    KESEY
          Nothing could be further from the
          truth. I'm not mocking the flag by
          wearing this, I'm celebrating it.
          Think about what this flag stands
          for. Freedom. Freedom of speech.
          Freedom of thought. Freedom to
          disagree with your government.
          Even the freedom to burn it. Think
          about how profound that is.
          Nowhere else in history has there
          ever been a flag that stands for
          the right for someone to burn it.

Kesey glances up at the clock.

                    KESEY (cont'd)
          Whoah, didn't realize it was this
          late. I gotta a flight to catch!

He packs his pencils, stamps, and ink pads into his battered
Day-Glo suitcase and presses the sagging duct tape tight to
the hinges. Ken heads toward the exit with long rapid
strides, along with the LIBRARIAN who organized the event.
David falls in beside him.

                    DAVID
          Ken, thank you for taking the time
          to talk to me.

Kesey stops and envelops David in a tight bear hug. Then
leans back, his two enormous hands on David's shoulders.
His electric blue eyes bore into the younger man.

                    KESEY
          I'm very sorry about the trouble
          you're having with your mother.
          But, you know, grief is a luxury.
          These people caught up in the civil
          wars in Bosnia and Sudan right now,
          where they're losing thousands
          every day -- they don't have the
          opportunity to grieve because their
          loved ones suddenly disappear,
          never to be heard from again. So
          try to make the most of the time
          you have left with your mother.
          Try to enjoy it and be thankful you
          have been given at least that.

Kesey continues on his way down the hall. David watches the
psychedelic Don Quixote with his battered suitcase full of
Day-glo dreams disappear through the door, and ruminates on
his advice.

INT. ENCHANTED HILLS RETIREMENT HOME - GLORIA'S ROOM - DAY

Gloria (63) sits on her bed staring at the gold-framed
picture of her mother and father. Behind her, a small COLOR
TV plays THE EVENING NEWS. David eases open the door.

                    DAVID
          Hi, Mom!

Gloria turns to him, lighting up with a big smile.

                    GLORIA
          Hello! I'm so happy to see you!

David sits beside her, puts his arm around her shoulders and
gently pulls her into a hug. She buries her head in the
crook of his shoulder and neck, like a child starved for
affection.

                    GLORIA (cont'd)
          I'll take it! I'll take it!

David gazes at the picture of her parents.

                    DAVID
          You've been looking at your
          parents?

She nods, regarding the photograph thoughtfully.

                    GLORIA
          Yes. Sometimes I talk to them.
          And they talk to me.

Behind them, on the TV, comes the familiar TICK-TICK-TICK of
the opening of *60 Minutes*. MIKE WALLACE appears on the
screen.

                    MIKE WALLACE (ON TV)
          Tonight, on *60 Minutes*, a report
          from the front lines of the brutal
          civil war in Bosnia, where last
          month the Serbian Army perpetrated
          one of the largest mass killings
          since World War Two in what the
          United States is calling a
          systematic campaign of genocide.

David grips his mother's hand tight and rubs her forearm.

                    GLORIA
               (softly)
          I'll take it.

ON THE TV: MIKE WALLACE narrates as a SERBIAN TANK rumbles
down a road firing its machine guns and then its cannon into
a dense forest.

                    MIKE WALLACE (ON TV)
          On July Sixth the Bosnian-Serb Army
          began advancing. Tens of thousands
          of Bosnian Muslims fled and were
          under siege in the town of
          Srebrenica, under the protection of
          600 lightly armed U.N.
          Peacekeepers.

REVEAL DAVID AND GLORIA, now lying on the bed, watching the
screen, still holding hands -- Gloria impassive, content to
have her son at her side; David, disturbed by...

ON THE TV: images of Serbian soldiers rounding up young
Muslim men at gunpoint.

                    MIKE WALLACE (cont'd)
               Faced with overwhelming firepower,
               the UN soldiers surrendered. The
               Serbians then rounded up all Muslim
               men between the ages of 12 and 77
               for what they claimed were
               "interrogations." The first
               killings began two days later.
               More than 8,000 Muslims were
               murdered in just five days, their
               bodies dumped in mass graves.

David shifts about on the bed, emotions roiling.

ON THE TV: images of Serbs shooting unarmed civilians and
heaps of bodies INTERCUT WITH BLACK AND WHITE FLASHES of
AMERICAN MARINES MACHINE GUNNING WAVES OF ATTACKING JAPANESE
SOLDIERS... WE ARE NOW IN...

INT. WEDDLE LIVING ROOM - DAY

SUPER: **1966**

TEN-YEAR-OLD DAVID sits on the floral patterned couch beside
46-YEAR-OLD JAMES WEDDLE as they watch *THE WORLD AT WAR* on
the GE COLOR TV. Jim is tense -- smoking, crossing and
recrossing his legs, obsessed by the imagery, possessed and
tormented and yet transfixed by it.

                    NARRATOR (ON TV)
               Wave after wave of Japanese
               soldiers charged the marines at
               Bloody Ridge, the night echoing
               with their animalistic cries of
               "Banzai!"

                    JIM
                 (to David)
               They'd run right over the backs of
               their dead, howling like hyenas...

                    NARRATOR (ON TV)
               Only to be cut down by the machine
               guns of the marines... Then came a
               new terror weapon.

ON THE TV: IMAGES OF JAPANESE ZEROS DIVING THROUGH ANTI-
AIRCRAFT FIRE STRAIGHT INTO AIRCRAFT CARRIERS AND DESTROYERS
AND EXPLODING.

                    NARRATOR (ON TV) (cont'd)
          The Kamikaze, which in Japanese
          means "Divine Wind," were a
          desperate effort to turn the tide
          of the war in Japan's favor.
          Japanese suicide pilots, chained in
          their cockpits, flew their planes
          straight into American ships...

                    DAVID
          Did you see them do that?

                    JIM
               (nods)
          Lost a lot of friends to those
          bastards. See, the Japs didn't
          value life the way we did. Didn't
          care whether they lived or died.

                    NARRATOR (ON TV)
          Most Japanese refused to surrender.
          Many jumped off cliffs to their
          deaths. Others holed up in the
          island's lava tubes and fought to
          the bitter end.

ON TV: A MARINE WITH A FLAME THROWER STRAPPED TO HIS BACK
CAUTIOUSLY APPROACHES THE MOUTH OF A CAVE.

                    JIM
          Only one way to deal with them...

ON TV: THE MARINE FIRES A RIPPLING COLUMN OF FLAME INTO THE
CAVE.

                    JIM (cont'd)
          Gotta burn 'em out.

ON TV: A JAPANESE SOLDIER STUMBLES OUT OF THE CAVE ON FIRE.
HE STAGGERS A FEW FEET THEN FALLS DEAD, STILL BURNING. THE
MARINES WATCH IMPASSIVELY.

                    JIM (cont'd)
          Burn 'em. It's the only way.

                    NARRATOR (ON TV)
          The fighting in the South Pacific
          was the most savage of the entire
          Second World War. As the marines
          pushed inland, they came upon
          American soldiers who had been
          mutilated by the Japanese.

                    JIM
          My patrol found the bodies of three
          of our guys, hands tied behind
          their backs, with their penises cut
          off and stuffed into their mouths.

                    DAVID
               (shocked)
          Seriously?...

                    JIM
          You bet your ass, I'm serious.

There's an anxiety beneath Jim's anger, a hint of panic.

                    NARRATOR (ON TV)
          Only a handful of Japanese
          surrendered.

ON TV: A GROUP OF MARINES CAPTURE A BLISTERED AND BLACKENED,
WEEPING JAPANESE SOLDIER.

Jim turns to David, his eyes strangely intense.

                    JIM
          We'd get orders to take 'em back to
          the base for interrogation. And
          guess what?

                    DAVID
          What?

                    JIM
               (with relish)
          None of 'em made it.

                    DAVID
          What happened to them?

                    JIM
          Shot while trying to escape. Only
          a couple ever got questioned and
          you know what they said?

David stares with big eyes, waiting.

                    JIM (cont'd)
          They thought they were on Catalina
          Island. Just a few miles off the
          coast of California. That's how
          primitive those people were.

OUTSIDE THE GLASS DOORS, a JAPANESE GARDENER mows the lawn.
David's gaze strays over to him, filled with questions.

PLATOON, 15
MARINE BARRACKS
PARRIS ISLAND, S.C.

PLAT. SGT. M. B. JOHNSTON
CPL. O. WILLIAMS
JULY 1938

                    NARRATOR (ON TV)
          Survivors of those vicious battles
          report atrocities committed by both
          sides.

A FORMER MARINE, in his mid-40s, APPEARS ON THE TV.

                    FORMER MARINE (ON TV)
                 (tears in his eyes)
          I saw a lot of Marines who went
          over the edge. They'd cut the ears
          off of dead Japanese, yank out
          their gold teeth. Even came across
          one guy who completely lost it. He
          was boiling a Japanese head in a
          bucket so he could keep the skull
          as a souvenir.

Jim erupts, bolting to his feet, spraying spit as he screams
at the screen.

                    JIM
          THAT NEVER HAPPENED! LYING SON-OF-
          A-BITCH!

Jim snaps the TV off. David watches THE IMAGE COLLAPSE INTO
DARKNESS.

INT. WEDDLE HOUSE - ENTRYWAY - DAY

ON THE OAK DOOR AS THE DOORBELL RINGS.

                    GLORIA (O.C.)
          David, can you get that?

A pause. THE DOORBELL RINGS AGAIN.

                    GLORIA (O.C.) (cont'd)
          David...

                    DAVID
          I got it!

David, dressed in different clothes because it's a different
day, opens the door to find a UPS DRIVER with a THICK PADDED
ENVELOPE AND A STEEL CLIPBOARD WITH A PEN.

                    UPS DRIVER
          Special delivery.

                    DAVID
          Thanks.

                    UPS DRIVER
          Sign here for it.

David does. The driver nods and heads off to his TRUCK.
David reads the envelope's label as he shuts the door.

                    GLORIA (O.C.)
          Who was it?

                    DAVID
          Delivery for Dad.

                    JIM (O.C.)
          Who's it from?

                    DAVID
          Saul Bass.

An excited Jim appears in a red shirt and plaid shorts.

                    JIM
          Oh great! It's the latest graphics
          for the marketing campaign.

Jim takes the envelope and rips it open. As he reaches in, a
HUGE BLACK COCKROACH leaps out, crawling up the hairs of
Jim's forearm. Jim jumps back, emitting small inarticulate
whines of panic as he slaps the bug off his arm. It skitters
across the tile. Jim jumps back with a strangled cry. David
stomps the bug flat.

                    DAVID
          It's okay. I got him.

ON THE VISCOUS BLOB OF PROTOPLASM that was the roach as David
wipes it away with a PAPER TOWEL.

                    DAVID (cont'd)
          I cleaned it up.

No answer from his father. David walks into...

INT. WEDDLE HOUSE - LIVING ROOM - DAY

David enters to find his Dad slumped in a chair, struggling
to breath, pale skin mottled and covered with sweat.

                    DAVID
          What's wrong?

Jim struggles to focus on his son. He gently grips David's
forearm.

                    JIM
          Can't take bugs.

                    DAVID
          I don't like 'em either.

Jim tries to slow his breathing.

                    JIM
          Can't let them near me.

                    DAVID
          Why?

                    JIM
          'Cause of the war. First year,
          they didn't bother me. But then...
          After a year of pulling ticks out,
          burning leeches off with
          cigarettes... I don't know... Got
          so I just couldn't take it anymore.
          Only so much... only so much you
          can take...

David strokes the thick black hairs of his father's forearm.

                    DAVID
          I'm sorry, Dad.

Jim pulls him into a tight embrace.

                    JIM
          I love you. You know that, don't
          you?

David nods. His eyes tear up. This is the father he longs
for. The one who always comes back to him after the fits of
rage.

EXT. WEDDLE HOUSE - BACK YARD - ANOTHER DAY

The Japanese gardener, TAKASHI (35), picks SNAILS off of
SHRUBS, dropping them into a bucket.

                    DAVID
                (awkward pronunciation)
          Kon'nichiwa...

Takashi turns to find David gazing at him with huge curious
eyes. Takashi smiles and bows his head slightly. Then
unleashes a TORRENT OF JAPANESE.

                    DAVID (cont'd)
          Sorry. That's the only word I
          know.

                    TAKASHI
          Where did you learn it?

                    DAVID
          School. Did you move here from
          Japan after the war?

                    TAKASHI
          No. I am American. I was born in
          Fullerton.

David's surprised. Doesn't quite know what to say next. He
nods to the bucket.

                    DAVID
          Can I help you?

                    TAKASHI
          Sure. Look for snails. When you
          find them, throw them into the
          bucket.

David watches Takashi's strong dexterous fingers pick off
snails. He imitates the technique, stealing curious glances
at Takashi.

EXT. WEDDLE HOUSE - DAY

ON AN AMERICAN FLAG ATOP A TALL POLE, FLAPPING AGAINST THE
BLUE CALIFORNIA SKY. MOVE DOWN FROM IT TO THE FRONT LAWN,
which features a HUGE GRANITE BOULDER and a brick walkway to
the oak slab of a front door. It opens. TRACEY (7) walks
out in sweats with a ROLLED UP BEACH TOWEL in her arms. She
is followed by GLORIA (35), Jim, David, and their Weimaraner,
KING.

                    GLORIA
               (to Tracey)
          Did you bring your bathing cap?

                    TRACEY
               (annoyed)
          Yes, Mom. We gotta go. If we're
          late, Coach Hooper will give me a
          fanny burner.

                    JIM
              (to David)
          Sure you don't want to come? This
          is a big swim meet for your sister.

                    DAVID
          No. Need to catch up on my math
          homework.

                    GLORIA
          That's for sure. Remember to walk
          King in the ice plant at four.

                    DAVID
          Got it.

                    JIM
          And feed him.

                    DAVID
          I know.

                    GLORIA
          Half a can of Alpo and a scoop of
          dry food.

                    DAVID
          Mom, I do it every day.

                    JIM
          Don't talk back to your Mother.
          Mix a little warm water in it. He
          likes it moist.

                    DAVID
              (defeated)
          Okay.

                    GLORIA
          And stir it.

                    DAVID
          Right.

                    JIM
          Wish your sister luck.

                    DAVID
          Good luck, Tracey.

Tracey shrugs irritably and climbs into the FORD COUNTRY
SQUIRE STATION WAGON. Gloria and Jim follow, Jim behind the
wheel. David waves as the station wagon pulls out. It heads
down the street.

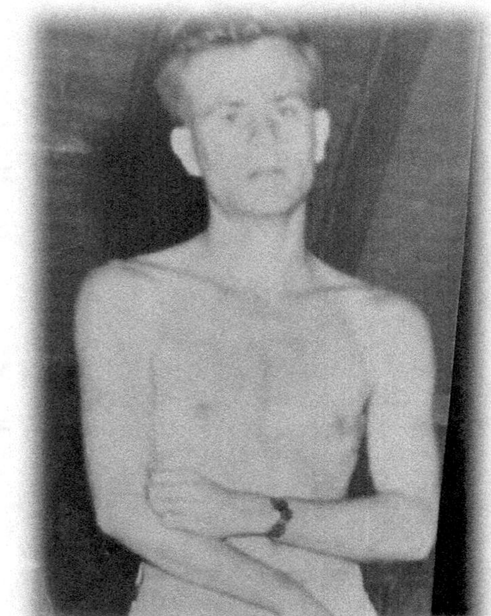

David walks to the sidewalk to make sure it won't turn back because someone forgot something. Once the car has disappeared from view, he pivots toward...

THE GARAGE. David hits a button hidden behind THE MAILBOX. THE GARAGE DOOR opens ponderously with a GROAN OF DUSTY SPRINGS.

INT. GARAGE - DAY

David pulls a set of KEYS from the pocket of his plaid shorts and moves to A LARGE WOOD CABINET SECURED BY A PADLOCK. He inserts a key and opens the cabinet. Sorts through some BOXES OF PAPERS bearing the logo of the FULLER PAINT COMPANY. He comes upon a MARINE GARRISON CAP with a black Marine emblem affixed on the left side. David reverently strokes the fabric, then sets the hat down.

Next is A PHOTO IN A CARDBOARD FRAME OF A PLATOON OF MARINES WHO HAVE JUST GRADUATED FROM BOOT CAMP ASSEMBLED ON A SET OF BLEACHERS. His 19-year-old father stands ramrod straight in his piss cutter hat at the apex of the back row. A white caption at the bottom of the picture says: **Platoon 15 -- Marine Barracks, Parris Island, July, 1939.**

David turns the cardboard frame over. Scrawled on the back are inscriptions to his father from his fellow marines.

David carefully sets the photo aside and reaches for a GREY STRONG BOX. Uses another key to open it. There is a neat stack of papers and A SMALL LEATHER CASE. David unfolds a yellowed TELEGRAM. Peruses the blue typed lines. It's addressed to Hilda Weddle at 1401 Union Avenue, McKeesport, PA. The message:

"I MADE THE MARINE CORPS. WILL SEE YOU VERY SOON. DON'T WORRY."

The words of an easy-going fun-loving boy that David never had the chance to meet. He gently folds the telegram and opens the leather case. Inside are TWO SILVER CAMPAIGN STARS attached to a PIECE OF WHITE POSTER BOARD. A BRONZE STAR. And an HONORABLE DISCHARGE PAPER.

David sets the leather case back in the strong box. Locks it and is about to set it back into place when he notices a DUSTY BROWN PHOTO ALBUM half concealed by a CARDBOARD BOX.

David opens the album. Faded PHOTOS OF MARINES on Guadalcanal are glued behind yellowed cellophane. Marines hanging out together at a SUPPLY DEPOT, arms slung over each other's lean shoulders, grinning like college students on spring break. Marines cavorting in the surf.

David turns the album page to another set of photos. A
SCORCHED BATTLEFIELD. Palm trees withered like burnt match
sticks, the charred superstructure of a Japanese Zero, the
indistinct forms of bodies scattered over the obsidian
earth...

A DEAD JAPANESE SOLDIER, staring up at the camera with dull
glazed eyes that seem to wonder how such a terrible thing
could have happened to him. David looks into them,
struggling to comprehend the mystery of death.

He turns the album to the next page and discovers...

HIS YOUNG FATHER, HOLDING A SEVERED JAPANESE HEAD BY THE
HAIR. Jim beams at the camera, as if displaying a fish he
just caught.

David slams the album closed. In a panic, restores
everything on the shelf to the positions he found them in.
Glances anxiously at the street, worried his father will
return and catch him in the act. Slams the cabinet door.
Drops the lock while trying to snap it closed. Finally
secures the cabinet, then stops, pressing his palms against
the door, as if trying to push the entire cabinet off the
face of the earth, his breathing fast and ragged.

EXT. RAVINE - DAY

MOVE ACROSS A GRASSY BLUFF OVERLOOKING PACIFIC COAST HIGHWAY
AND DOWN INTO A RAVINE, THROUGH THE TWISTS AND TURNS UNTIL WE
COME UPON...

FOUR TEN-YEAR-OLD BOYS -- BILL, SCOTT, BOB, and David --
scrambling around the muddy edges of a WATER HOLE fed by a
small CREEK. They have a STEEL BUCKET with them.

MOVE CLOSER to see the mud is alive with TINY BROWN FROGS
leaping frantically as the boys chase them. David nabs one
the size of match box and puts it in the bucket where FIVE
OTHER FROGS scramble in a couple of inches of water, vainly
seeking an avenue of escape.

                    BILL
          Okay, we got enough.

ON A DRY PATCH OF DIRT, the boys gingerly arrange PIECES OF
PRICKLY PEAR CACTUS to form a circle around a dug out PIT
that looks like a miniature arena. Scott cries out, dropping
a piece of cactus.

                    SCOTT
          Ahh! Got a needle in my finger.

                    BILL
          Told you to be careful.

Bill pushes the cactus pieces around with a stick, closing
the gaps in the circle. He adopts the pretentious voice of a
Roman Emperor

                    BILL   (cont'd)
          The preparations are complete. Let
          the games begin.
               (to David)
          Bring me the first contestant.

David reaches into the bucket and pulls out a frog. He holds
it close, looks into its stoic green eyes.

                    DAVID
          Hear me well, gladiator. You will
          be placed in the center of the Ring
          of Death. Should you leap beyond
          the Dragon Teeth to safety, you
          will be returned to your homeland
          to live out your life in peace.
          Should you fail, your remains will
          be consumed in the crematorium.

                    BILL
          How's the fire coming?

REVEAL SCOTT AND BOB feeding dry sticks to A SMALL CRACKLING
FIRE.

                    BOB
          All is in readiness, my Liege.

                    BILL
               (to David)
          Place the contestant in the Ring of
          Death.

David carefully sets the frog into the center of the pit.
Its green eyes look up at him, its emotions impossible to
fathom.

                    BILL (cont'd)
          Now turn him loose.

David lets go. The frog hesitates, uncertain of which
direction to take.

                    SCOTT
          What's he doing?

                    BILL
          Shhh.

The frog leaps. Once. Twice. Now at the lip of the cactus
ring, he pauses. The soft white skin beneath his lips
bulging and receding as he breathes. He blinks his moist
green eyes, delicate webbed feet clutching the dry earth.

                    SCOTT
               (to the frog)
          What are you stopping for?

                    BOB
               (to the frog)
          Don't you want to be free and
          return to your friends? Jump!

                    BILL
               (to David)
          Give him a nudge.

David's suddenly filled with apprehension. He doesn't want
to go through with this, but the expectant eyes of the others
are on him and he's not strong enough to defy them. David
carefully reaches in and touches the frog's rear end.

The frog leaps. For a moment it looks like he might clear
the needles, but gravity has other plans. He falls short and
impales himself on the cactus. A THORN PUNCTURES HIS SOFT
WHITE UNDERBELLY. BLOOD SQUIRTS FROM THE HOLE.

The other boys laugh, giddy from the grisly spectacle. But
David falls silent, his forehead taut and jaw tightening.

                    SCOTT
          Gnarly!

                    BOB
          Oh, look, he's still trying to get
          free!

David's filled with remorse as he watches...

The frog tries to climb over the needles, but only further
impales himself -- thorns lacerating his delicate webbed
feet, ripping open his belly, stabbing his right eye and
jerking it free from the socket.

                    SCOTT
          Oh man, look at his eye!

                    BOB
          He's gonna need a white cane after
          this!

David can't stand it. He grabs the cactus and the frog and
throws them into the fire.

                    BILL
          What're you doing? He might've
          made it.

Before David can muster an answer...

                    SCOTT
          Guys, look!

IN THE FIRE, THE FROG ATTEMPTS TO CRAWL FROM THE FLAMES, his
skin sizzling and oozing like bacon on a skillet.

David turns and runs away from the group, tears spilling from
his eyes. The others watch in astonishment.

                    BILL
          Where the hell are you going?

                    BOB
          Crybaby.

David arrives at the water hole and falls to his knees in the
mud, FROGS LEAPING all around him. He looks at his hand,
STIPPLED WITH CACTUS NEEDLES. David slowly closes his
fingers into a fist, pressing the needles deeper into his
flesh.

EXT. WEDDLE HOUSE - DAY

David crosses the driveway, beneath the gently flapping
American flag, relieved to see the Country Squire Station
Wagon is not there.

INT. WEDDLE HOUSE - ENTRYWAY - DAY

David enters. King bounds in from the backyard, barking
until he sees the intruder is David. He wags his stubby tail
furiously and pants with excitement. But David's in no
condition to pet him. He calls out apprehensively.

                    DAVID
          Hello? Anybody home?

No answer. Good.

INT. WEDDLE HOUSE - KITCHEN - DAY

As he passes the refrigerator, David notices a NOTE on a
piece of paper embossed with the words: **From the Desk of
James O. Weddle.** The note's in HIS MOTHER'S GRACEFUL
HANDWRITING. **"Went to the Bay Club to see your sister swim.
We'll be home in time for dinner."** David's relieved. He
heads off to...

INT. WEDDLE HOUSE - BATHROOM - DAY

ON DAVID'S HAND. Most of the CACTUS NEEDLES have been
removed, leaving red puncture marks across his palm.
TWEEZERS slowly approach a remaining NEEDLE and yank it free.
David registers relief and drops the needle in a WASTEBASKET.
THE PHONE RINGS.

INT. WEDDLE HOUSE - KITCHEN - DAY

The PHONE is attached to the wall in a built-in NOOK with a
WOODEN LEDGE painted bright yellow to match the FLOWER-
PATTERNED WALLPAPER. David grabs a BIC PEN and a PAD OF
PAPER EMBOSSED with: **From the Desk of James O. Weddle.** Picks
up the phone and answers as he has been trained to do...

                         DAVID
               Weddle residence. David Weddle
               speaking. Who's calling, please?

A deep, unfamiliar voice responds.

                         VOICE (ON PHONE)
               James Weddle.

                         DAVID
                    (confused)
               Uh... I'm sorry. James Weddle
               isn't here right now.
                    (let's try it again)
               Who shall I say is calling?

The voice is tight. Angry. Stark.

                         VOICE (ON PHONE)
               James Weddle.

                         DAVID
                    (distressed)
               I... He's not here right now.
               Who... Who are you?

                         VOICE (ON PHONE)
               James Weddle.

                         DAVID
               I don't... I'm sorry, who are you
               calling for?

                         VOICE (ON PHONE)
               James Weddle.

                         DAVID
               Okay, fine. But what's your name?

                         VOICE (ON PHONE)
               James Weddle.

David slams the phone down and bursts into tears. He starts
to flee the kitchen then stops, hyperventilating. Paces a
tight circle. Picks up the phone. Dials. The other end of
the line RINGS TWICE. An OPERATOR answers.

                         OPERATOR (ON THE PHONE)
               Balboa Bay Club. How may I help
               you?

                         DAVID
               Can you please page James... No,
               sorry. Gloria Weddle. Please page
               Gloria Weddle at the main pool.
               Hurry, please!

                         OPERATOR (ON THE PHONE)
               One moment, please.

DAVID'S INDEX FINGER wraps the phone cord around it until the
cord's bunched in a series of ugly knots. MOVE UP to David's
anxious face as he grips the receiver in his sweaty hand.

                         DAVID
                    (murmurs)
               Come on!... Come on!

Finally, a CLICK.

                         GLORIA (ON THE PHONE)
               Hello?

                         DAVID
               Mom, it's me. A strange man just
               called. He was really, really
               weird.

                         GLORIA (ON THE PHONE)
               What do you mean?

                    DAVID
          He said his name was James Weddle
          and he was calling for James
          Weddle. And when I asked him to
          explain he wouldn't say anything.
          Should I call the police? I'm
          afraid he's going to --

                    GLORIA
          David, it's okay.

                    DAVID
          What do you mean it's okay? He
          said he has the same name as Dad
          and --

                    GLORIA
          He does.

                    DAVID
               (baffled)
          What?

                    GLORIA
          He has the same name.

                    DAVID
          Who is he?

                    GLORIA
          Your brother.

                    DAVID
          Brother... I have a --

                    GLORIA
          I'm coming home now. I'll explain
          everything. Just wait there for
          me. You're perfectly safe.

INT. WEDDLE HOUSE - DAVID'S ROOM - DAY

David sits on his bed with his mother.

                    GLORIA
          Before your father met me, he had
          another wife.

                    DAVID
          Why?

Gloria chooses her words carefully.

                    GLORIA
          Well, you see, he met her when he
          was very young. Before the war.
          And he had two children with her.
          Jimmy and Jeanne.

                    DAVID
          So I have another sister, too?

                    GLORIA
          That's right.

                    DAVID
          How come Dad didn't stay married to
          this other lady?

                    GLORIA
          Because when he came back from the
          war... Well, it changed him. And
          his wife had changed, too. So
          eventually, they decided to get a
          divorce.

                    DAVID
          How come I never met my brother
          before this?

                    GLORIA
          You did.

                    DAVID
               (astonished)
          When?

Gloria reaches into a MANILLA ENVELOPE she has brought with
her.

                    GLORIA
          Your brother and his sister came to
          spend the summer with us in Cape
          Cod.

Gloria produces a snap shot of a long-legged 13-year-old boy
with blond hair, his arm wrapped around two-year old David.
They're in swim trunks, sitting in white sand. David wears a
sailor's hat.

                    GLORIA (cont'd)
          That's you and your brother, Jim.

David carefully studies the photo.

                    DAVID
          I... I don't remember this.

                    GLORIA
          Well, you were only two. And we
          never saw Jim or Jeanne after that.

                    DAVID
          How come?

                    GLORIA
          Your Dad and their mother got into
          an argument about child support.

                    DAVID
          What's that?

                    GLORIA
          The money a father has to pay to
          the mother of his children after a
          divorce. It was a pretty bad
          argument. After that, well, your
          Dad said, "That's it. I won't see
          them anymore."

                    DAVID
          Is he still mad at them?

                    GLORIA
          No. Jimmy came to see your Dad and
          they worked it all out.

David processes this. Then shrugs.

                    DAVID
          Okay. When do I get to meet him?

                    GLORIA
          Tonight. He's coming over for
          dinner.

David studies the photo of himself and his brother. MOVE IN
ON THE IMAGE UNTIL IT FILLS THE FRAME.

                    TRACEY (PRE-LAP)
          Does he get in bad moods, like Dad?

REVEAL WE ARE NOW IN...

INT. WEDDLE HOUSE - TRACEY'S ROOM - DAY

Tracey has a large CANOPY BED and blue carpet. Her shelves
are lined with DOZENS OF PLASTIC HORSES. David is showing
her the photo.

                    DAVID
          Maybe not.

                    TRACEY
          Why?

                    DAVID
          He wasn't in a war. Least, not as
          far as I know.

                    TRACEY
          I hope he doesn't get in bad moods.
          One Dad is enough.

THE DOORBELL RINGS.

                    DAVID
          There he is!

They race off to...

INT. WEDDLE HOUSE - ENTRYWAY - DAY

David and Tracey rush in as their father opens the door to
reveal JIMMY WEDDLE, a tall, lanky 20-year-old with sandy
blond hair and the chiseled features of a young Peter Fonda.
A TRIUMPH MOTORCYCLE is parked on the driveway beside the
COUNTRY SQUIRE STATION WAGON. Jim grips his eldest son's
hand with manic enthusiasm.

                    JIM
          Hello! This is David and Tracey.

                    JIMMY
               (smiles)
          Hey there.
               (to David)
          That was you I spoke to on the
          phone this afternoon?

                    DAVID
          Yeah.

                    JIM
          Yes.

                    DAVID
          Yes.

Jimmy clocks the fear David has for their father.

                    JIMMY
          Sorry if I scared you.

                    DAVID
          No biggie.

Tracey won't be kept in background a moment longer.

                    TRACEY
          So you're my new brother?

                    JIMMY
          Well, not new, exactly. But new to
          you, I guess.

Jimmy throws a pointed look at his father. Jim's again eager
to change the subject.

                    JIM
          Come on, let me fix you a face
          tightener. Gloria! Jimmy's here!

INT. WEDDLE HOUSE - DINING ROOM - NIGHT

They have finished eating. Jim is regaling Jimmy with war
stories.

                    JIM
          I'll never forget the day I found
          out your sister was born. I ever
          tell you about that?

                    JIMMY
          No.

Jim grabs the JACK DANIEL'S BOTTLE on the table.

                    JIM
          Here. Let me top off your tank.

                    JIMMY
          Ah, that's okay... I...

Jim has already filled the glass.

                    JIM
          It was on Guadalcanal. I was
          coming back from a push -- that's
          what we called our offensives.
          Anyway, I'm trudging down this
          muddy road, covered with ticks and
          leeches and jungle rot --

                    GLORIA
          Jim, we're at the dinner table.

                    JIM
          Oh, that's okay. They don't mind.
          And we come upon a relief column
          heading the opposite way. This
          marine I know spots me and calls
          out, "Hey, Slim Jim, you're a
          father! I just heard it over the
          Mosquito Network."

                    DAVID
          The what?

                    JIM
          Mosquito Network. Special Services
          recorded messages back in the
          States from soldiers' wives,
          parents, kids, what have you. Then
          they shipped the recordings to the
          islands and broadcast them so we
          could get news from our families.
               (to Jimmy)
          Your mother sent a message, and
          that's how I found our your sister
          was born.

                    JIMMY
               (pointed)
          You should call her.

                    JIM
          Who?

                    JIMMY
          My sister. You didn't go to her
          wedding. Didn't send a present or
          even a telegram.
               (firmly)
          You should call her.

Gloria, David, and Tracey are unbearably tense. They are
used to Jim being an absolute dictator. No one ever talks to
him this way. But to their astonishment, Jim doesn't blow
up. Instead, he shifts uneasily then nods.

                    JIM
          I will.
               (off Jimmy's look)
          I'll call her.

                    JIMMY
          When?

                    JIM
          Tomorrow.

                    JIMMY
          Why not now?

                    JIM
          It's late there.

                    JIMMY
          She's still up.

                    JIM
          Don't have her number.

                    JIMMY
          I'll give it to you.

                    JIM
          Okay, uh, Gloria, can you --

Gloria already has a PAD and PEN in hand. She places it
before Jimmy. He writes the number on the pad and slides it
before his father.

                    JIMMY
          There you go.

                    JIM
          Okay. I'll call her right now.

Jim gets up and walks toward the kitchen.

                    JIMMY
          That wasn't so hard. Was it?

Jim meekly disappears into the kitchen. The others are
astonished by Jimmy's ability to bend his father to his will.

                    JIMMY (cont'd)
          By the way, Gloria. The salmon was
          fantastic.

INT. WEDDLE HOUSE - DAVID'S ROOM - NIGHT

David lies in bed, in the dark, his door slightly ajar.
Across the hall, light spills from his parent's bedroom.

                    JIM (O.C.)
          Maybe I didn't see them, talk to
          them. But I thought about them
          every single day.

                    GLORIA (O.C.)
              (wearily)
          I know...

David rolls this over in his mind.

EXT. BALBOA BAY CLUB - DAY

ON THE BACK OF A SABOT SAILBOAT. It is bright blue with
WHITE LETTERS proclaiming the vessel's name: ***DAVE'S WAVE.***
MOVE UP to David wearing a pair of Hawaiian Hang Ten Jams,
sitting inside the small boat as he rigs the sail. The
vessel is brand new with shiny brass cleats and a tall
aluminum mast. His brother, Jimmy, stands on the cement dock
in aviator sunglasses and a brand new pair of Hang Ten Jams,
his tall lean torso as pale as that of a stripped down
farmer.

                    DAVID
          Okay, hand me the rudder and
          tiller.

Jimmy hands the polished teak rudder assembly to David. As
David fastens it in place, Jimmy lights a CIGARETTE and turns
to take in...

The panorama of The Balboa Bay Club. A restaurant with
tinted windows that offer a view of Newport Harbor.
Adjoining it, a broad white cement deck shaded by navy blue
UMBRELLAS fringed with white tassels. Beneath them, wealthy
CLUB MEMBERS in sports jackets and cocktail dresses sip
BLOODY MARYS and RAMOS FIZZES. RED JACKETED WAITERS attend
to their every need. On a nearby white sand beach, CLUB
MEMBERS brown their Coppertone-basted bodies beneath the
California sun.

                    JIMMY
          Gotta say, this is a pretty sweet
          set-up. How long you belonged to
          this club?

                    DAVID
          About four years, I guess. Ever
          since we moved to California. Have
          you been sailing before?

                    JIMMY
               (shakes his head)
          We don't live near the water.

                    DAVID
          Where's your house?

                    JIMMY
          Maryland. But we don't live in a
          house. We live in an apartment.

                    DAVID
          How come?

Jimmy's face clenches with resentment.

                    JIMMY
          My Mom can't afford one. Pretty
          tough to buy a house on a
          secretary's salary.

This embarrasses David. He struggles with a desire to drop
the subject, but his curiosity wins out.

                    DAVID
          I heard Dad got in a fight with
          your mom over money.

                    JIMMY
          They had many fights.

                    DAVID
          Didn't Dad send you enough?

                    JIMMY
          He never sent us a goddamned dime.

                    DAVID
          Oh... sorry.

                    JIMMY
          Why? You didn't do it. You didn't
          even know I was alive until
          yesterday.

                    DAVID
          Yeah, but, I mean...
               (gestures to the club)
          I got all this, and you...

David's too uneasy to finish the thought.

                    JIMMY
          It's okay. I don't begrudge you.
          Squeeze him for all you can get...
          Besides, I think you got the short
          end of the stick.

                    DAVID
          What do you mean?

                    JIMMY
          Living under him all the time --
          that's gotta be tough.

David fidgets -- profoundly uncomfortable.

                    DAVID
          Ah, it's okay. He gets in bad
          moods, but he loves me.

                    JIMMY
               (pointed)
          That doesn't make it easier. That
          makes it harder.

David gingerly approaches a topic he's burning to know more
about.

                    DAVID
          So you lived with him right after
          he came back from the war?

Jimmy nods and lights A FRESH CIGARETTE off the one in his
mouth. He tosses the used butt into the water.

                    DAVID (cont'd)
          What was he like then?

                    JIMMY
          A raving lunatic. That's why my
          mother threw him out.

David mulls this over then decides to confess something.

                    DAVID
          He's got an album in a closet in
          the garage. Has a picture of him
          holding a Jap head.

Jimmy laughs. But it is a strange, dry laugh. There's no
humor in it. And his eyes look ready to cry.

                    JIMMY
          Jesus Christ. He promised my
          mother he threw all those away.

                    DAVID
          So there were more?

                    JIMMY
          Ask him.

                    DAVID
          He doesn't know I found the
          picture.

                    JIMMY
          So tell him. Make him explain it
          to you.

This idea terrifies David. He changes the subject.

                    DAVID
          So how'd you find him after all
          these years?

                    JIMMY
          Bill.

                    DAVID
          Uncle Bill?

                    JIMMY
          You've met him?

                    DAVID
          A couple of times. He seems nice.

                    JIMMY
          Bill came to my sister's wedding.
          So I went up to him and asked where
          my father was. And he gave me
          Dad's business card. I knew he'd
          never answer a telephone call. So
          I drove out here. Went straight to
          his office, walked up to his
          secretary and said, "Tell him his
          son is here."

David's eyes widen. He's amazed by Jimmy's audacity.

                    DAVID
          Weren't you scared?

                    JIMMY
          Of what? That he'd throw me out?
          I hadn't seen him eight years. If
          he kicked me to the curb, I'd be no
          worse off than I was before.

                    DAVID
          So what'd he do?

                    JIMMY
          Kept me waiting for 45 minutes.

                    DAVID
          And then?

                    JIMMY
          The secretary said, "He'll see you
          now." I walked into his office and
          asked: "So, where ya been?"

David laughs. Jimmy looms 40 feet tall in his eyes.

                    DAVID
          What'd he do?

                    JIMMY
          He got all flustered and took me
          into other offices to meet the
          members of his sales team. He was
          scared to be alone with me.

David erupts with liberated laughter.

                    DAVID
          That is so bitchen!

                    JIMMY
               (grins)
          I thought so.

EXT. WEDDLE HOUSE - DAY

Jim, Gloria, Tracey, and David stand in the driveway beneath
the gently flapping AMERICAN FLAG. King sniffs a bush and
lifts his leg. They are bidding Jimmy farewell. Jim shakes
his eldest son's hand and Jimmy discovers two $100 BILLS have
been pressed into his palm.

                    JIMMY
          Thanks.

                    JIM
          Say hello to your sister for me.

                    JIMMY
          You do it. You got her number now.

                    JIM
               (shifts uncomfortably)
          I will.

Tracey grabs Jimmy's leg, bursting into tears.

                    TRACEY
          I don't want you to go!

                    JIMMY
          I have to. Gotta go back to
          school, just like you.

                    TRACEY
          So go here! You can live with us!

Gloria gently pries Tracey off of Jimmy's leg.

                    GLORIA
          Tracey, let Jimmy go. Say good-
          bye.

                    TRACEY
               (sniffling)
          Bye.

                    JIMMY
          Jeanne's married to an aerospace
          engineer. They're supposed to move
          out here next summer. So I'll be
          back. Promise.

                    DAVID
               (sad)
          I hope so.

Jimmy squeezes his little brother's shoulder, speaking gently
to him.

                    JIMMY
          Take care of your Mom and sister,
          okay?

                    DAVID
          Sure...

Jimmy puts on his AVIATOR SUNGLASSES, throws a leg over his
TRIUMPH MOTORCYCLE, but doesn't put on a helmet because no
law requires him to. Kicks the bike to life with a
TREMENDOUS ROAR, turns out of the driveway and onto the road.
Waves to them, then rockets away in a cloud of blue exhaust.
David watches his retreating figure with the forlorn
expression of a homesteader watching a Western hero ride into
the sunset.

EXT. CORONA DEL MAR - HOBBY SHOP - DAY

David approaches his religious mecca. The window is crammed
full of a 10-year-old boy's treasures. MODELS FOR UNIVERSAL
MONSTERS -- Dracula, Frankenstein, the Wolfman -- MODELS FOR
WORLD WAR II BATTLESHIPS AND TANKS, MODELS OF 707 JETS, THE
STARSHIP ENTERPRISE, and A KLINGON BIRD OF PREY.

BAKING SODA POWERED ROCKETS, LIONEL TRAINS, ALCOHOL POWERED MINIATURE AIRPLANES. David pushes the door open, the BELL attached to it tinkles.

INT. HOBBY SHOP - DAY

David wanders down an aisle, stops when he sees... A CELLOPHANE PACKET CRAMMED WITH RUBBER BUGS of all shapes and sizes. The label proclaims: CREEPY CRAWLIES! COCKROACHES, SCORPIONS, BEETLES and LIZARDS! David's eyes brighten with devious inspiration.

INT. WEDDLE HOUSE - MASTER BEDROOM - DAY

David stealthily approaches the SLIDING MIRRORED DOORS to his parents' closet. Casts a wary eye to the hall behind him, listening for signs of his mother or sister. Hears nothing. The coast is clear.

Slides open the closet door. Beneath the neat array of his father's BUSINESS SUITS and LEISURE WEAR sits a long line of polished DRESS SHOES and CONVERSE SNEAKERS. David kneels, reaches into his pocket and removes the BAG OF RUBBER BUGS. He begins to carefully place bugs on the shoes.

EXT. NEWPORTER INN - HELIPORT - SUNSET

Gloria's in a loose flowing flowered Moo-moo. Tracey wears a fluffy white dress with puffed sleeves. David's got on a white button-down shirt and slacks with wingtip shoes. Tracey excitedly points to a GREY DOT in the sky.

                    TRACEY
          There it is!

The gray DUAL PROP HELICOPTER grows larger. The RUNWAY LIGHTS SWITCH ON AROUND A MODEST PATCH OF ASPHALT.

THE HELICOPTER descends from the heavens, the THRUM OF ITS BLADES growing louder. WIND BUFFETS David and Tracey. Gloria struggles to hold her sprayed hair in place. THE HELICOPTER'S WHEELS TOUCH DOWN. THE ROTORS SLOW.

The door opens and a CO-PILOT UNFOLDS A SET OF STAIRS. BUSINESS EXECUTIVES begin descending to the tarmac.

                    DAVID
          There he is!

Tracey and David dash across the tarmac toward Jim, who steps
down from the ladder in a business suit with a BRIEFCASE and
TWO CARDBOARD BOXES UNDER HIS ARM. Tracey wraps herself
around his leg.

                    TRACEY
          Daddy! I love you so much! What'd
          you bring me!

                    JIM
          Oh, just a little something I
          thought you might like.

He hands her a CARDBOARD BOX WITH A PICTURE OF A BARBIE IN A
COWGIRL OUTFIT.

                    TRACEY
          A cowgirl Barbie! Wow! She can
          ride my plastic horses! Thank you!
          You're the best Daddy in the whole
          wide world!

David hangs back, pretending to be above such material hunger
as he eyes the other package in his father's arm. Jim
swivels his gaze to his son.

                    JIM
          Here, Chief, this is for you.

He hands David a similar box. This one features a PICTURE OF
G.I. JOE WITH A SUBMACHINE GUN IN HIS HANDS.

INT. WEDDLE HOUSE - ENTRYWAY - EARLY EVENING

David and Tracey burst through the door and race to...

INT. WEDDLE HOUSE - HALL - EARLY EVENING

Tracey dashes into her bedroom. The shelves are full of
PLASTIC HORSES of every color. David continues on to...

INT. WEDDLE HOUSE - DAVID'S ROOM - EARLY EVENING

David runs into his room. The Buster Keaton poster remains
on the cork board. BOOKS SIT ON A SHELF above his bed: *THE
FILMS OF LAUREL AND HARDY* BY WILLIAM K. EVERSON, *W.C. FIELDS -
- HIS FOLLIES AND HIS FORTUNES* by Robert Lewis Taylor, a TIME-
LIFE SERIES ON WORLD WAR II. There is also AN IMPRESSIVE
ARRAY OF MODEL TANKS, all of them from World War II. In the
corner sits a big PLASTIC MACHINE GUN ON A TRIPOD.

David carefully opens the box of his GI Joe. His parents'
voices drift over from the open door to their bedroom across
the hall.

                    GLORIA (O.C.)
          So how'd it go?

                    JIM (O.C.)
          Dragonne was laying for me.
          Everyone's terrified of him, 'cause
          he's got an MBA from Harvard. They
          knew he was gonna shoot holes in
          our marketing plan and I could see
          them losing their nerve.

                    GLORIA (O.C.)
          So what'd you do?

                    JIM (O.C.)
          Started pounding my fists on the
          conference room table until finally
          Norton Simon asked what was going
          on.

                    GLORIA (O.C.)
          Jesus. And what did you say?

The sound of the CLOSET DOOR SLIDING OPEN reverberates from
across the hall. But David doesn't hear it because he's too
enraptured with his new G.I. Joe.

                    JIM (O.C.)
          I said, "That's the sound of
          everybody's balls dropping off
          before the meeting starts."

                    GLORIA (O.C.)
          Jim, why would you do that? Simon
          must've thought --

                    JIM (O.C.)
          Fuck it! Who cares what he
          thought. Someone has to have the
          guts to tell it like... like...

Jim emits a blood curdling scream.

                    GLORIA (O.C.)
          What is it? What's wrong?

                    JIM (O.C.)
          HOLY FUCK!

David's listening now, suddenly full of apprehension as a
MUFFLED POUNDING reverberates from his parents' bedroom.

                    JIM (cont'd)
          Jesus! They're everywhere!

                    GLORIA (O.C.)
          What is? Let me see.

David listens keenly as the sounds from his parent's room
cease. A long silence seems to stretch into eternity,
until...

                    GLORIA (cont'd)
          DAVID! GET IN HERE RIGHT NOW! DO
          YOU HEAR ME?

Like a condemned prisoner walking the long last mile, David
heads out the door to...

INT. WEDDLE HOUSE - MASTER BEDROOM - EARLY EVENING

David enters to find his father lying on his back on the bed,
bathed in cold sweat, eyes disoriented, gasping like a hooked
fish on a hot dock.

His mother holds a RUBBER TARANTULA in her hand. RUBBER
COCKROACHES, BEETLES AND WASPS are scattered on the shag
carpet, along with a CHAOTIC TANGLE OF SHOES. Gloria wags
the spider at her son, the legs wiggling frantically, and
speaks through pursed lips.

                    GLORIA
          Did you do this?

                    DAVID
             (choked voice)
          Yes, Ma-am.

                    GLORIA
          Why?

                    DAVID
          It was...

                    GLORIA
          Was what?... Speak up!

                    DAVID
          A joke.

                    GLORIA
          A joke? You know how your Dad
          feels about insects. What would
          ever possess you to think this was
          funny?

                    DAVID
          I don't know.

                    GLORIA
          That's not an answer. Go to your
          room. You're not getting any
          supper tonight.

                    JIM
          No. Don't do that.

Gloria turns, incredulous.

                    GLORIA
          What?

Jim sits up, wiping the sweat from his face.

                    JIM
          A Weddle's got to be able to take a
          joke.

Gloria's bewildered when Jim holds his hand out to his son.

                    JIM (cont'd)
          Good one. You really got me.

David grasps his Dad's hand.

                    DAVID
               (grins)
          Can't believe it worked so well.

                    JIM
               (begins laughing)
          You shoulda seen me. Was trying to
          smash them with my shoes. But the
          harder I hit 'em, the higher they
          bounced!

They both burst into hysterical laughter. A dismayed Gloria
shakes her head.

                    GLORIA
          I'm living in a lunatic asylum.
          Gonna go get dinner ready.

She walks out as father and son howl unhinged laughter.

INT. COUNTRY SQUIRE STATION WAGON/EXT. LAGUNA BEACH - DAY

SUPER: **1969**

Jim (49) drives, Gloria (38) rides shotgun, David (13) and
Tracey (10) are in the back. Jim's hair is streaked with
grey and he's developed a large pot belly. Gloria's face and
body are rounder and heavier. They pass a colorful wooden
sign: *Welcome to Laguna Beach!*

                    TRACEY
          After the movie, can we go to the
          Snack Shop for dinner?

                    GLORIA
          That's the plan.

                    TRACEY
          Yay! Can I have a Top Hat?

                    GLORIA
          If you eat all of your supper.

Tracey bounces up and down in her seat.

                    TRACEY
          I will! You'll see!

They descend a hill on Pacific Coast Highway that leads into
the downtown area of this bohemian beach community. ON THE
RIGHT: TANNED TEENAGERS in skimpy bathing suits play
VOLLEYBALL or stroll the boardwalk. ON THE LEFT: the
commercial district. SHOPS sell local artwork, handmade
pottery, and beach souvenirs. But their windows are obscured
by CROWDS OF HIPPIES. The town has become a mini-Haigh-
Ashbury. Frayed sleeping bags take up much of the sidewalk.
Long-haired young men loiter in suede and tie-dyed outfits,
and braless girls in halter tops and cut-off jeans that
expose butt cleavage. They exchange JOINTS, play GUITARS,
HARMONICAS, and AFRICAN DRUMS as they sing counterculture
anthems. Others peddle HANDMADE LOVE BEADS AND "INDIAN"
JEWELRY to passing MIDDLE-AGED TOURISTS.

David and Tracey press their noses to the windows, fascinated
by the gaudy spectacle. Jim and Gloria are filled with
revulsion.

                    JIM
          Hippies. Look at 'em! <u>Filthy</u>!
          They <u>smell</u>! One day they'll wake
          up to find out they're 30 years old
          and have never finished high school
          or held a job. Their lives will be
          ruined. Ruined!

                    TRACEY
          Why don't they go to school or
          work?

                    JIM
          'Cause they live on a higher
          spiritual plane. But their
          stomachs don't. Empty bellies play
          hell with enlightenment.

                    DAVID
          How do they support themselves?

                    GLORIA
          They panhandle. Like bums.

                    JIM
          Which is what they are. Look at
          their bare feet. <u>Black with filth</u>!

David looks. Many of their feet are indeed filthy.

                    GLORIA
          They're probably covered with lice.

                    JIM
               (to his kids)
          Don't you ever come home looking
          like that. You do and I'll throw
          your ass back on the street so fast
          your head'll spin!

David gazes at the hippies with both revulsion and longing.

EXT. LAGUNA TWIN CINEMAS - DAY

AN OLD 1930'S ERA CINEMA has been converted to two smaller
theaters. Tracey and David stand before the glass-encased
photos for the two movies.

Tracey's focused on *THOROUGHLY MODERN MILLIE*, starring Julie
Andrews, Mary Tyler Moore, and Carol Channing. The graphics
feature the stars cavorting in 1920s flapper outfits, and the
slogan: **The Happiest Movie of the Year!**

David stands before a POSTER for *THE WILD BUNCH*. It offers
silhouettes of nine western outlaws armed with rifles walking
away from camera into a blood red landscape jagged with
Spanish ruins. THE CAPTION: **Unchanged men in a changing
land. Out of step, out of place, and desperately out of
time. Suddenly a new West had emerged. Suddenly their day
was over. Suddenly the sky was bathed in blood.**

                    TRACEY
          Hope mine has some good songs.

                    DAVID
          Looks like this'll have great
          shootouts. Like *The Good, the Bad,
          and the Ugly.*

Jim and Gloria walk away from the box office, each with a
pair of TICKETS in their hands.

                    GLORIA
               (to Jim)
          Okay, ours gets out before yours,
          so we'll be in that art gallery
          over there.

                    JIM
          Sounds like a plan.

Gloria and Tracey disappear into the theater on the right.

Jim leads David to the doors on the left. Hands the tickets
to a MALE USHER (66). The old man hesitates, scrutinizing
David.

                    USHER
          You sure you want to take a young
          boy in to see a movie like this?

                    JIM
          Why not?

                    USHER
          It's pretty intense. May not be
          appropriate for --

                    JIM
          He's my son! I'll decide what's
          appropriate for him!

INT. THEATER LOBBY - DAY

David waits in the red carpeted antechamber. His father
joins him, arms laden with luscious ITEMS FROM THE SNACK BAR.
He hands David a BOX OF RAISINETS AND A BUTTERFINGER.

                    JIM
          Here ya go, Chief. I get your
          order right?

                    DAVID
          Yeah, thanks!

                    JIM
          And I got a large Coke. And a
          large popcorn. Figured we could
          share it.

                    DAVID
          Boss!

Silence, as they wait for the current show to end so they can
enter the theater. Now having second thoughts, Jim shifts
uneasily.

                    JIM
          Now, David... Apparently there may
          be some things in this movie that
          may be...

                    DAVID
          It's okay, Dad. Don't worry. I'm
          ready!

INT. MOVIE THEATER - DAY

FLUORESCENT MARINE CREATURES -- OCTOPUSES, SWORDFISH, AND
SMILING DOLPHINS -- decorate the walls. David and Jim sit in
red velvet seats. David devours his Raisinets. Jim takes a
bite from his HERSHEY BAR WITH ALMONDS and leans close to his
son.

                    JIM
          How many lights are up there on the
          ceiling? Just take a guess.

                    DAVID
          Eighteen.
             (off his Dad's surprise)
          Knew you were gonna ask, so I
          counted them on my way in.

Jim smiles, pleased that he's taught David well. THE LIGHTS
DIM. Jim and David fall silent, instantly attentive. THE
WIDE SCREEN FILLS WITH A HIGH CONTRAST STILL PICTURE OF
HORSEMEN RIDING THROUGH A BLEAK LANDSCAPE, EMBLAZONED WITH
THE WARNER BROTHERS LOGO. It dissolves to a Panavision image
of William Holden leading his outlaw band, disguised in U.S.
Army uniforms, into the withered fringes of a dust-choked
town. They come upon a group of giggling children squatting
barefoot and ragged in the dirt. As his horse pulls abreast
of them, Holden glances down at the object of their mirth and
the camera catches a wink of horror and premonition in his
stoic gaze.

The children grin tauntingly as he spurs his horse onward,
then turn to the miniature arena they've constructed out of
sticks and dried mud. Inside it, several scorpions writhe on
a teeming anthill.

                         BOY
                      (giggles)
                  Turn 'em over!

A poking stick flips the scorpions, their stingers twitching
spasmodically at thousands of tiny red tormentors. A
haunting melody slips beneath the heavy percussion
soundtrack, tying an eerie connection between the scorpions
succumbing to the sea of red and the destiny of Holden and
his men.

IN THE AUDIENCE, David has forgotten the candy. Pinned to
his seat, he feels strangely exposed, naked -- as if the
movie is looking at him instead of him watching it. Jim sits
motionless, mesmerized. Clearly this is no ordinary Western.
It's unlike any western, any movie he has seen before.

ON THE SCREEN: Holden and his men stride into a Railroad
Office. The manager -- a gray haired gentleman in a vest --
turns toward Holden.

                        CLERK
                 Yes, sir. Can I help you?

Holden yanks him out of his chair and throws him against the
wall. The other clerks are also thrown there by members of
the gang.

                        HOLDEN
                If they move... Kill 'Em!

Holden's face turns to a high contrast image and a title
appears with a sinister riff from a guitar: **Directed by Sam
Peckinpah.**

The gang opens the safe and throws sacks of cash into their
saddle bags.

A Mexican member of the gang, Jaime Sanchez, moves to a
window that looks out on the street. Down the unpaved
thoroughfare a commotion stirs up dust. A parade of citizens
with a band of trumpets, tubas and drums playing a hymnal --
women with delicate parasols, children laughing and holding
hands, righteous church goers in dark suits and derbies
holding aloft a banner that declares themselves members of a
South Texas Temperance Union.

                    SANCHEZ
          People marching and singing, coming
          down the street. They're going to
          pass by the horses.

                    HOLDEN
          We'll join 'em.

Holden's second in command, ERNEST BORGNINE, emits a manic
high-pitched giggle.

                    BORGNINE
          The Temperance Union?

On the roof of a nearby building, a group of unbathed and
deranged bounty hunters watch the railroad office, salivating
over the violence to come. Their leader, a world weary
Robert Ryan, turns in disgust to Albert Dekker, the self-
righteous railroad man who set up this ambush. Ryan nods to
the approaching parade of innocents.

                    RYAN
          They should've been told.

                    DEKKER
          Told what? How long do you think
          anyone in this manure pile could
          keep his mouth shut?

In the railroad office, Holden grabs the head clerk and
presses him close to the door. Glances at his gang.

                    HOLDEN
          When I kick him out, blast 'em!
          We'll make a run for it.

Holden heaves the clerk out the door. He stumbles across the
freight platform and falls into the street. The bounty
hunters open fire on the clerk, blasting blood spewing holes
in him as he jerks this way and that.

IN THE AUDIENCE, David and Jim are disoriented. Who are the
good guys and who are the bad?

                    JIM
          Jesus...

He grabs his son's forearm, holding on for dear life.

ON THE SCREEN: A little boy and girl embrace in the middle of
the street as mayhem swirls all around them. Outlaws gallup
past, horses' hooves thundering on the dirt. Bullets whizz
by them. A man wrenched forward and then back as slugs tear
holes into him, blood geysering.

IN THE AUDIENCE: People in front of David and Jim get up and
head out of the theater.

                         WOMAN
                Disgusting!

Jim still grips his son's forearm. David winces.

                         DAVID
                Dad, you're hurting me.

Jim realizes what he's doing and lets go, leaving red marks
on David's arm. And yet, they are unable to tear their eyes
from...

THE SCREEN: On the roof top, a nauseated Robert Ryan yanks
the barrel of a bounty hunter's rifle skyward.

                         RYAN
                They've cleared out, for chrissake!

In the street, townspeople rush to their loved ones who lie
bleeding, moaning, dying and dead in the dirt. Wails of
grief rise to the blue sky above.

Two bounty hunters, L.Q. Jones and Strother Martin, run
amongst the corpses, grinning like famished hyenas. Martin
points to a dead man.

                         MARTIN
                Take him.

L.Q. rushes to relieve the body of its valuables. Martin
heads for another blood-soaked corpse.

                         MARTIN (cont'd)
                He's mine!

They quickly strip the dead.

But walking down the street, Ryan sees the townspeople crying
over the mutilated bodies of their loved ones, his slumped
shoulders weighed down by their anguish.

IN THE AUDIENCE: Jim leans close to his son and murmurs.

                         JIM
                You see? The others can live with
                it. But he can't. And never
                will...

It's a naked confession, filled with torment. David glances
at his father, sees tears in his eyes.

Dad has never made an admission like this before and David
doesn't know what to do with it.

ON THE SCREEN, Ryan watches a group of kids forming their
hands into imaginary guns and yelling "Bang! Bang!" as they
shoot pretend bullets at the gore drenched bodies in the
street.

IN THE THEATER: David and Jim watch in stunned silence as the
violence of one generation is passed on to the next.

INT. WEDDLE HOUSE - KITCHEN - NIGHT

Jim, Gloria, David, and Tracey sit before PLATES OF SPAGHETTI
AND MEATBALLS. A TRAY OF GARLIC BREAD rests in the center of
the pinewood table. The SONY PORTABLE TV on the kitchen
counter delivers the nightly news.

ON THE TV: ANCHOR CHET HUNTLEY addresses the camera.

                    HUNTLEY (ON TV)
               And now, a report from California
               on the bizarre Hippy Love Cult that
               may be behind the murders of
               actress Sharon Tate, and four other
               people....

Black and white 16mm footage plays of the Spahn Movie Ranch
in Simi Valley. Ramshackle buildings that simulate a town in
the Wild West. Emaciated horses, run-down cars and trucks
litter the arid boulder-strewn landscape.

                    HUNTLEY (ON TV) (cont'd)
               This is where they lived, among the
               stables, barns, and phony buildings
               of a run-down movie location, 20
               miles from Los Angeles. They
               called themselves "The family."

An image of a mattress lying in the dirt between the
boulders, strewn with discarded clothing.

                    HUNTLEY (ON TV) (cont'd)
               People who worked on the ranch said
               they were heavy users of drugs.

Jim pounds his fist on the table.

                    JIM
               I knew it!

ON THE TV: a leathery woman in a cowboy hat speaks to camera.

                    WOMAN (ON TV)
          They were constantly taking dope,
          stealing cars.

A DISTRICT ATTORNEY appears, wearing horn-rimmed glasses and
a flattop haircut.

                    D.A. (ON TV)
          Most of them appeared to be quite
          frankly, hippie types.

Gloria looks at her children.

                    GLORIA
          You see where that lifestyle leads?

INT. WEDDLE HOUSE - DINING ROOM - ANOTHER NIGHT

THE WEDDLE FAMILY WEAR DIFFERENT CLOTHES. MEATLOAF AND
MASHED POTATOES GRACE THE TABLE. They're glued to the TV.

                    WALTER CRONKITE (ON TV)
          Outside the courtroom today,
          members of the Manson family who
          are still at large have carved X's
          into their foreheads to emulate
          their leader.

ON TV: THREE YOUNG WOMEN SIT ON THE SIDEWALK, smiling
serenely at REPORTERS. One of them speaks into a
journalist's microphone.

                    MANSON FOLLOWER (ON TV)
          Charlie will be out soon. All the
          people will be out. Angela Davis
          will be out. Bobby Seale will be
          out. There's a revolution coming.

                    REPORTER (ON TV)
          When do you expect this revolution?

                    MANSON FOLLOWER (ON TV)
          Soon. Very soon. A bloody
          revolution. You are next. All of
          you.

IN THE DINING ROOM: Jim's jaw tightens.

                    JIM
          Let 'em come here. Let 'em try.

INT. WEDDLE HOUSE - LIVING ROOM - ANOTHER NIGHT

The Weddles wear different cloths. They sit on the flower
print sofa, eating ICE CREAM, captivated by...

ON THE G.E. COLOR TV: Chet Brinkley looks solemnly into the
camera.

                    BRINKLEY (TV)
          Manson spoke before the court in
          his own defense for more than an
          hour today. He said, in part, "I
          never went to school, so I never
          growed up to read and write too
          good, so I have stayed in jail and
          I have stayed stupid, and I have
          stayed a child while I have watched
          your world grow up, and then I look
          at the things that you do and I
          don't understand. My father is the
          jailhouse. My father is your
          system... I am only what you made
          me. I am only a reflection of you.

The Weddles each process this in their own way.

INT. WEDDLE HOUSE - KITCHEN - NIGHT

ON THE WALL CLOCK, it's after midnight. The kitchen is dark
and deserted. The only sound, the whir of the refrigerator.
MOVE OUT OF THE KITCHEN, past the huge oak dining room table
and into...

INT. WEDDLE HOUSE - HALLWAY - NIGHT

MOVE DOWN THE HALL PAST PHOTOS ON THE WALL: GLORIA'S PARENTS
IN THE GOLD FRAME, GLORIA AS A STEWARDESS, PROFESSIONAL
PORTRAIT PHOTOS OF JIM AND GLORIA SITTING TOGETHER IN SEMI-
SILHOUETTE, A SILHOUETTE OF GLORIA IN PROFILE, A PHOTO OF
DAVID AND TRACEY TOGETHER, AND ANOTHER OF THE FOUR OF THEM.

MOVE INTO...

INT. WEDDLE HOUSE - MASTER BEDROOM - NIGHT

Jim and Gloria lie asleep.

King sleeps at the foot of the bed. His gray ears perk up.
King raises his head, brown eyes focused on the sliding glass
door that leads to the backyard.

A growl comes to a slow boil deep in his throat. His ears twitch and King leaps to his feet, charging to the glass door and barking frantically.

Jim and Gloria stir.

      GLORIA
    (alarmed)
  What... what is it?

Jim jumps out of bed in his pajamas, struggling to clear his head.

      JIM
    (hisses)
  Quiet!

He goes to the door. FLIPS ON A SPOTLIGHT that illuminates the backyard. King howls frantically, bouncing off his paws with each bark.

      GLORIA
  Is something there?

      JIM
  I don't...

The BOUGAINVILLEA lining the top of the fence RUSTLES.

      JIM (cont'd)
  Wait...

A YOUNG MAN (16) with long hair and torn jeans vaults over the top of the fence.

      JIM (cont'd)
  Jesus Christ!

The teenager runs across the backyard, followed by A SECOND TEEN, who scrambles over the fence and across the patio.

      JIM (cont'd)
  Fuck!

      GLORIA
    (panicked)
  What? What's going on?

Jim scrambles into a pair of pants, but leaves his pajama top on.

      JIM
  They're in our yard!

                    GLORIA
          Who is?

                    JIM
          No fucking idea!

INT. WEDDLE HOUSE - HALLWAY - NIGHT

Jim rushes out of the bedroom. David and Tracey stand
outside the doors to their rooms blinking sleep from their
puffy eyes.

                    DAVID
          What is it?

                    JIM
              (to David)
          Get your clothes on!
              (to Tracey)
          You stay with your mother.

David ducks into his room. Tracey races into the master
bedroom.

EXT. WEDDLE HOUSE - BACK YARD - NIGHT

Jim strides into the yard with King, who barks and sniffs the
air. The yard appears empty. Jim turns to a stack of GARDEN
TOOLS behind a PLANTER. Grabs a HAND RAKE. David appears,
now dressed.

                    DAVID
          See anyone?

                    JIM
          No. They must've hopped the other
          fence.

He hands David a SHOVEL.

                    JIM (cont'd)
          Here, take this. Come on.

He leads David back into the house.

                    JIM (cont'd)
          Anyone comes at you, give 'em a
          taste of your shovel.

EXT. WEDDLE HOUSE - FRONT YARD - NIGHT

Jim steps out of the front door. David follows his father,
who holds King on a leash in one hand and the hand rake in
the other.

                    DAVID
          Who were they?

                    JIM
          No idea. But I sure as hell am
          gonna find out.

They walk around the corner along the fence that encloses
their backyard, approaching the house behind theirs.

FOUR COP CARS are parked at the curb, their SWIRLING LIGHTS
SENDING RED BEAMS ACROSS THE ASPHALT. A PAIR OF COPS walk
TWO TEENAGE BOYS IN HANDCUFFS toward the squad cars.

MORE TEENAGERS file out of the house under direction from
ANOTHER COP.

Jim approaches an OFFICER standing beside one of the squad
cars.

                    JIM (cont'd)
          What the fuck's going on here?

                    COP #1
          And who are you, sir?

                    JIM
             (points)
          I live in that house. Two guys
          came over our fence and ran through
          the back yard.

                    COP #1
          I see. Nothing to get too worked
          up about.
             (nods to this house)
          Parents are out of town. So junior
          gets the bright idea to throw a
          party. We got complaints, so we're
          shutting it down.

At another squad car a cop confronts a teenager.

                    COP #2
          Empty your pockets.

The teenager reluctantly does so, producing a joint and a
bent package of matches. The cop takes the joint and holds
it before the boy's eyes.

                    COP #2   (cont'd)
          What's this?

                    TEENAGER
          Cigarette. I like to roll my own.

The cop sniffs it.

                    COP #2
          That's marijuana. Possession is a
          felony. You're looking at a year
          in juvie, my friend.

                    COP #1
             (to Jim)
          It's all under control now, sir.

                    JIM
          It better be. 'Cause anyone comes
          on my property again, I'll put 'em
          down. Understood?

                    COP #1
          They're just teenagers.

                    JIM
          So was the Manson family.

                    COP #1
             (firmly)
          Go home and put those tools away
          before you get yourself into
          trouble.

Jim's profoundly dissatisfied with this response.

INT. WEDDLE HOUSE - HALLWAY - NIGHT

MOVE DOWN THE DARK DESERTED HALL past the pictures.

SUPER: **TWO NIGHTS LATER**

MOVE AROUND THE CORNER INTO...

INT. WEDDLE HOUSE - MASTER BEDROOM - NIGHT

Gloria, Jim, and King are fast asleep. Suddenly, Gloria
gasps and bolts upright.

                    GLORIA
          Someone's in the yard!

                    JIM
               (wakes with a start)
          What?

                    GLORIA
          Someone's in the backyard! I heard
          them whispering. Giggling!

Jim sits up in his pajamas. Reaches under his bed and comes
up with a WINCHESTER RIFLE.

INT. WEDDLE HOUSE - HALLWAY - NIGHT

Jim strides into the hall. David and Tracey stand outside
their doors, blinking at him.

                    DAVID
          What is it?

                    JIM
          Your Mom heard someone in the yard.

                    TRACEY
          Again?

                    JIM
               (to Tracey)
          Go to your Mom.
               (to David)
          Grab a flashlight.

Tracey rushes into the master bedroom, David heads for the
kitchen. Jim strides toward...

EXT. WEDDLE HOUSE - BACKYARD - NIGHT

Jim steps out on the back patio, scanning the shadows. David
arrives with a LONG STEEL FLASHLIGHT. King sniffs the air,
venturing an exploratory bark.

                    JIM
          Who's there?

Something rustles in the bougainvillea along the top of the
fence. Jim levers a bullet into the Winchester's chamber in
one swift lethal motion. He points the rifle at the
bougainvillea.

                    JIM (cont'd)
          Over there! Give me some light!

David shines the flashlight at the hedge.

                    JIM (cont'd)
          Okay, you son-of-a...

He falls silent as the light falls upon...

A POSSUM in the greenery, staring back at them with it's pale
alien face.

Jim lowers the rifle and turns, swinging the barrel toward
David, who darts out of the way.

INT. WEDDLE HOUSE - KITCHEN - DAY

Father and son re-enter the house, Jim now pointing the rifle
barrel toward the ceiling. Gloria and Tracey wait
apprehensively.

                    GLORIA
          Did you see anyone?

                    JIM
          Just a possum on the fence. You
          sure you heard voices?

                    GLORIA
                (confused)
          Thought I did... Maybe...

                    JIM
          Maybe what?

                    GLORIA
          Maybe it was just a nightmare.

Jim sighs, both relieved and irritated. David and Tracey
relax.

EXT. SUBURBAN STREET - WEDDLE HOUSE - DAY

SUPER: **1970**

David (14) rides his TEN-SPEED BIKE home from school, a
CANVAS BACKPACK slung over his shoulders. He practices
riding with no hands, doing pretty well until he sees...

An unfamiliar BUICK SKYLARK parked in his driveway, and next
to it, his brother's TRIUMPH MOTORCYCLE, resting in the
rippling shadow of his father's AMERICAN FLAG fluttering atop
its steel pole.

Excited, David sails into the drive and jumps off his bike.
Heads up the brick path to the front door and pushes it open.

                    DAVID
          Jim --

The call out to his brother catches in his throat when a six-
foot-tall WOMAN (28) with long brown hair appears.

                    JEANNE
          Hi! You must be David.

                    DAVID
          Uh... yeah. Who are --

                    JEANNE
          I'm your sister, Jeanne.

David instantly transitions from shock to excitement.

                    DAVID
          Oh... Hi!

His brother, JIMMY (24), appears behind her. The four years
since David last saw him have brought changes. Jimmy has
hair down to his shoulders. He wears a brilliantly colored
TIE-DYED SHIRT, a PUKA SHELL NECKLACE with a QUARTZ MEDALLION
cut and polished into the shape of a Mandala, and a pair of
large round GOLD FRAMED GLASSES like those worn by John
Lennon.

                    JIMMY
          Looking for me, little brother?

David races to embrace him.

                    DAVID
          No one told me you were coming.

                    JIMMY
          We like to surprise Dad. After all
          the curve balls he's thrown us --

                    JEANNE
          Turnabout's fair play.

Jeanne hugs David. Another man, STEVE (29) appears. He's
taller than both Jeanne and Jim, and barrel chested.

                    STEVE
          Hello, David.

                    JEANNE
          This is my husband, Steve.

                    DAVID
          Nice to meet you.

David shakes his hand.

INT. WEDDLE HOUSE - LIVING ROOM - DAY

GLORIA (39) brings out a CUTTING BOARD full of SALAMI,
CHEESE, AND TRISCUITS. Jim (50), Jimmy, Jeanne, Steve,
Tracey (11), and David sit around a coffee table crowded with
BUDWEISER CANS, an OPEN BOTTLE OF JACK DANIELS, and HALF-
FILLED GLASSES. Jeanne emits a peal of infectious laughter.

                    JEANNE
          -- oh Dad, of course I remember!
          The day you came home from the war,
          I thought, "Who is this strange
          person kissing <u>my mother</u>?"

                    JIM
          How do you think I felt? Your
          brother hadn't been born yet.
          Between you, your mother, and your
          grandmother, I was surrounded by
          women.
               (to the others)
          During the four years that I was
          gone, Jeanne had been babied and
          coddled, and if she didn't get her
          way she'd throw fits you wouldn't
          believe.

                    JEANNE
               (laughs)
          I was pretty bad, wasn't I?

                    JIM
          Bad? Bad doesn't begin to describe
          it.
               (to the others)
          She'd bounce off the walls.
          Literally! Screaming like a
          banshee. And her mother would
          say...
               (adopts a sweet voice)
                    (MORE)

                    JIM (cont'd)
          "Now, Jeanne, I know you are
          frustrated, but let's try to calm
          down and discuss this."
               (back to his own voice)
          And Jeanne would continue to scream
          bloody murder until she got her
          way.

                    JEANNE
               (laughs warmly)
          But you straightened me out quick,
          didn't you, Dad?

                    JIM
               (smiles)
          With the horseradish.

Jeanne and her father erupt with conspiratorial laughter.

                    TRACEY
          I don't get it. What happened?

                    JIM
          Tell 'em, Jeanne.

                    JEANNE
          No, Dad, you tell 'em.

Jim pours some more whiskey into his glass, warming to the
assignment.

                    JIM
          Well, I'm sitting listening to the
          ball game on the radio one day,
          spreading this very hot horseradish
          on some salami and a cracker. When
          I say hot, you could use this stuff
          to strip paint off a wall. I broke
          out in a sweat, eating it. Then
          all of a sudden...
               (gestures to Jeanne)
          This vision of loveliness appears
          before me and says, "I want some."
          I said, *you can't have it. It's
          too hot.*

                    JEANNE
               (laughs)
          But I wouldn't take no for an
          answer.

                    JIM
          Talk about a Category Five
          Hurricane!
               (MORE)

                    JIM (cont'd)
She jumps up and down screaming, "I
want it! I want it! I want it!"
So I said, *okay, you want some.
Here!* And I shoved a cracker full
of that horseradish into her mouth.

                    STEVE
               (to Jeanne)
What'd you do?

                    JEANNE
Ran into the toilet and threw up.
Took a bucket of ice to stop the
burning.

                    GLORIA
               (horrified)
Charming.

Jeanne laughs, looking at her father.

                    JEANNE
Nana didn't think so.

                    JIM
               (pantomimes a shiver)
Oh, no she didn't. But that woman
hated me already.

                    JEANNE
She sure did.

                    JIMMY
Gee, I wonder why. Who could
possibly take a dislike to such a
scintillating personality?

Jimmy says it with a sharp laugh. His father feels the cut
and looks into his eldest son's challenging gaze from behind
those John Lennon glasses. Jeanne attempts to break the
tension by changing the subject.

                    JEANNE
So, David, I hear you make movies.

                    DAVID
Yeah, I just got a new movie
camera, a Yashica Super 800 with an
electric zoom.

                    JEANNE
What kind of movies do you make?

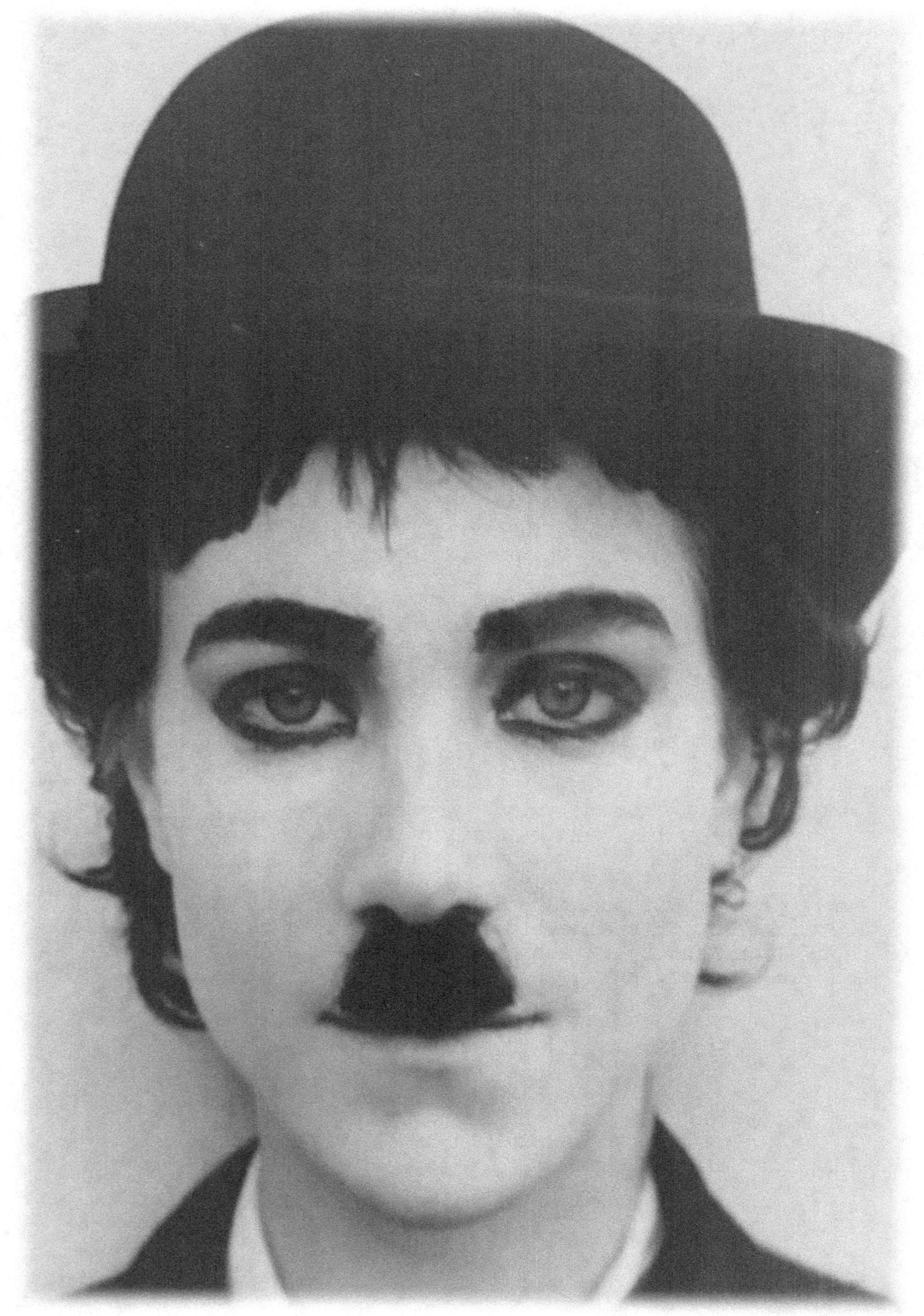

                    DAVID
          Silent comedies.
               (sudden inspiration)
          You want to be in one?

                    JEANNE
          Sure!

                    JIM
          What about me? Can I be in it?

                    DAVID
          Maybe you can all be in it.

EXT. WEDDLE HOUSE - BACKYARD - DAY - HOME MOVIE

THE ACTION IS IN BLACK AND WHITE, SIX FRAMES FASTER THAN
NORMAL SPEED, WITH A SCOTT JOPLIN MUSICAL SCORE.

A TITLE CARD APPEARS IN THE FORM OF A WHITE PIECE OF PAPER
WITH LETTERING IN BLACK MAGIC MARKER: **RETURN OF THE TRAMP.**

Tracey shuffles around a corner dressed as Charlie Chaplin's
tramp character: black derby, vest, a baggy jacket and pants,
oversized shoes, a dab of black mustache, and a bamboo cane,
which she deftly twirls. Her resemblance to Chaplin's iconic
character is startling.

TITLE CARD: **The lonely tramp seeks companionship in a
sidewalk cafe.**

Tracey duckwalks past a table where Gloria and David, in
formal wear, portray a couple enjoying COCKTAILS. Tracey
continues on to...

A BAMBOO BAR. Jim plays the bartender, in a white button
down shirt and vest. Painfully self-conscious with the
camera on him, Jim can't stop laughing as he fills a SERIES
OF SHOT GLASSES with WHISKEY. The bottle runs empty, so Jim
ducks behind the bar to retrieve another. Quick as a
striking snake, Tracey downs one of the shots, puts the empty
glass back on the bar, then turns as if fascinated by the
activity in the cafe. Jim rises with a fresh BOTTLE, sees
the empty shot glass and peers suspiciously at Tracey's back.

Meanwhile, Tracey's captivated by...

TITLE: **Lil, the Dance Hall Queen.**

Jeanne appears in a crazy curly beehive wig that defies the
laws of gravity. Jeanne makes eyes at the Tramp and rolls
her shoulders provocatively.

Tracey-the-Tramp looks over her shoulder to make sure Jeanne
isn't flirting with someone else. Realizing Jeanne is
looking at her, Tracey returns Lil's smile and approaches.

Tracey-the-Tramp asks Jeanne for a dance. Jeanne quickly
agrees. The Tramp and the Dance Hall Queen sashay across the
patio. The Tramp's baggy pants keep slipping down because
they have no belt. The Tramp spots a COIL OF ROPE on the
ground.

Jimmy, wearing a broad-brimmed Stetson and cowboy boots,
plays another patron of the cafe. He asks Jeanne for a
dance. She refuses. While they argue, Tracey-the-Tramp
picks the rope off of the ground and deftly ties it around
the waist of her trousers.

Jeanne rebuffs Jimmy and she and the Tramp resume their waltz
across the concrete. But the Tramp discovers the solution to
one problem creates another. The other end of the rope is
tied around King's neck. The dog trails after the Tramp,
despite the Tramp's efforts to kick him away. Suddenly, King
spots something OFF CAMERA, barks and gives chase, yanking
the Tramp to a humiliating pratfall on the pavement.

Before Tracey-the-Tramp can recover, Jimmy swoops in to
embrace the Dance Hall Queen, arguing in pantomime that she
should dump this loser and come away with him. Jeanne laughs
in agreement and they prance away together.

When Tracey-the-Tramp rises to her feet, she finds herself
alone in the world once more. For a moment she is
devastated. Then she shrugs off her defeat, kicks her feet
behind her, like a dog dispensing with a turd, and walks AWAY
FROM CAMERA. THE IMAGE SLOWLY FADES TO BLACK.

TITLE: **THE END**

INT. WEDDLE HOUSE - LIVING ROOM - NIGHT

The room vibrates with laughter and applause as the TAIL OF
THE FILM runs out of David's EUMIG MARK S810 PROJECTOR and
flaps around the take-up reel. Gloria snaps on the lights to
reveal Jim, Jimmy, Jeanne, Steve, Tracey, and HERB and LOUISE
PINTARD seated on the couch and overstuffed chairs. [Note:
The Weddles are all in different clothes -- this is a couple
of weeks after the previous scene in the living room.]

                    HERB
          David, that was fabulous!

                    LOUISE
          Tracey, can't believe how much you
          looked like Charlie Chaplin!

                    TRACEY
          I know, it's weird. I wanted to be
          the Tramp for Halloween. So Mom
          helped me make the costume.

                    GLORIA
          I re-blocked an old hat of Jim's,
          took up the legs on a pair of his
          trousers, and stuffed newspaper
          into the toes of his wingtips.
          Used zinc oxide to whiten her face,
          and cut up a brush for the
          mustache.

                    DAVID
          She was the spitting image. So I
          said, "Let's make a Charlie Chaplin
          movie!"

                    LOUISE
          Well, you certainly did!

                    HERB
               (to Jim Sr.)
          The only flaw was you, Jim. You
          kept cracking up.

                    DAVID
          I know! I did a bunch of takes,
          but I couldn't get Dad to keep a
          straight face.

Jim's embarrassed and a little humiliated. He's unable to
admit how much he wanted to do well as an actor. It has been
a secret dream of his since he was a kid.

                    JIM
          Don't know what got into me -- just
          couldn't stop laughing.

Tracey sees her father topping off everyone's drinks from the
ARRAY OF LIQUOR BOTTLES on the coffee table. Worried that
the hour of the wolf may be approaching, she gets up.

                    TRACEY
          Thanks for watching, everybody. I
          gotta go do homework.

                    HERB
          Jimmy, I gotta say, you seemed a
          little out of place. With that
          long hair and those glasses, you
          didn't exactly fit the period. You
          look like someone out of Woodstock.

                    JIMMY
          I am.

                    LOUISE
          I'm afraid I don't understand.

                    JIMMY
          I was there. From the first notes
          played by Richie Havens on Friday
          afternoon, till Monday morning when
          Jimi Hendrix played the Star
          Spangled Banner.

Herb looks at Jim, his eyes silently asking, "Did you know
about this?" Jim shifts uncomfortably, irritation spreading
like a rash over the top of his sweaty head.

                    JIM
               (downs his whiskey)
          I heard that on the news. Didn't
          sound like any Star Spangled Banner
          I ever heard.

                    JIMMY
          That's what made it so beautiful.

                    JIM
               (testy)
          That a fact.

                    HERB
          I saw some of that news footage,
          too. All the rain and mud. Looked
          like a living hell.

                    JIMMY
          Quite the contrary. It was a warm
          summer rain. When the sun broke
          through those clouds and everyone
          resumed dancing, it was really
          groovy.

                    JIM
               (sarcastic)
          Oh yeah, groovy. Far out, man.

                    JIMMY
          It was. Three days of peace and
          love. It was the single most
          beautiful experience of my life.
          Just extraordinary.

                    HERB
          Saw all those hippy chicks swimming
          nude in the lake. You get any of
          that action?

                    LOUISE
          Herb!

                    JIMMY
               (smiles)
          Wouldn't you like to know.

Jim can no longer contain his agitation.

                    JIM
          Saw a picture of one of your long-
          haired brethren with an American
          flag sewed on the ass of his jeans.
          What's the meaning of that?

                    JIMMY
          You'd have to ask him.

                    JIM
          I'm asking you.

                    JIMMY
          Just a fashion statement.

                    JIM
          What's the statement? That he
          wanted to wipe his ass with the
          flag?

                    JIMMY
          I wouldn't go that far.

                    JIM
          Oh yeah? Just how far would you
          go?

Everyone's tense now. David busies himself with rewinding
his film. Herb glances at his watch, searching his mind for
an excuse to leave, but before he can find it...

                    JEANNE
          Dad, come on. Let's not make a big
          deal of this.

                    JIM
          Oh, it's not a big deal to you?
          Because the flag's just a big joke
          to you and your entire generation?

                    JIMMY
          It's not a joke to us, but it's
          true doesn't have the same meaning
          as it does for --

                    JIM
          Don't you dare denigrate the flag!

                    JIMMY
          I'm not denigrating it. If you'll
          just shut up for a moment and let
          me explain --

Jim leaps to his feet.

                    JIM
          Don't tell me to shut up in my own
          house! I don't have to sit here
          and listen to you tell me the flag
          has no meaning. That people can
          burn it, shit on it --

                    JIMMY
               (stands)
          That's not what I said! Stop
          twisting my words!

But Jim isn't listening anymore. Something deep and buried
has been brought to the surface. There is more than rage in
his eyes -- there is fear. He's like a man flailing in a
whirlpool, a vortex dragging him back to those islands in the
Pacific and the things he did there.

He grabs his oldest son by his shirtfront and slams him
against the wall.

                    JIM
          I saw people die for that flag!
          And you want... you want --

                    JIMMY
          What I want is truth from this
          government!

Gloria sits in abject horror. David jumps up and runs from
the room, terrified. Jeanne tries to pry the two men apart.

                    JEANNE
          Dad, stop!

                    JIM
          Truth? Truth about what?

                    JIMMY
          Vietnam! I have friends who died
          too! For that flag of yours!

INT. TRACEY'S ROOM - NIGHT

Tracey is not studying. She's curled in the fetal position
under the covers with her STUFFED DOG, Froffy. David bursts
into the room and slams the door behind him.

                    TRACEY
               (alarmed)
          What's going on?

                    DAVID
               (barely able to talk)
          Jimmy...

                    TRACEY
          What about him?

                    DAVID
               (in disbelief)
          He talked back to Dad. About the
          flag.

                    TRACEY
               (flabbergasted)
          Why'd he do that?

David notices that the shouting from the living room has
stopped. An eerie silence has settled over the house. He
motions for Tracey to be quiet and slowly cracks the door
open to peek out at...

INT. WEDDLE HOUSE - HALLWAY - NIGHT

Jim stalks down the hall, vibrating with rage. With sudden
ferocity, he punches the closed door to David's bedroom,
putting his fist through the particle board and leaving A
JAGGED HOLE.

INT. WEDDLE HOUSE - TRACEY'S ROOM - NIGHT

David closes the door, praying Dad didn't see him.

                    TRACEY
          What?

David holds a trembling finger to his lips and Tracey falls
into petrified silence as their father stalks past.

THE DOOR TO THE MASTER BEDROOM SLAMS. Funereal silence.
David and Tracey look at each other.

                    TRACEY (cont'd)
          You can sleep in here tonight.

INT. WEDDLE HOUSE - KITCHEN - NIGHT

LATER. David cautiously treads out from the hall to find the
lonely figure of his mother WASHING DISHES, and sipping a
TALL GLASS OF VODKA.

                    DAVID
          Mom... you okay?

                    GLORIA
              (shakes her head)
          Just don't understand why these
          things happen. Everyone seemed to
          be having such a good time.

                    DAVID
          Where's Jeanne and Jimmy?

                    GLORIA
          They just left.

EXT. WEDDLE HOUSE - NIGHT

David rushes out to find Jimmy leaning in the open passenger
window of the Buick, talking to Jeanne. David waves to them.

Jeanne says something to Steve, who's behind the wheel with a
grim expression. He backs the car out of the driveway as
Jeanne raises her window. David stops short, crestfallen.
Waves forlornly at Jeanne. She waves back and he sees she is
crying.

The Buick drives off. Jimmy heads for his Triumph
motorcycle. David intercepts him.

                    DAVID
          You okay?

Jimmy throws a leg over his bike, offering a Nihilistic grin.

                    JIMMY
          Never better. Let the good times
          roll.

                    DAVID
          I thought he was gonna hit you.

                    JIMMY
          I wish he had.

                    DAVID
          Why?

                    JIMMY
          'Cause it woulda freaked him out.
          Well, can't have everything.

Jimmy kickstarts the bike. The ENGINE ROARS to life.

                    DAVID
          You're leaving again?

                    JIMMY
               (nods)
          Not going far this time. I
          enrolled in Cal-State Long Beach.
          Got an apartment on the Balboa
          Peninsula. If things get rough,
          call me.

                    DAVID
          I don't have your phone number.

                    JIMMY
          Six-four-four, two-four-seven-nine.

As his older brother rockets out of his life once again,
David wonders if he will be free to leave too, one day.

                                        FADE OUT.

                    END OF EPISODE FOUR

The Nose Knows

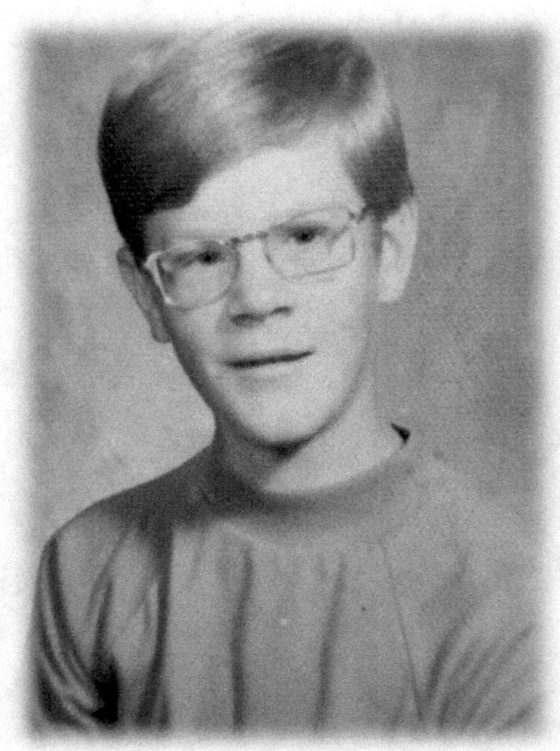

INT. OPTOMETRIST'S EXAM ROOM - DAY

DAVID (14) stares through a PHOROPTER at AN EYE CHART on the
opposite wall.

                    DAVID
          This one.

The optometrist, GREGORY MURPHY, is a cadaverous man with
pale bloodless hands, thin fingers with long talon-like
nails, and huge and vaguely unsettling owl eyes. He switches
the phoropter to a new lens.

                    DR. MURPHY
          And again... Which is sharper?
          This one... or this?

He switches to a another lens. David squints.

                    DAVID
          The first one.

Dr. Murphy swings the phoropter away and makes a note on a
FORM ON HIS CLIPBOARD.

SUPER: **1970**

                    DR. MURPHY
          Very good, David.

INT. OPTOMETRIST'S SHOW ROOM - DAY

Dr. Murphy stands behind a counter, explaining the results to
a concerned Gloria (39).

                    DR. MURPHY
          Your son is severely near-sighted.
          20/70, as a matter of fact. Which
          means he would have trouble reading
          a classroom blackboard.

                    GLORIA
               (to David)
          Why didn't you tell us?

                    DAVID
          I didn't know. I mean, I knew it
          was bad, but... not that bad... I
          I see close up great. No trouble
          reading, so...

                    GLORIA
          Yeah, but if you can't read the
          blackboard. No wonder your grades
          have been slipping.

                    DR. MURPHY
          The good news is we can have a set
          of lenses ready next week that will
          give him 20/20 vision. All you
          need to do is pick out a pair of
          frames.

ON A HUGE RACK OF EYE GLASS FRAMES in every conceivable shape
and size.

                    GLORIA
          These are nice.

She pulls a pair of BLACK HORN-RIMS from the rack.

                    DR. MURPHY
               (eager to close a sale)
          The classic horn-rims. They never
          go out of style.

David slips them on and turns to the MIRROR -- horrified by
the face staring back at him.

                    DAVID
          I look like a brainiac.

                    GLORIA
          Why would it be bad for people to
          see you as smart?

                    DAVID
               (removes the frames)
          No one likes an egghead. Besides,
          I'm not smart.

                    GLORIA
          Don't say that about yourself.

Gloria picks out a pair of TORTOISE SHELL FRAMES.

                    GLORIA (cont'd)
          These are a little more subtle.

David grimly slides them on and stares at himself in the
mirror.

                    GLORIA (cont'd)
          Those look fabulous!

                    DR. MURPHY
          The prep school look. Serious, and
          yet more relaxed and fun-loving.
          You can wear them with corduroy
          slacks or bellbottom jeans.

                    DAVID
               (removes them)
          No.

                    GLORIA
          Why not?

                    DAVID
          They're brainiac lite.

David moves down the rack of frames until he comes upon...

A PAIR OF LARGE ROUND GOLD FRAMES -- identical to the ones
worn by John Lennon, and his brother, Jimmy.

                    DAVID (cont'd)
          I want these.

He tries them on. Looks in the mirror, loving them.

                    DR. MURPHY
          Excellent choice. Those are very
          popular with young people. We can
          hardly keep them in stock.

Gloria's horrified. Her mouth puckers.

                    GLORIA
          Absolutely not.

She snatches them off of David's nose.

                    DAVID
               (crestfallen)
          Why?

                    GLORIA
          Your father will hit the roof if
          you come home in those.

                    DAVID
          Jimmy has them.

                    GLORIA
          Exactly. Your Dad will throw you
          out in the street before he allows
          another pair in his home.

                    DAVID
               (grief stricken)
          I'm the one who has to wear them.
          Why do I have to get frames that
          make me look like an old man?

Gloria's torn between her son's desire and her husband's
wrath. She scans the rack of frames for an acceptable
compromise and sees...

A RECTANGULAR PAIR OF GOLD FRAMES.

                    GLORIA
          How about these?

David realizes he will have to make a concession. He slips
them on, looks in the mirror and tries to like them.

INT. WEDDLE HOUSE - KITCHEN - NIGHT

Jim (50), David, and Tracey (11) sit at the pinewood table as
Gloria dispenses SALAD FROM A LARGE WOODEN BOWL.

                    GLORIA
          ...and the optometrist says that's
          why David may be struggling in
          school.

                    TRACEY
          Or maybe he's just retarded.

                    JIM
          Hey. Don't ever say that about
          your brother.

Tracey sullenly drops her eyes to her plate.

                    TRACEY
          I was just joking.

The inward curve of David's shoulders reveal he suspects
Tracey is right.

                    GLORIA
          That's not something to joke about.
               (to Jim)
          So, anyway, they're making the
          lenses. And David picked out some
          frames.

Jim hears the tension in her voice, sees David's rigid body
language, and senses another shoe is about to drop.

                    JIM
          What kind?

                    GLORIA
          Well, they're gold-framed and --

BAM! Jim slams his fist on the table, RATTLING THE
SILVERWARE.

                    JIM
          Absolutely not! He can walk around
          blind for all I care! He's not
          wearing those fucking Beatle
          glasses!

David withers like a burning leaf. But Gloria has rehearsed
a defense for her son and quickly launches into it.

                    GLORIA
          They're not Beatle glasses --

                    JIM
          Bullsh --

                    GLORIA
          Would you please listen? They're
          not round. They're rectangular.
          And they're not large. They're
          normal size. In fact, they look
          like the glasses people used to
          wear when we were kids. Not at all
          modern.

Jim takes this in. Sees David staring dejectedly at his
salad. He doesn't like the fact that the frames are gold
anymore than David likes the fact that they rectangular.

                    JIM
          Well... okay. As long as they
          don't look like that fucking
          Beatle, it's fine, I guess.

David looks up, smiling stiffly.

                    DAVID
          Thanks, Dad.

EXT. USC CAMPUS - DAY

Jim pulls his green FORD CAPRI FASTBACK to a stop on a leafy
street lined with WOODEN BUNGALOWS dating back to the 1930s.
David's in the passenger seat. They get out and walk toward
one of the bungalows.

SUPER: **UNIVERSITY OF SOUTHERN CALIFORNIA, 1976.**

Jim's now 56 years old -- his brown hair shot through with
gray, belly ballooning over his snakeskin belt with a silver
buckle. He wears a white button down shirt, a Camel hair
sports jacket and tan slacks. David (20) is now 5'10" and
lanky, his bushy red hair spilling over his ears. He wears a
white button-down shirt, khaki pants, Oxford saddle shoes,
and the same gold-framed glasses, though the lenses are now
Coke bottle thick.

They ascend the steps of the bungalow, which is NUMBERED 64.
A BRASS NAMEPLATE BEARS THE INSCRIPTION: **PROFESSOR MORT
ZARCOFF.** Jim knocks, then grasps David's shoulder and gently
maneuvers him into the forward position. The door's opened
by MORT ZARCOFF (50), a thin man with gray hair and a goatee,
wearing jeans, a plaid shirt, and desert boots. He smiles
and extends his hand.

                    ZARCOFF
          Hello. You must be David Weddle.

                    DAVID
          I am, sir. Thank you for taking
          the time to see me.

                    ZARCOFF
          You're early. I like that... And
          you must be Jim.

Zarcoff shakes Jim's hand. Then he gestures for them to
enter the bungalow.

INT. USC BUNGALOW - DAY

Mort sits behind his desk. He's polite, but he's not
enthused about this meeting because he was pressured into
taking it.

                    ZARCOFF
               (to David)
          So, you're a friend of Art Swenson.

                    DAVID
          Yes. I've been going to Cal-State
          Fullerton, and working at Mr.
          Swenson's plant in the summer.

                    ZARCOFF
          So he told me. Says you're a hard
          worker. Wishes he had 50 more like
          you.

                    JIM
          Art's known David since he was a
          kid.

                    ZARCOFF
          Mr. Swenson's been a great friend
          to this University over the years,
          so we take a recommendation from
          him very seriously.

David eyes a POSTER ON THE WALL THAT FEATURES A SILHOUETTE OF
A CINEMATOGRAPHER PEERING THROUGH A 35MM MOVIE CAMERA. BELOW
IT IS A LOGO: **USC SCHOOL OF CINEMA.** To David it symbolizes
the Promised Land. He desperately wants to be part of it.

But Jim's attention is drawn to a FRAMED PHOTO on another
wall. It is A STILL FROM BUSTER KEATON'S *SHERLOCK JR.*
Buster stands in a steel-lined projection booth circa 1924,
holding a strip of 35mm film in his hands. Behind him are
two enormously complex Rube Goldberg-like silent movie
projectors. Jim nudges David.

                    JIM
          You see what he's got there?

Mort gives them a quizzical look.

                    JIM (cont'd)
          My son's a huge Buster Keaton fan.

Mort glances at the photo.

                    ZARCOFF
          Interesting.
              (feigning it)
          I forget what movie that's from...

                    DAVID
          Sherlock Jr. Made in 1924. It was
          the first picture where Buster took
          sole credit as the director.

                    ZARCOFF
          Oh right. Thank you for refreshing
          my memory. So you've studied his
          films?

                    DAVID
          Whenever I can. They're hard to
          find. I saw *Sherlock* at the Fine
          Arts Theater in Beverly Hills last
          year. And *Our Hospitality* a couple
          of months ago at Chapman
          University.
                        (MORE)

                    DAVID (cont'd)
They also have a print of *Seven
Chances* at Chapman. Saw that two
years ago.

                    ZARCOFF
I was at that screening.

                    JIM
David also owns quite a few prints
of Keaton's movies.

                    ZARCOFF
On 16mm?

                    DAVID
No, Super Eight.

                    ZARCOFF
Which movies?

                    DAVID
Oh, let's see. *One Week, Cops, The
Playhouse, The General, Steamboat
Bill, Jr...*

                    ZARCOFF
Where did you get them?

                    DAVID
Mail order houses in Iowa,
Argentina, and Europe.

                    ZARCOFF
Well, you certainly seem passionate
about film.

                    DAVID
It's everything to me.

                    ZARCOFF
You interested in directing?

                    DAVID
I'd like to direct my own stuff,
maybe.

                    ZARCOFF
Your own stuff?

                    DAVID
My own scripts. I'm most
interested in screenwriting.

                    ZARCOFF
          That's refreshing. Seems like all
          the students these days want to sit
          in that director's chair. They
          think that's the whole game. Don't
          meet many who want to write.

Jim has been trying to let his son take the lead. But he can
contain himself no longer.

                    JIM
          He writes all the time. Ever since
          he was a kid. Since he saw a
          production of...

Jim realizes he's overshadowing David and reins himself in.

                    JIM (cont'd)
               (to David)
          You tell him.

                    DAVID
          When I was 12, I saw a production
          of John Steinbeck's *Of Mice and Men*
          on TV. Starring George Segal and
          Nicol Williamson. It had a
          powerful effect on me... So I got
          the book from the library and after
          reading it...
               (can't articulate it)
          ...Decided I wanted to write.

                    ZARCOFF
          What did you find so compelling
          about that television production?

                    DAVID
               (struggles for words)
          The loneliness of the characters, I
          guess. It really caught that.
          It's the most faithful adaptation
          ever done. They didn't try to
          "improve" the story. They just
          shot the novel verbatim.

                    ZARCOFF
          Yes, I remember that version. It
          was produced by David Susskind, and
          directed by...

                    DAVID
          Ted Kotcheff. He's a Canadian.
          Did a wonderful movie a couple of
          years ago, *The Apprenticeship of
          Duddy Kravitz.*

Mort no longer considers this meeting a chore. He's leaning
forward, engaged.

                    ZARCOFF
          And what did you like about that
          film?

David thinks for a moment.

                    DAVID
          The relationship between Richard
          Dreyfuss and Jack Warden, who
          played his father.

                    ZARCOFF
          Why did that strike a chord?

                    DAVID
          Dreyfuss was desperate to please
          his father. It drove him to
          achieve a lot, but it cost him
          dearly on a personal level.

                    ZARCOFF
               (nods)
          That's an overlooked movie. Didn't
          get wide distribution. How'd you
          happen to see it?

                    DAVID
               (shrugs)
          Read a review in the *Los Angeles
          Times.* Found the one theater it
          was playing at in Orange County.

                    JIM
          He goes to movies three or four
          nights a week. Disappears on
          weekends altogether. Goes into a
          multiplex at noon and doesn't come
          out until midnight.

                    DAVID
          I've seen every film released in
          the United States over the last two
          years.

Mort tries to maintain a poker face, but he's impressed.

EXT. USC CAMPUS - DAY

Jim and David walk back to the Capri.

                    JIM
          How do you think you did?

                    DAVID
          Don't know.

                    JIM
          Are you kidding? You blew him out
          of the saddle. You can bet your
          ass he hasn't interviewed another
          kid who knows as much about movies.
          You're gonna be accepted. Mark my
          word.

Jim touches the side of his mangled proboscis.

                    JIM (cont'd)
          The nose knows. I can smell it.
          I'm never wrong about these things.
               (off David's brooding)
          You don't believe me, do you?

                    DAVID
               (shrugs)
          It's the best cinema school in the
          country. People compete from all
          over the world to get in. And I've
          only got a 3.2 grade average.

                    JIM
          But your SAT scores are sky high.

                    DAVID
          Not sure that's enough to put me
          over the top.

They have arrived at the car. Jim places a hand on his son's
shoulder.

                    JIM
          Look at me.
               (David does)
          So you're weak in math and foreign
          languages. So what? You think
          that professor doesn't have weak
          points? I guaran-fucking-tee you
          he does. We all do. But you have
          something that matters more than
          grades or test scores. You know
          what that is?

David shakes his head. Jim leans close and taps his temple
with an index finger now knotted with arthritis.

                    JIM (cont'd)
          A <u>creative mind</u>. I know. I've
          seen your movies. Read all of your
          stories since you started writing
          them when you were 12 years old.
          Believe me, if I thought you didn't
          have what it takes, I would be the
          first one to tell you to forget it.
          Get a real estate license.

                    DAVID
          That's what Mom thinks I should do.
          Go into real estate, or insurance.
          Get a business degree and --

                    JIM
          <u>She's wrong</u>. You have what it
          takes to do this. If I didn't
          believe that with every fiber of my
          being I wouldn't shell out the
          money for you to go here.

                    DAVID
          That's what worries me. This new
          job of yours doesn't pay as well.
          Maybe I should just stay at Cal-
          State Fullerton and continue to pay
          my own tuition so I don't stress
          you out.

                    JIM
          I'm not stressed, and I'm not gonna
          be stressed. You let me worry
          about the money. You're going to
          USC. <u>End of discussion</u>.

Jim gets in the car. David follows suit, his spirits buoyed
by his father's faith. He glances back at Zarcoff's
bungalow, allowing himself to feel excited for the first
time.

EXT. WEDDLE HOUSE - DAY

David's packing his POSSESSIONS into a powder blue 1968 FORD
MUSTANG -- DUFFLE BAGS FULL OF CLOTHES; OLD POTS AND PANS his
mother donated to him; A NEW TOASTER OVEN, STILL IN ITS BOX;
his SMITH-CORONA PORTABLE TYPEWRITER; MOVIE CAMERA,
PROJECTOR, AND A HIGH END CASSETTE TAPE RECORDER; ROLLED UP
MOVIE POSTERS, etc.

Gloria (45) -- her hair now cut short and curled -- and
Tracey (17) -- with long blond hair -- stand on the lawn
under the flapping FLAG. A new WEIMARANER, BRUTUS, watches
the proceedings with curiosity, oblivious to the fact that
this is a huge turning point in the family's history.

Jim sprays the Mustang's windshield with WINDEX and rubs A
PAPER TOWEL on the glass with manic intensity.

David stands back to survey the possessions in his car.

                    DAVID
          I think that's... oh shit, almost
          forgot...

He runs back into the house.

TIME CUT: ON THE FRONT DOOR as David dashes out of the house
again with a CLAY REPLICA OF THE MALTESE FALCON, shiny with a
black coat of Tester's Model Paint.

                    DAVID (cont'd)
          Okay, I think that's it.

Gloria's emotional. Her first born is leaving home, forever
altering the dynamics of her world. She covers it with
maternal advice.

                    GLORIA
          Now be careful driving on those
          freeways.

                    DAVID
          I will.

                    GLORIA
          They had a report on the news last
          night about a woman on the 405.
          Got distracted, drove into the back
          of a truck carrying steel pipe.
          Decapitated her instantly. Her
          head rolled down an offramp. Took
          them hours to find it.

                    DAVID
          Thanks for that upbeat sentiment.

                    GLORIA
          Just trying to point out what could
          happen at any time.

                    DAVID
          Message received.

                    GLORIA
          And don't go walking around that
          neighborhood at night. It's in the
          middle of Watts.

                    DAVID
          Not quite. But I get your point.

                    GLORIA
          I read an item in the paper about a
          student who was raped the other
          night, by three men --

                    TRACEY
          Enough, Mom! You want him to never
          leave home?

Part of her does, but she can't admit that.

                    GLORIA
          Just trying to make sure you're
          careful.

                    DAVID
          I will be. Promise.

He hugs his mother. Uncomfortable with intimacy, Gloria pats
David's back as if he is too hot to hold. Gloria pivots to a
PACKAGE resting on the large rock on the front lawn.

                    GLORIA
          Here. Made you some garlic bread.
          Know how much you like it.

                    DAVID
          I do. Thanks!

David tosses it in the car then turns to his sister.

                    DAVID (cont'd)
          Well, you're finally rid of me.

                    TRACEY
          Thank god.

                    DAVID
          Now you get to help Dad with the
          yard work on the weekends. Should
          be a bonding experience.

                    TRACEY
          Your concern for my welfare is
          heartwarming. Please go, before I
          bawl my eyes out.

David turns to his father who has completed cleaning the
windshield.

                    DAD
          Okay, remember to wash this car
          every week and wax it once a month.
          Otherwise this paint job will go to
          hell on you.

                    DAVID
          Got it.

                    DAD
          You'll call when you get there?
          Let us know you're all right? Not
          that I give a shit. But your
          mother will worry.

                    DAVID
          I'll call.

                    DAD
          Don't be a stranger. Come home to
          visit every once and a while.

                    DAVID
          I will.

                    DAD
          When?

                    DAVID
          I don't know. Soon.

                    DAD
          How about next weekend?

                    DAVID
          I don't think so.

                    DAD
          Why? You have such a packed social
          schedule you can't be bothered to
          come home and tell us how your
          adjusting?

                    DAVID
          I think I have to spend some time
          there to adjust. It's going to be
          a whole new life.

                    DAD
          New life? You're going to college.
          No need to get so dramatic about
          it.

                    DAVID
          Okay.

                    DAD
          So when can we expect to see you?

                    DAVID
          In a few weeks, maybe.

                    DAD
               (crestfallen)
          A few weeks?

                    DAVID
          Dad, I gotta go.

                    JIM
               (dying inside)
          Okay... Good luck.

He shakes his son's hand. David discovers he has pressed
SEVERAL $20 BILLS into his palm.

                    DAVID
          Thanks, Dad. See you soon.

David climbs in his car and backs out of the driveway.
Glances out the window and sees his father, mother, and
Tracey standing beneath the flag, waving. His eyes fill with
tears as he hits the gas.

EXT. JEWEL MANOR - DAY

David pulls his Mustang up to a run-down apartment building
with a wrought iron gate that protects the inner courtyard
and a small oval SWIMMING POOL. A DOZEN INNER CITY KIDS play
FOOTBALL in the middle of the street. David gets out to
compare the address with the one on his housing contract.
Yeah, this must be it. He opens the trunk of his car and
grabs a SONY TRINITRON TV. He turns toward the building.
BONK! The football bounces off his head, nearly causing him
to drop the television. A kid rushes to retrieve the ball,
taking no notice of David, who continues on to...

INT. JEWEL MANOR - COURTYARD - DAY

THE MANAGER, RANDY, examines David's paperwork. David has
set the TV down. Light blue water laps at the edges of the
pool, dilapidated PATIO FURNITURE scattered haphazardly
around it.

                    RANDY
               (points)
          Apartment 11, on the second floor
          there. You're the first one. Your
          roommates have yet to arrive.
          Welcome to USC.

David shakes his hand.

INT. JEWEL MANOR APARTMENT - LIVING ROOM/KITCHEN - DAY

The kitchen and living room flow together into one small
enclosure filled with A CHEAP COUCH AND OVERSTUFFED CHAIRS, a
wobbly COFFEE TABLE, and a BATTERED DINETTE SET.

A SERIES OF JUMP CUTS as David puts the TV on a small
DRESSER, a STEREO on a nicked TABLE, and his POTS AND PANS
into the kitchen drawers.

As he puts some MISMATCHED DISHES into an overhead cabinet, a
COCKROACH SCURRIES OUT. Already prepared to deal with this
inner city pest, David reaches into a box and pulls out a CAN
OF RAID. He sprays it into the cabinet. To his surprise and
then growing horror, COCKROACHES STAMPEDE out of the cracks
in the cabinets. David meets them with more spray. DOZENS
THEN HUNDREDS OF COCKROACHES POUR OUT. David sprays wildly
in a blind panic as ROACHES DROP ON THE STOVE TOP AND FLOOR,
a hailstorm of writhing, spasming insects. David sprays and
sprays and still more come, bouncing off the discolored
linoleum.

INT. JEWEL MANOR APARTMENT - DAVID'S ROOM - DAY

The small bedroom is furnished with A PAIR OF BUNK BEDS and
TWO DESKS. David's SMITH-CORONA TYPEWRITER sits on one of
the desks. A POSTER OF BUSTER KEATON IN *THE GENERAL* has been
thumbtacked to the wall above the desk. Next to it, David
finishes HAMMERING A NAIL into the wall. Then he hangs a
PHOTO FROM *THE LEBANESE COBRA,* a movie he made in high
school. It features David and two friends, Jim Hilliard and
Doug Dietz, dressed in 1940's film noir garb, grouped around
a black plaster statue of a cobra.

                    DANA
          Oh, you're a movie fan, too.

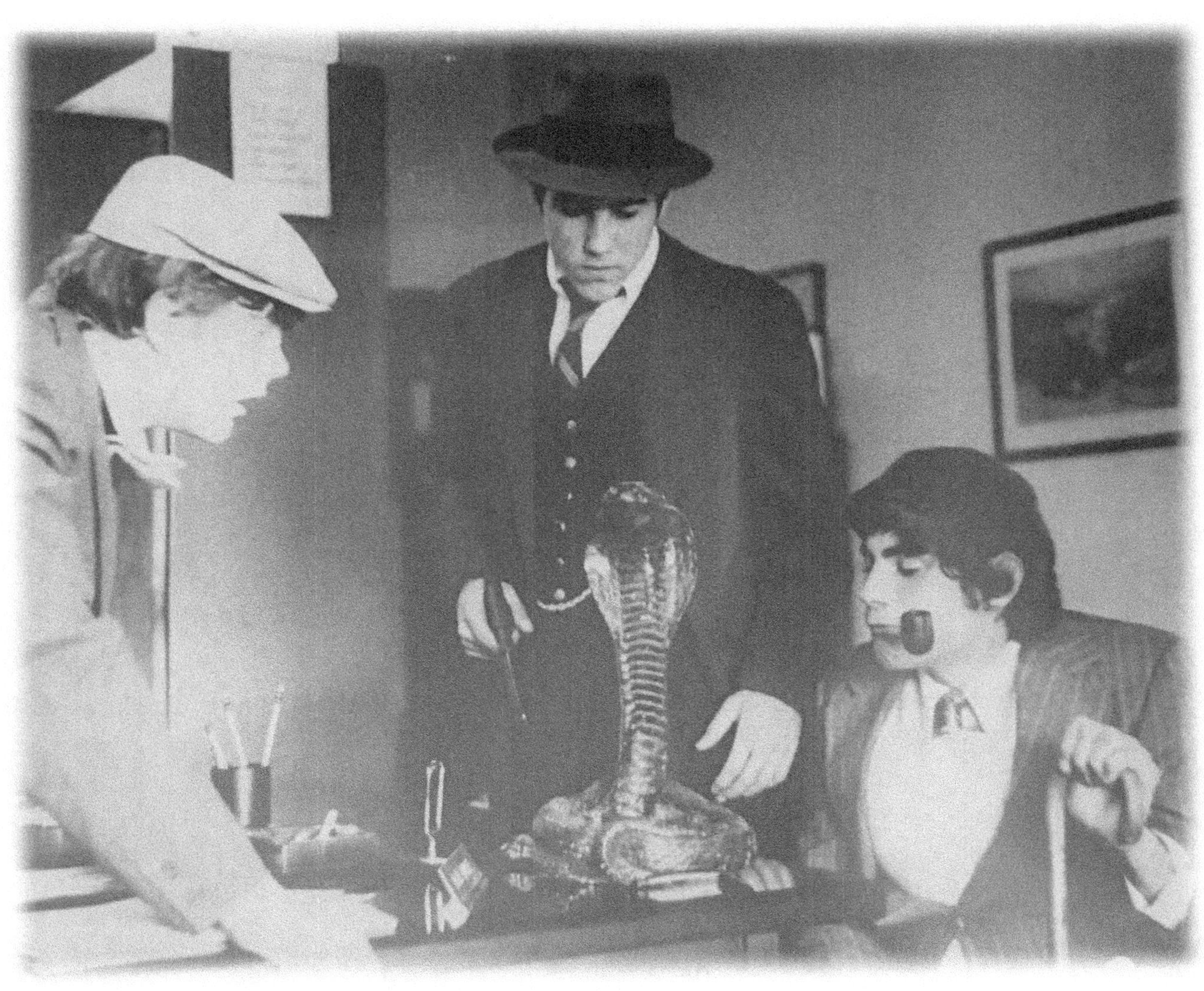

David turns to see DANA ZENKA (20), a handsome blond with an
athletic build, standing behind him with a CARDBOARD BOX FULL
OF BELONGINGS.

                    DAVID
          Uh, yeah.

Dana puts the box on the lower bunk bed and presents his
hand.

                    DANA
          Dana Zenka. I just drove up from
          Laguna Beach.

                    DAVID
               (shakes his hand)
          David Weddle. I'm from Corona del
          Mar.

                    DANA
          Awesome! I guess we were neighbors
          all our lives and didn't know it.
               (excited)
          Hey, I've got a poster of the
          greatest movie ever made.

                    DAVID
          Cool. Let's see it.

He turns to his box. David wonders what it will be. *Citizen
Kane? Stagecoach? Lawrence of Arabia? The Wild Bunch?*
Maybe he and Dana will become fast friends.

Dana unfurls a POSTER OF *STAR WARS*. David's heart sinks.
He's not a fan. Dana hums the *Star Wars* theme.

                    DANA
          Did that movie kick butt, or what?

                    DAVID
          Definitely what.

                    DANA
          Hey, you going to the mixer
          tonight?

                    DAVID
               (anxiety spike)
          What mixer?

                    DANA
          Here in the courtyard. They're
          gonna have a keg. You see the
          chicks moving into this place?
               (MORE)

                              DANA (cont'd)
                    Bonerama time! Play your cards
                    right and you could get righteously
                    laid tonight.

David's still a virgin, a dark secret that fills him with
self-loathing -- that and the ACNE pustules that stud his
back, forehead, and neck.

                              DAVID
                    That sounds totally awesome.

David wonders how Dana's voice suddenly ended up in his
throat.

INT. JEWEL MANOR APARTMENT - BATHROOM - NIGHT

LOUD MUSIC AND RAUCOUS LAUGHTER drift under the door from the
courtyard. David has his shirt off. He sprays RIGHT GUARD
DEODORANT on his armpits until his underarms burn, his eyes
water, and he's forced to wave away the fumes. Grabs the
LISTERINE BOTTLE, takes a giant swig, swishes it around in
his mouth until he scalds his taste buds. Spits it out,
gasping.

EXT. JEWEL MANOR - COURTYARD - NIGHT

David descends the cement stairs toward the glimmering
SWIMMING POOL. He wears a pair of yellow corduroy pants that
are too short, a blue and white striped *Hang Ten* shirt with
little gold footprints over his right breast, and tan
Hushpuppy shoes.

THE ROLLING STONES pound away on a STEREO. COUPLES DANCE,
DRINK BEER, LAUGH AND CHATTER AWAY. A CURLY BLEACHED BLONDE
GIRL in a halter top and hot pants gyrates with a tall dark-
haired CHISEL-CHINNED BOY. David's so captivated by her
moves, he slips on the stairs and almost falls.

                              DAVID
                    It's all right! I'm okay!

No one seems to have noticed. They carry on as if he's
invisible.

He heads to the BEER KEG. Grabs a PLASTIC CUP and tries to
get the spigot to work. Turns the lever this way and that.
Nothing happens. Decides it must be broken and walks away.
A DARK HAIRED GIRL steps up the keg and effortlessly fills
her cup. David sighs, heads for...

A BUFFET TABLE FILLED WITH SHRIVELED HOT DOGS, POTATO CHIPS,
AND CHEETOS.

                    DANA
          Hey, Weddle.

David turns to find Dana talking with a VOLUPTUOUS GIRL in a
mini skirt and low cut blouse. As he approaches them, Dana
holds out a SMOLDERING JOINT.

                    DANA (cont'd)
          Panama Gold. Have a hit.

David stiffens. He's never smoked pot.

                    DAVID
          Uh, no thanks. I'm cool.

The girl emits a blast of derisive laughter.

                    GIRL
          Oh yeah. You're cool all right.
          Fucking Four-eyed Opie.

Dana laughs and passes the joint to her.

Crushed, David fights the impulse to jump in his car and
drive home to his parents.

INT. USC CLASSROOM - DAY

Written on a CHALKBOARD in precise letters: **ADVANCED CREATIVE
WRITING - PROFESSOR GEOFFREY BLOOM.**

PROFESSOR BLOOM (40) sits behind a desk -- pale, frizzy
unkempt hair, white hands with long expressive fingers. He
wears a suit and tie, but it is rumpled and coffee stained.

Before him are 15 CREATIVE WRITING STUDENTS. They are the
polar opposite of the fraternity/sorority crowd. Long
sloppily combed hair, worn jeans (Levis not Jordache) fraying
at the knees not because a designer cut a calculated hole,
but because of wear and tear. Rock and Roll t-shirts abound,
and shirts with portraits of Albert Einstein, Che Guevara,
and Gertrude Stein.

                    GEOFFREY
          All right... David. I believe
          you're the only one who hasn't
          read. Would you, if you please?

David sits up, adjusts his square, gold framed glasses with
Coke bottle lenses. Clears his throat nervously. Adjusts
his typed pages on his desk top with cold sweaty fingers.

                    DAVID
          Okay, this is called *Private Dick*.

A SMATTERING OF LAUGHTER from the students.

                    DAVID (cont'd)
                  (reading)
          I had a hard day pounding the
          streets of Bay City. I was tired,
          dog tired. You see, I'm a gumshoe,
          a flat foot, a private dick. I
          carry a heater. Not the kind made
          by General Electric, the kind made
          by Smith and Wesson.

TITTERS of amusement from the students.

                    DAVID (cont'd)
                  (reading)
          What I needed was a shower and a
          shave. I turned on the water. It
          ran against the tile, like the rain
          pounds against the streets of Bay
          City. Rain, washing all the puss
          out of this scum-ridden town. As
          the water pummeled my tanned
          leathery body, I gazed out the
          window at the city. The lights
          twinkled merrily. Gee, they looked
          pretty. Pretty as your horse when
          it finishes a winner at 5 to 1
          odds.

The LAUGHTER BEGINS TO GROW in the class.

                    DAVID (cont'd)
                  (reading)
          I spread the soapy lather across my
          shoulders, then let my hands run
          across my breasts. The nipples
          rippled between the crevices of my
          fingers. I felt all goose pimply.
          My nipples swelled with delight and
          my mouth watered as my hands
          slipped down to my crotch. Ahh!
          That's the ticket!

This wins a BIG LAUGH from his audience.

                    DAVID (cont'd)
          I dried myself with a fluffy,
          terrycloth towel. Now for a shave.
                  (MORE)

                    DAVID (cont'd)
          I spread lather over my skin like
          you spread mustard over hot
          pastrami. My hand moved the razor
          in the same deft way that it busts
          teeth so they crack like dried
          matzahs. I made a long stroke from
          my calf to my thigh. That's right,
          you guessed it. I'm a dame. But I
          got balls.

David looks up from his pages. The students burst into
applause. He soaks in his triumph, hardly able to believe it
is happening. STEVE, a surfer poet with long curly hair,
claps David on the shoulder.

                    STEVE
          What the fuck, dude? That was
          wild!

                    GEOFFREY
          Indeed it was.
               (to David)
          A very novel approach to the
          assignment. You were asked to
          explore how gender manifests in the
          voice of a character. And to, what
          else?

                    DAVID
          Write in a voice that's the
          opposite of my gender.

                    GEOFFREY
          And yet you chose to write in a
          voice that inhabits neither gender.

                    DAVID
          Because it is both. Male and
          female.

                    GEOFFREY
          Why did you make that choice?

                    DAVID
          I don't know. I thought it would
          be fun. And more challenging.

                    GEOFFREY
          Fair enough. A very adroit piece
          of writing, Mr. Weddle.

A BELL RINGS, signifying the end of the class period. The
students rise, gathering THEIR BELONGINGS. Professor Bloom
points to a stack of HANDOUTS on the corner of his desk.

                    GEOFFREY (cont'd)
          Okay, be sure to pick up next
          week's assignment on your way out.

David puts his story into a FOLDER, and the folder into a
BOOK BAG, trembling as he comes down from the adrenalin rush
of reading.

                    SARAH
          So, you're a Raymond Chandler fan.

David looks up to find SARAH SLACK (20) standing before him.
She has long curly brown hair, piercing intelligent blue
eyes, round moist lips, and wears a white and blue SAILOR'S
BLOUSE with baggy sleeves that dangle about her long slender
arms.

                    DAVID
          Oh yeah. You ever notice how there
          are almost no straight descriptions
          in his prose? It's all in the form
          of metaphors or similes. And
          they're so over the top they're
          almost satiric.

David notices professor Bloom slip out the door.

                    DAVID (cont'd)
          But I guess I didn't really fulfill
          the assignment.

                    SARAH
          Fuck that. It's the most original
          thing anyone's written in this
          class.

Ever since David started writing at the age of 12 he's
dreamed of the moment when a beautiful woman would recognize
his genius. Suddenly, the moment has arrived. Sarah sticks
out an elegant, slender-fingered hand.

                    SARAH (cont'd)
          My name's Sarah, by the way. Sarah
          Slack.

David shakes her hand, racking his brain for a literary bon
mot to toss off. But he comes up empty.

                    SARAH (cont'd)
          You in the writing program?

                    DAVID
          Yes... Well, no, not in the English
          Department. I'm a cinema major.
                    (MORE)

                    DAVID (cont'd)
But I'm specializing in screen
writing.

                    SARAH
               (disappointed)
I guess everyone wants to make
movies these days. You working on
a script?

                    DAVID
Yeah.

The others have left. David and Sarah are alone in the
classroom. Should he get up? Begin to walk out? What if
the next class starts coming in? But he's afraid to make a
move that will break the spell.

                    SARAH
What's it about?

                    DAVID
What? Oh, my script. It's about
Buster Keaton. I'm obsessed with
him.

                    SARAH
You're kidding! I love Buster
Keaton!

                    DAVID
Really? What's your favorite film
of his?

                    SARAH
Our Hospitality. That train ride
across country. So poetic and
strangely poignant. Eat your heart
out John Ford.

                    DAVID
I know. They talk about Ford's
iconic imagery of the west. But
Keaton did it first.

                    SARAH
What's your favorite film?

                    DAVID
Steamboat Bill, Jr.

                    SARAH
               (nods)
The tornado sequence at the end.
It's so surreal, nightmarish.

                    DAVID
          And permeated with imagery from his
          past.

                    SARAH
          You're talking about the ruins of
          the vaudeville theatre. Like the
          ones he performed in with his Mom
          and Dad.

                    DAVID
          Oh yeah. It's filled with all
          these specific memories.

                    SARAH
          Diving into the canvas backdrop.

                    DAVID
          The ventriloquist dummy, like the
          one that scared him when he was six
          years old.

                    SARAH
          Wow. You really do know a lot
          about him. Sounds like your script
          will be amazing...

An awkward pause inserts itself between them as the excited
rush of words runs dry. David wonders if she is waiting for
him to ask her out. Or is she simply admiring him on an
elevated creative plane, and if so, would he ruin it if he --

                    SARAH (cont'd)
          Well, see you next Monday.

                    DAVID
          Yeah, next Monday. Right on.

David cringes inside. *Right on? What a dumb fucking thing
to say! You idiot!* She vanishes through the classroom door
and David plunges from the heights of ecstasy to unchartered
depths of despair. *I should've asked her out. She was
waiting for me to. You blew it, you gutless wonder. But
wait... hold on. It's not too late, shithead. Show some
courage for once!*

He scrambles to his feet and heads out the door to...

INT. USC HALLWAY - DAY

David blasts out of the classroom then forces himself to slow
down. *Don't run, idiot!*

He slaloms through streams of STUDENTS heading toward their
next classes. Cranes his neck, but doesn't see Sarah. He
bursts through a glass door to...

EXT. USC CAMPUS - DAY

David hurries into a quad of bustling STUDENTS. No sign of
her. Despite his effort to remain calm, he begins to run,
around a corner to...

EXT. DOHENY LIBRARY - DAY

David races around the next corner and comes face to face
with Sarah. He skids to a stop, trying to control his
breathing. She smiles, amused by the spectacle.

                    SARAH
          Well, hello again. Didn't expect
          to see you so soon.

                    DAVID
          Yeah, well, I...

*FUCK! WHERE THE HELL ARE MY WORDS! WHAT'S HAPPENED TO MY
TONGUE? IT WON'T MOVE! What if she's late for class and she
just wants me to stop harassing her?*

                    DAVID (cont'd)
          I... I mean, I wanted to ask you if
          you want to --

A tall blond broad shouldered boy, DREX (22) charges between
them and sweeps Sarah into his arms. She drops a BOOK,
laughing giddily.

                    SARAH
          Drex, what're you doing?

                    DREX
          You miss me?

David watches them, his heart breaking.

                    SARAH
          Put me down!

                    DREX
          Only when you admit you missed me.

                    SARAH
          Okay, okay, I missed you.

He sets her down.

                    DREX
          That was fun, the other night.

                    SARAH
          What was?

                    DREX
          You repressed it already, huh?

                    SARAH
          Guess so. Oh, Drex, this is...

Sarah turns to introduce David, but he's gone.

EXT. USC - DOHENY LIBRARY - LAWN - DAY

David flees across the lawn -- passing STUDENTS talking,
throwing FRISBEES, and making their way to their next
classes. He dashes up the library steps to...

INT. DOHENY LIBRARY - RECEPTION DESK - DAY

David runs past the desk, drawing a disapproving glare from a
LIBRARIAN. He rushes into...

INT. USC - DOHENY LIBRARY - MEN'S ROOM - DAY

David explodes through the door. Drops his CANVAS BOOK BAG
and leans against the sink, fighting the urge to vomit.
Looks into the mirror at his acne-stippled face, half hidden
by his ridiculous square framed glasses with their coke
bottle lenses.

                    DAVID
               (repulsed)
          STUPID! FUCKING! IDIOT!

His saliva sprays the mirror. David rips the glasses from
his face, leaving a RED MARK on his nose. He crumples them.
The lenses pop out in his hands.

INT. USC - COUNSELING CENTER - NIGHT

A GROUP OF EIGHT STUDENTS sit in a circle on FOLDING CHAIRS.
David wears a new pair of AVIATOR GLASSES. They could look
cool, if not for the heavy thick lenses. The group is a
scruffy bunch. All the kids who don't fit in on Frat Row, or
anywhere.

The lost kids, searching for a way to belong, to accept
themselves. It is a very hard task. Sometimes it feels
impossible.

At the moment, one of them, ALICE (24) -- a graduate student
with unruly blond hair, and a face that might be beautiful if
it wasn't in so much torment -- sits on the floor in the
center of the circle. She wields a BATAKA -- a thickly
padded club used in group therapy so people can vent their
anger during role playing exercises. Alice glares into the
eyes of STEVE (21), a tall strong man with a buzz cut. He's
playing the part of her father as Alice pounds the floor with
the Bataka and screams.

                    ALICE
          YOU FUCKING ASSHOLE!

The group leader, MARIANNE (35) -- a slim red-haired woman
with penetrating blue eyes, wearing jeans and a checkered
blouse -- gently coaxes Alice.

                    MARIANNE
          Maintain eye contact.

Alice refocuses on Steve.

                    MARIANNE (cont'd)
          Good. Now tell him how you feel.

                    ALICE
          All those years you made me think
          it was my fault. Made me feel
          unclean, unfit for other men, unfit
          to live, when all along it was you!
          YOU WERE THE FILTHY ONE, NOT ME!
          YOU FUCKING PERVERT!

Alice drops the Bataka and begins to wail. Tears stream down
her face, snot drooling from her nostrils. The sound coming
from her is Shakespearean. Primal. A torment that reaches
all the way to her groin.

MOVE ALONG THE FACES OF THE GROUP. Many are also crying --
chins trembling, noses running. ARRIVE AT DAVID not crying,
but profoundly uneasy. He shifts about in his chair, unable
to find a comfortable position. Alice's catharsis stirs up a
maelstrom inside him that David struggles to subdue. He
feels his mouth moving of its own accord as his cheeks
contract, forcing the corners of his lips upward.

MIKE -- another member of the group wearing beat-up hiking
boots, a hole ridden Grateful Dead t-shirt, and a scruffy
beard -- notices David. His eyes harden with distaste.

                         MIKE
               What's so funny?

Everyone looks at David. It feels as if a white hot
spotlight has been turned on him.

                         DAVID
               You talking to --

                         MIKE
               Yeah, I'm talking to you, David
               Weddle. You look like you're going
               to laugh.

                         DAVID
               No... it's just...

Alice regards him with disgust.

                         ALICE
               You think the fact that my father
               molested me is funny?

                         DAVID
               No. I just... don't know how to
               react.

                         MIKE
               I've been watching you. We've been
               coming here, what, two weeks now.
               You never make eye contact. As
               soon as the group ends, you don't
               talk to anyone, or even acknowledge
               them, and you get the hell outta
               here as fast as you can. I bet you
               don't even know our names.

David stares back helplessly. Mike's correct. He doesn't.

                         MIKE (cont'd)
               Go on. Go around the circle. Tell
               us our names.

                         DAVID
                    (choked voice)
               You're right, okay? I don't...

                         MIKE
               How come?

Marianne holds up her hand, signaling Mike to back off. She
turns her piercing gaze on David.

                    MARIANNE
          What's going on with you right now?

                    DAVID
               (barely able to talk)
          Going on?

                    MARIANNE
          What are you feeling?

                    DAVID
          I'm... look, I admit I'm shaken by
          what happens in here.

                    MARIANNE
          You mean all of the cathartic
          emotion.

David nods, his throat so tight he can hardly breath. His
eyesight seems to be tightening down too, almost to tunnel
vision.

                    MARIANNE (cont'd)
          Why are you shaken by it?

                    DAVID
          It's different.

                    MARIANNE
          I don't think it's just because
          you're not used to it. I think
          there's something else going on.

                    DAVID
          Like what?

                    MARIANNE
          I don't know. But I can tell you
          this. From the first time you
          stepped into this room and shook my
          hand, I sensed a great deal of
          sadness in you. Am I right about
          that?

David's rattled by this observation, but tries to deny it.

                    DAVID
          I don't know. I may be tense, but
          I can't see myself as some sort of
          tragic figure.

                    MARIANNE
          I didn't say you were tragic. But
          come to think of it, that is a good
          word for you.

David senses eyes drilling into him from all directions. He
feels light-headed. Pin pricks of sweat force their way out
of the pores on his forehead.

                    DAVID
          It's true I feel ill at ease, most
          of the time.

                    MARIANNE
          Why?

                    DAVID
          I think... it has to do with my
          feelings about others.

                    MARIANNE
          And what are those feelings?

                    DAVID
          Intimidated... I'm intimidated by
          people...

A TEAR escapes from the corner of David's right eye and rolls
lethargically down the side of his face.

                    MARIANNE
          Tell me more about how that feels.

                    DAVID
          Cut off. I'm so cut off from...
          everyone. Never belong...

                    MIKE
          And who's fault is that? You're
          the one who chooses not to talk to
          us.

                    DAVID
          Yeah... if anyone does try to get
          close, I withdraw.

Mike starts to respond, but Marianne motions him to be quiet.

                    MARIANNE
          Why?

                    DAVID
          I don't know.

                    MARIANNE
          If you did know, what would you
          say?

                    DAVID
          It scares me.

                    MARIANNE
          It's dangerous to get close, isn't
          it?
               (off his nod)
          If you were to get close to
          someone, what are you afraid might
          happen?

                    DAVID
          I might lose control... Get hurt.

Marianne leans in, speaking in a low, hypnotic voice.

                    MARIANNE
          Who did that to you, David? Who
          did you love who hurt you?

Another tear escapes David's eye. *God damn it! Stop it!
Fucking crybaby! Stop crying or I'll give you something more
to...*

                    DAVID
          I don't know.

                    MARIANNE
          I think you do.

                    DAVID
          I don't! Swear to god, I don't.

Marianne assesses the impasse, makes a decision.

                    MARIANNE
          Feel like trying something with me?

                    DAVID
               (alarmed)
          What?

                    MARIANNE
          Just a little exercise. It might
          help you. Want to try it?

                    DAVID
          I don't know.

                    MARIANNE
          Look at me, David.

He meets her brilliant blue eyes.

                    MARIANNE (cont'd)
          Do you trust me?

                    DAVID
          I don't... I think so.

                    MARIANNE
          Okay, Alice, can you take your
          seat? We'll return to you in a few
          moments. David, can you sit in the
          center of the room there?

Alice takes her seat. David awkwardly sits on the floor, in
the crossfire of all those pointed eyes.

                    MARIANNE (cont'd)
          Can I have your glasses?

                    DAVID
          Why?

                    MARIANNE
          I think they form a barrier between
          you and us.

                    DAVID
          But I'm practically blind without
          them.

                    MARIANNE
          You don't need to see us for this.
              (off his hesitation)
          Trust me.

David reluctantly removes his glasses and hands them to
Marianne. She sets them on a TABLE beside her chair.

                    MARIANNE (cont'd)
          Now close your eyes.

David apprehensively complies. Marianne's voice takes on a
hypnotic cadence.

                    MARIANNE (cont'd)
          I want you to go back in time. You
          are six years old... What are you
          wearing?

David's silent for a moment. Then...

                    DAVID
          My cowboy pajamas.

                    MARIANNE
          And where are you?

                    DAVID
          My bedroom.

                    MARIANNE
          Describe it to me.

                    DAVID
          I've got shelves with my toys.

                    MARIANNE
          What toys?

                    DAVID
          Mr. Machine. He's a wind-up robot.
          My favorite.

                    MARIANNE
          What else?

                    DAVID
          My model of Fireball XL-5. It
          hangs over my bed.

THE PERCUSSIVE SOUNDS OF *THE DRUMS OF BORA BORA* reverberate
in David's ears.

                    MARIANNE
          What else?

                    DAVID
          My poster of Buster Keaton...

THE DRUMS BEAT LOUDER. HIS FATHER'S VOICE can be heard
faintly. "Shake it, Peg! Shake it!"

                    MARIANNE
          What else do you see?

                    DAVID
          The light from the hall, leaking
          beneath my door.

THE DRUMS THUNDER. "Shake it! You may never pass this way
again!"

                    MARIANNE
          Imagine you see a shadow in the
          light beneath the door. Someone's
          there. They're opening the door.

Sweat runs down David's brow. THE DRUMS DEAFENING,
PUNCTUATED BY GUTTURAL POLYNESIAN CRIES. "Come on, Herb!
Let's see some moves!"

Marianne grabs the padded Bataka and smacks David across the
face. Again and again, then more blows to his body.

                    MARIANNE (cont'd)
          GODDAMN YOU, DAVID! YOU NO GOOD
          PIECE OF SHIT! WHO DO YOU THINK
          YOU ARE, HUH? YOU'RE NOTHING! YOU
          HEAR ME! NOTHING!

A red hot rod of pain pierces David's brain, ramming all the
way up from the base of his skull to his forehead. He
crumples to the carpet, sobs exploding from his chest.
Marianne drops the Bataka and puts her hand on his back as
David pounds his fist on the floor, spit flying from his
mouth.

                    DAVID
          FUCKING IDIOT! STUPID! STUPID!
          STUPID! WHY DON'T YOU THINK, HUH?

He begins savagely punching the side of his face, over and
over.

                    DAVID (cont'd)
          THINK! THINK! THINK!

Marianne tries to restrain him.

                    MARIANNE
          David, stop.

                    DAVID
          THINK!

He punches himself again.

                    MARIANNE
          Everyone, I need your help. We
          need to hold him down.

The group moves swiftly, following Marianne's gestures to
secure David's limbs and chest, pinning him to the floor.
David screams like a wild animal.

                         DAVID
          I AM SUCH A FUCKING ASSHOLE!
          ASSSSSHOOOOOLLLLE!

                         MARIANNE
                    (with authority)
          Stop it! It's not you! It never
          was. Put the blame where it
          belongs for once!

The words cut through his mind like a scalpel. David's
hysteria ebbs. He opens his eyes, staring at Marianne
through his tears. She strokes his sweat-slick brow. Wipes
the tears from his cheeks with the back of her hand. A
switch has been thrown. The implications sink in. He says
nothing because he now knows what he must do.

INT. WEDDLE HOUSE - DINING ROOM - NIGHT

ON A 25-POUND TURKEY AS AN ELECTRIC CARVING KNIFE SLICES
THROUGH ITS ALREADY WHITTLED DOWN BREAST.

                         JIM
          Gloria, what can I say? You've
          done it again.

REVEAL Gloria, Tracey, JEANNE (34), and her husband, STEVE
(35), sitting around the big oak table.

                         JIM (cont'd)
          David, get your plate over here.

David hands his plate to his mother, who presents it to Jim.
Jim slides two fat turkey slices onto David's plate.

                         JIM (cont'd)
          Okay, everybody got turkey?

The others ad-lib affirmatives.

                         JIM (cont'd)
          Let the obscene gorging begin.

Jim places the turkey platter on a SIDEBOARD next to DISHES
OF MASHED POTATOES, STRING BEANS, CREAMED CORN, AND SWEET
POTATOES.

                         JIM (cont'd)
          I want to say once again how
          wonderful it is to have us all
          together. Just wish Jimmy could
          join us.

Jeanne raises her GLASS OF WINE. She's already sloshed.

                    JEANNE
          He'll be here next year, I'm sure.
          Gloria, you did an amazing job, as
          always. Thank you for all the hard
          work that went into this lovely
          meal.

                    GLORIA
          Oh, it was nothing. Is the turkey
          too dry?

                    TRACEY
          Are you kidding, Mom? It's so
          moist and flavorful. Just
          fantastic.

                    GLORIA
          Oh good, I'm glad.

                    TRACEY
          I'm going to get some more skin.

Tracey carries her plate to the sideboard.

                    STEVE
          Hey Jim, did you see that the
          Supreme Court refused to hear
          William Calley's appeal?

                    GLORIA
          I thought we agreed not to discuss
          politics. It's Thanksgiving.

                    JIM
               (to Steve)
          Yeah, heard about that. It's
          bullshit.

                    DAVID
          Why is it bullshit?

Jim's caught off guard. David rarely challenges his
political opinions.

                    JIM
          Because the Supreme Court are
          nothing but a bunch of liberal hand-
          wringers who are too worried about
          pleasing the Fourth Estate to do
          the right thing.

                    DAVID
          Six of those justices served in the
          military during World War Two, just
          like you.

Jim's surprised David's pressing the point. It makes him
uneasy and defensive.

                    JIM
          But none of them were in the
          Marines. They have no idea what
          it's like to fight in the jungles.

                    DAVID
          Calley's platoon wasn't in a
          jungle. They were in a village
          full of civilians.

                    JIM
          Not civilians. They were Viet
          Cong. Get your facts straight
          before you --

                    DAVID
          That's not what the soldiers in
          Calley's unit said. They testified
          that there were no Viet Cong at My
          Lai. Only women and children and
          old people.

Growing very uptight, Jeanne seeks to divert the
conversation.

                    JEANNE
          Gloria, this creamed corn is to die
          for. How do you --

                    JIM
               (to David)
          Oh really? I didn't realize you
          were such an expert in guerrilla
          warfare. Refresh my memory. When
          did you graduate from West Point?

                    GLORIA
          Jim, please --

                    JIM
               (to David)
          By all means, enlighten us with
          your vast combat experience. Oh
          wait, that's right, you've never
          been in combat, never even worn a
          uniform.
                    (MORE)

                    JIM (cont'd)
You've just watched war movies.
Well, let me tell you, kid, it
ain't like the movies.

                    DAVID
I don't need to have served in the
military to know that gunning down
women and children is murder.

                    JIM
Murder? Are you fucking kidding
me? Have you read the accounts?

                    DAVID
Yeah, I have. Read more of them
than you have, apparently. Maybe
because you didn't want to know
what was in them.

                    JIM
They were Viet Cong, wise ass!
They send women up to our soldiers
offering to sell trinkets and they
have grenades hidden in their
dresses.

                    DAVID
No one did that at My Lai. Our
soldiers herded women and children
into ditches and shot them at point
blank range.

                    JIM
That's not --

                    DAVID
They gang raped women, girls as
young as ten years old, bayoneted
infants. Why? Because they
thought those babies had grenades
in their diapers?

                    JIM
I don't know. I wasn't there.

                    DAVID
Exactly. You weren't there.

                    JIM
     (to Gloria)
See what happens when you send them
off to college? They come back
brainwashed. Pink to the core.

                    DAVID
          Maybe you were the one who was
          brainwashed. By the Marine Corps.
          They trained you to kill.

Jim leaps to his feet, filled with fury and... terror.

                    JIM
          I AM NOT A FUCKING MURDERER!

                    GLORIA
          Jim, take it easy. That's not what
          he --

Jim wheels on her with venom.

                    JIM
          SHUT UP!

                    DAVID
               (quietly)
          You treat her like shit.

Jim spins back to his son, who's still seated.

                    JIM
          Who?

                    DAVID
          My mother.

Jim leans forward, sticking a knotty index finger in David's
face.

                    JIM
          You're about to go through the
          roof.

David leaps to his feet, breathing rapidly as he stares deep
into his father's eyes.

                    DAVID
          You beat the shit out of me when I
          was a kid. You want to beat the
          shit out of me now. YOU'RE FUCKED!

Jim turns chalk white and falls silent. He pivots, walks
away from the table and down the hall. After a moment, they
hear THE DOOR TO THE MASTER BEDROOM CLOSE. Everyone looks at
David in amazement. He has slayed the monster.

                    JEANNE
          Oh, David, I'm so sorry.

                         STEVE
               It's my fault.

                         DAVID
                    (serene)
               It's nobody's fault. It needed to
               happen.

     Tracey wipes her mouth with a NAPKIN and pushes her chair
     back, eyes glassy and traumatized.

                         TRACEY
               Gotta stomach ache. I'm going to
               bed.

     Tracey heads off. Steve glances at his watch.

                         STEVE
               It's getting late.

                         JEANNE
               Yeah, we'd better go.

                         GLORIA
                    (dismayed)
               I don't understand what happened.
               Everyone was having such a nice
               time.

     INT. WEDDLE HOUSE - DAVID'S ROOM - DAWN

     David lies wide awake in the bed he grew up in. The
     bookshelves are empty. HIS OLD BUSTER KEATON POSTER IS STILL
     THUMBTACKED TO THE CORK ON THE CLOSET DOOR, ITS EDGES
     CURLING. A FEW FRAMED MOVIE STILLS adorn the walls -- ERROL
     FLYNN FENCING WITH BASIL RATHBONE IN *ROBIN HOOD*; HUMPHREY
     BOGART SMOKING A CIGARETTE NEXT TO THE MALTESE FALCON; LAUREL
     AND HARDY TRYING TO PUSH A PIANO UP AN IMPOSSIBLY STEEP SET
     OF STAIRS. Overhead, the MODEL OF FIREBALL XL-5 dangles from
     the ceiling.

     David glances at the WESTCLOX on his bedside table, the
     plastic face yellowed and cracked. It reads 5am. He sighs,
     realizing he's not going to sleep anymore. Gets up and
     begins to pull on his clothes.

     INT. WEDDLE HOUSE - HALLWAY - DAWN

     David steps out of his room with his DUFFLE BAG. Casts a
     wary glance at his parents' bedroom. The door's shut tight.
     He makes his way down the hall to...

E NEST

INT. WEDDLE HOUSE - LIVING ROOM/ENTRYWAY - DAWN

David's surprised to find his father sitting in a chair in
his pajamas with a MANILLA ENVELOPE in his hands. Jim looks
like hell, his red eyes raw and vulnerable.

                    JIM
          Heading back to USC?

                    DAVID
               (nods)
          You're up early.

                    JIM
          Never went to sleep. Couldn't.
               (stands)
          David, I don't know what to say,
          except I have an incredible
          capacity to ruin a great day or
          evening and hurt the ones I love
          most in this world.

David just watches him. Jim presents the manilla envelope.

                    JIM (cont'd)
          Went out to my cabinet in the
          garage and got this.

David suddenly remembers...

SUBLIMINAL FLASH

**THE PHOTO OF HIS YOUNG FATHER, BEAMING AT THE CAMERA AS HE
HOLDS A SEVERED JAPANESE HEAD BY THE HAIR.**

David tentatively takes the envelope.

                    DAVID
          What is it?

                    JIM
          When I was being interviewed for
          the job at Fuller Paint they made
          me sit down with a psychologist.
          He wrote this report afterwards.
          Maybe it'll help explain why I am
          the way I am.

David takes the report, profoundly moved by the gesture.

INT. JEWEL MANOR APARTMENT - LIVING ROOM - DAY

ON A STEREO AMPLIFIER. A COCKROACH SLITHERS AROUND INSIDE
THE FM DIAL.

                    DAVID
          God fucking damn it!

David picks up the amplifier -- shakes it, bangs the side,
trying to dislodge the cockroach. It crawls a bit to the
left, but remains inside the dial.

                    DAVID (cont'd)
          Come outta there motherfucker or I
          swear to god I will --

The PHONE RINGS. David sets the amplifier down and answers
it.

                    DAVID (cont'd)
          Yeah?

                              INTERCUT WITH:

INT. INSURANCE SALES OFFICE - ALBUQUERQUE - DAY

JIMMY WEDDLE (30) sits at a metal desk. On the wall behind
him is a LOGO for his company, THE INDEPENDENT ORDER OF
FORESTERS. POSTERS WITH UPBEAT SALES SLOGANS PLASTER THE
OTHER WALLS: **LIFE INSURANCE PROTECTION FOR YOU AND YOUR
FAMILY! PLAN TODAY FOR YOUR FAMILY'S FUTURE! DON'T WAIT FOR
OPPORTUNITY -- CREATE IT! SUCCESS IS NO ACCIDENT!**

Jimmy has on a handsome ready-to-wear suit. His hair still
dangles at his shoulders, but it is professionally cut and
neatly manicured. A FAT ROLODEX sits on his desk, along with
WEEKLY SALES REPORTS.

                    JIMMY
          Hey there, little brother.

                    DAVID
               (brightens)
          Oh, hi Jim.

                    JIMMY
          Jeanne told me about Thanksgiving.
          Sorry I missed all the fun.

TIM (30), a salesman with a giant ball of fuzzy hair and
LARGE HORN-RIMMED GLASSES, interrupts Jimmy.

                    TIM
          I'm going out on some calls.

                    JIMMY
          How many appointments you got?

                    TIM
          Three.

                    JIMMY
          Remember --

                    TIM
          Close 'em, close 'em, close 'em!

                    JIMMY
               (laughs)
          Good hunting.

Tim departs. Jimmy returns his focus to David.

                    JIMMY (cont'd)
          Yeah, wish I could have been there.

                    DAVID
          Another heartwarming holiday with
          the Weddles. Did Jeanne tell you
          about the psychologist's report?

                    JIMMY
          Was just gonna ask about that.
          What'd it say?

                    DAVID
          Nothing earth shattering. It
          mostly focused on Dad's qualities
          as a leader, whether or not he was
          fit to be a Vice President. Wasn't
          an in-depth psychological profile.

                    JIMMY
          If it was, he never would have
          gotten the job.

                    DAVID
          It did say he was egotistical.

                    JIMMY
          No shit. Who could've guessed?

                    DAVID
          I'll tell you something though...
          He stayed up all night looking for
          it. And when he gave it to me, if
          you coulda seen his face...

                    JIMMY
          What about it?

                    DAVID
          He looked so lost. Couldn't help
          feeling sorry for him. I mean,
          that war, it really warped him.

                    JIMMY
          So? He coulda gotten his ass into
          therapy and dealt with his
          problems. He chose not to.

David realizes Jimmy is right.

EXT. USC CINEMA SCHOOL - DAY

David walks Tracey through a ramshackle MAZE OF WOODEN
BUNGALOWS surrounding a small INNER GRASS-COVERED COURTYARD.
It's RAINING. WATER STREAMS out of ancient steel gutters and
splashes onto the ASPHALT WALKWAYS.

They pass an DOOR with a sign: **CAMERA DEPARTMENT.** A STUDENT
stands at the DOOR'S OPEN WINDOW, checking out a LIGHTING
PACKAGE from another STUDENT inside a CAVERNOUS ROOM HOUSING
SHELVES PACKED WITH CAMERA EQUIPMENT.

                    DAVID
          That's the camera department.
          They've got 16mm Bolexes and
          Arriflexes, and all kinds of
          lighting equipment. We get to use
          it for free, but we have to buy our
          own film stock.

Tracey nods. She's tense. Something's on her mind, but she
hasn't found the right moment to give voice to it.

David leads her to ANOTHER OPEN DOOR. Inside it is ANOTHER
LARGE ROOM filled with STUDENTS EDITING 16MM FILM ON
MOVIOLAS.

                    DAVID (cont'd)
          This is the editorial department.
          We can reserve a Moviola any time
          we want.

They approach an OPEN DOOR to A SMALL PADDED ROOM containing
THREE AMPEX MULTITRACK REEL-TO-REEL TAPE RECORDERS.

                    DAVID (cont'd)
          This is a recording stage, where we
          can mix complex sound tracks. One
          of my favorite spots. I'm really
          getting into sound design.

                    TRACEY
          Cool.

INT. USC CINEMA SCHOOL - SOUNDSTAGE - DAY

David escorts Tracey into a huge room with heavily insulated
walls. A LIVING ROOM SET takes up the center of the space,
surrounded by PAINTED PLYWOOD FLATS that simulate apartment
walls.

                    DAVID
          And this is our soundstage. I
          haven't used it. Don't know if I
          ever will. I prefer practical
          locations because --

Tracey screams.

                    DAVID (cont'd)
               (startled)
          What?

She points to a FAT RAT scurrying along one of the OVERHEAD
BEAMS.

                    DAVID (cont'd)
          Oh yeah. Sorry. Should've warned
          you. This used to be a barn. And
          the whole complex was a horse
          stables, once upon a time. All
          that feed for the livestock drew a
          slew of rodents, and they've never
          been able to get rid of the
          tenacious motherfuckers.

EXT. USC CINEMA SCHOOL - DAY

David and Tracey sit on a worn wooden bench beneath an eave,
watching the rain pummel the courtyard.

                    DAVID
          So what do you think?

                    TRACEY
          I don't know. The best cinema
          school in the country... I expected
          something more... sophisticated, I
          guess.

                    DAVID
          I like it. Has a nice bohemian
          feel. Much rather be here than in
          some big modern antiseptic complex.
               (off her silence)
          So... you given any more thought to
          where you want to go?

                    TRACEY
          UCLA. They've got an incredible
          theater program. Sue Lorbach's
          going there. Says she can get me
          into a sorority.

                    DAVID
          You sure you want to do that? The
          Greeks at USC are a bunch of raving
          assholes.

                    TRACEY
          So you told me. Sue says it's
          totally different at UCLA. They're
          really mellow and laid back. Help
          each other study, and support you
          if you have a problem. Makes for
          an easier transition.

David's not convinced, but decides not to press the point.

                    DAVID
          Cool. We'll be crosstown rivals.
          I'll boo you from the other side of
          the Coliseum.

Another awkward silence blooms. Tracey decides to take the
plunge.

                    TRACEY
          When's the last time you talked to
          Dad?

                    DAVID
          Few weeks ago, I guess.

                    TRACEY
          He misses you.

Instantly irritated, David tenses up.

                    DAVID
          What're you, some kind of
          clairvoyant? Able to channel his
          emotions at any given --

                    TRACEY
          I talked to him. Last weekend.
          He's worried.

                    DAVID
          About what?

                    TRACEY
          You and he used to be such close
          pals. Best friends. Now you never
          call, hardly ever come home, and
          when you do, you keep him at a
          distance.

                    DAVID
          I see. So he appointed you to be
          his special envoy, did he?

David gets up and walks away, down an eave-covered asphalt
path, WATER STREAMING OUT OF THE GUTTERS. Tracey catches up
to him.

                    TRACEY
          Why you getting so angry?

                    DAVID
          This family.

                    TRACEY
          What about it?

                    DAVID
          Nobody talks to anyone directly.
          They send messengers. "Dad wants
          you to know blah blah blah." It's
          so manipulative. If he wants to
          tell me how he feels why doesn't he
          do it himself?

                    TRACEY
          Why don't you ask him yourself?
          Instead of asking me.

INT. JEWEL MANOR APARTMENT - LIVING ROOM - DAY

A STEEL BOX on the apartment's front door houses its
mechanical doorbell. Someone presses the exterior button and
the box emits a METALLIC CHIME.

David -- dressed in shorts, a t-shirt featuring BUSTER
KEATON'S FACE, and flip-flops -- opens the door.

Gloria and Jim stand on the outside walkway. He wears a blue
blazer, a white button-down shirt, a blue and gold tie, and
khaki slacks. Gloria has on a pair of pearl earrings and
matching necklace, a gold and white patterned dress, and high
heels. She takes the lead; he hangs back,
uncharacteristically quiet and self-conscious.

                    GLORIA
          Hello, hello! Well, the big day's
          finally here. We're so proud of
          you!

She hugs David, patting his back as if he's too hot to hold.

                    DAVID
          Thanks, Mom.

Jim starts to hug David. His son sticks out his hand. Jim
quickly abandons the hug and switches to a stiff handshake.

                    JIM
          Very proud.

David nods then gestures to the sagging plaid couch.

                    DAVID
          Have a seat.

They sit gingerly, as if afraid it might infect them with a
communicable disease. Gloria unsnaps her BLACK PATENT
LEATHER PURSE.

                    GLORIA
          We got you a card.

                    DAVID
          That wasn't necessary.

                    GLORIA
          Of course it was.

She hands him an ENVELOPE. He rips it open. Reads the card.
Jim studies him carefully, hoping for a gushing response.
David cooly looks at his mother.

                    DAVID
          Very nice. Thank you.

Jim feels a stab in the chest. He gestures to the window.

344

                    JIM
          Look outside.

                    DAVID
               (puzzled)
          Uh, okay.

David steps to the window of the second story apartment and
looks down at the street. Parked in front of the building is
A BRAND NEW CANARY YELLOW FORD ESCORT WITH A SUN ROOF. Jim
comes up behind David.

                    JIM
          Bought you a new car. For a new
          beginning. Paid for it in cash.
          It's yours, free and clear.

Gloria notes David's subdued reaction.

                    GLORIA
          Don't you like it?

                    DAVID
          Yeah, it's beautiful... It's just,
          my Mustang, I paid for half of it
          myself...

Jim struggles to subdue his irritation.

                    JIM
          You paid for this one too, with all
          your hard work. Finished Cinema
          School in just two years. That's
          quite an accomplishment.
               (off David's silence)
          But if you don't want it --

David sees how much it means to his father and makes a forced
show of enthusiasm.

                    DAVID
          No, no, I do want it. It's great.
          Thank you so much.

Jim hands him the KEY ON A FORD ESCORT KEYCHAIN.

                    JIM
          Here you go, then.

David takes the key. Another awkward pause.

                    DAVID
          Well, ceremony's in 45 minutes.
          Better get changed.

David heads off to his bedroom.

A FEW MINUTES LATER, Gloria and Jim sit on the couch in
strained silence.

David appears from his room in a graduation cap and gown.

                    DAVID (cont'd)
          Ta-da! What do you think?

                    GLORIA
          Ahem...

She points to his feet. He's still wearing the flip-flops.

                    GLORIA (cont'd)
          You're not going in those.

                    DAVID
          Why not?

Gloria can't believe she has to spell it out.

                    GLORIA
          You're graduating from college.

                    DAVID
          So? It's just a bullshit ceremony
          to impress the alumni so they'll
          donate more money, as if USC really
          needs it.

Gloria's mouth puckers.

                    GLORIA
          Did it occur to you that it's
          important to us?

David blinks. It did not.

                    GLORIA (cont'd)
          We never had the opportunity to go
          to college. So we gave that
          opportunity to you.

David's mortified. He glances at his Dad. Jim has sagged
into the couch, his shoulders slanted off kilter, no
discernible expression on his face.

                    DAVID
          Okay. I get it. Sorry. Be right
          back.

INT. JEWEL MANOR APARTMENT - DAVID'S ROOM - DAY

David opens his CLOSET and looks down at a PAIR OF SNEAKERS,
and a PAIR OF OXFORD SADDLE SHOES. He starts to reach for
the sneakers then changes his mind and grabs the saddle
shoes.

INT. JEWEL MANOR APARTMENT - LIVING ROOM - DAY

David emerges wearing the saddle shoes.

                    DAVID
          Okay. All set.

                    GLORIA
               (smiles)
          Thank you.

David looks at his father, sitting listlessly on the sofa,
his eyes glazed.

                    DAVID
          Dad, are you okay?

Jim looks at his son. His eyes flood with tears. He speaks
in the strangled voice of a small child.

                    JIM
          I love you.

Suddenly there are tears in David's eyes, too. He crosses
the room, puts his hand on the back of his father's head and
rubs the short bristly hair there.

                    DAVID
          Hey, hey, hey. Come on. It's
          gonna be okay. I'm really happy
          you're here.

Jim's eyes search David's, wondering if he really means it.

                    DAVID (cont'd)
          I am. Honest. Come on now.

David gestures for his Dad to stand and Jim does. Father and
son embrace, both crying. Gloria dabs at her moist eyes with
a HANDKERCHIEF. Finally, David releases his Dad.

                    DAVID (cont'd)
          All right. Shall we go?

Jim nods, pulling himself together.

                         JIM
               Lead the way, Kemohsabe..

They head out the door, closing it behind them.

MOVE AWAY FROM THE DOOR TO THE SONY TRINITRON TV on a nearby
TABLE. It suddenly TURNS ON. *60 Minutes* commentator ANDY
ROONEY fills the screen with his curmudgeon jowls and wild
wiry eyebrows.

                         ANDY ROONEY (ON TV)
               I don't use foul language and I
               don't like to hear anyone else use
               it, either. It doesn't make me a
               wonderful person, but I like this
               about myself or I wouldn't be
               telling you about it...

INT. ENCHANTED HILLS RETIREMENT HOME - GLORIA'S ROOM - DAY

David (39) and Gloria (63) sit on her bed, holding hands and
watching the television.

SUPER: **1995**

                         ANDY ROONEY (ON TV)
               You don't hear bad words on
               television very often, except on
               cable and satellite, because 30
               years ago the Federal
               Communications Commission banned
               their use in broadcasting. Later
               this year, the Supreme Court will
               decide which broadcasters should be
               fined by the FCC for the brief use
               of those dirty words -- they call
               them fleeting expletives. I was in
               the army for four years. I know
               all of the four-letter words. I
               just don't want to be reminded of
               them on broadcast. But I don't
               want a lot of government agencies
               trying to regulate what I can say
               or hear on the air, either.
               Language is one of the best tools
               ever invented for anything. And
               English is by far the best
               language. We should be careful
               using it, though. So I'll damn
               well decide for myself what I can
               say and what I can't say.

ON THE TV: Rooney smiles into camera. The images cuts to
Mike Wallace sitting on a stool. A huge stop watch behind
him ticks down the final seconds of the hour.

                    MIKE WALLACE (ON TV)
          I'm Mike Wallace. We'll be back
          next week with another edition of
          60 Minutes.

David looks at his mother.

                    DAVID
          I've got to get going.

                    GLORIA
               (bewildered)
          You mean you are leaving? Oh, I
          don't believe you. Pulling a stunt
          like this.

                    DAVID
          I know, it's a rotten deal, but I
          have get home. Got work to do.

David stands at the foot of the bed.

                    DAVID (cont'd)
          Can I have a hug goodbye?

                    GLORIA
               (smiles)
          Don't I know it.

Gloria gets up and steps close. David envelopes her thin
fragile body in his arms.

                    GLORIA (cont'd)
          I'll take it. I'll take it!

David cradles her fuzzy-haired head.

                    DAVID
          You never got held much, did you,
          Mom?

                    GLORIA
          The corn needs to be buttered.

She rests her head deep in the crook of his shoulder. They
stand like that for a long moment, mother and son luxuriating
in each other's presence, David realizing the time with her
is growing short. He leans back, looking into her eyes.

                    DAVID
          I love you.

                    GLORIA
          I'll take it.

He kisses her on the forehead then steps away.

                    DAVID
          I'll be back Wednesday. Risa and I
          will take you to dinner. Won't
          that be fun?

                    GLORIA
          I should say! The hamburger is
          very American.

David slips out the door.

EXT. DAVID'S TRAILER - PARADISE COVE - NIGHT

David pulls his HONDA ACCORD into the gravel driveway beside
his single wide. He gets out wearily.

INT. DAVID'S TRAILER - PARADISE COVE - NIGHT

David steps into his office. Walks past the posters of
Buster Keaton and Ken Kesey to a shelf holding AN AMERICAN
FLAG immaculately folded and contained within a TRIANGULAR
GLASS CASE. David picks up the case. A SMALL PLAQUE is
affixed to the bottom: **This flag flew over the former
headquarters of Admiral William Halsey on Guadalcanal Island.
As Director of The Guadalcanal War Museum, I hereby bequeath
it to James O'Neal Weddle for taking part in the liberation
of the island from the Japanese. Kevin Rymer, April 16th,
1986.**

On David's conflicted face, reflected in the glass of the
flag case, we...

                                        FADE OUT.

                    <u>END OF EPISODE FIVE</u>

The Birds That Fly Backwards
drawn by Abigail Weddle Crouse, David Weddle's granddaughter in 2026.